Titles in the DISCOVERING CIVIL WAR AMERICA series:

*Protecting the Flank: The Battles for Brinkerhoff's Ridge
and East Cavalry Field, Battle of Gettysburg, July 2-3, 1863,*
by Eric J. Wittenberg

*A Little Short of Boats: The Fights at Ball's Bluff and
Edwards Ferry, October 21-22, 1861,* by James A Morgan, III

*"No Such Army Since the Days of Julius Caesar": Sherman's
Carolinas Campaign from Fayetteville to Averasboro,*
by Mark A. Smith and Wade Sokolosky

"No Such Army Since the Days of Julius Caesar"

Sherman's Carolinas Campaign from Fayetteville to Averasboro

Volume 3 of the
Discovering Civil War America Series

To:
Chester
Best Wishes

Mark A. Smith and Wade Sokolosky

© 2005

*I offer neither pay, nor quarters, nor
provisions; I offer hunger, thirst,
forced marches, battles and death.
Let him who loves his country in his
heart, and not with his lips only, follow me.*

Giuseppe Garibaldi

To every Patriot who picked up a rifle in the defense his country.

Dedicated to:

*Pvt. Benjamin Sarver - Co. F. 78th Pennsylvania Volunteer
Infantry Regiment
Sgt. Lawrence M. Smith, Jr. - Tank Destroyers WWII
SSG. John Sokolosky – 1st Bn. 244th Coastal Artillery WWII &
979th Engineer Maintenance Co. WWII*

Mark A. Smith and Wade Sokolosky
No Such Army Since the Days of Julius Caesar:
Sherman's Carolinas Campaign from Fayetteville to Averasboro

Library of Congress Cataloging-in-Publication Data

Smith, Mark A. (Mark Anthony), 1961-
    No such army since the days of Julius Caesar : Sherman's
    Carolinas campaign : from Fayetteville to Averasboro /
    Mark A. Smith and Wade Sokolosky.
        p.   cm. —
    (Discovering Civil War America series ; v. 3)
    Includes bibliographical references (p. 280) and index.
    ISBN 13:978 0-9673770-6-3
    ISBN 10:0-9673770-6-4
    1. Sherman's March through the Carolinas. I. Sokolosky, Wade.
II. Title. III. Series.
    E477.7.S64 2005
    973.7'38—dc22

Printed in the United States of America

Ironclad Publishing, Inc.
PO Box 175614
Ft. Mitchell, KY 41017

Contents

Acknowledgments

This is the story of the Carolinas Campaign, fought in the closing days of the Civil War and perhaps its most difficult, longest, and most remarkable campaign. Soldiers on both sides battled, not only each other, but rains, flooding, swamps, isolation from support, and the scarcity of food and supplies. It is a story told, as much as possible, in the words of those soldiers. We have sought only to provide a narrative framework to hold their stories.

Because of the focus of this book, we did not discuss Sherman's "secret weapon," his engineers/pioneers, in any great detail. Their ingenuity made this campaign successful. It is noteworthy that, with the goal of keeping the army moving constantly, Sherman had instilled in his army the mindset that every man was an engineer/pioneer.

Sherman's troops were so successful in keeping his army moving that Wheeler's cavalry gave up felling trees in roadways in an effort to slow its advance, as the Union soldiers removed them in less time than it took to cut them down. To read more about the remarkable feats and accomplishment of Sherman's engineers, we recommend Dr. Philip Lewis Shiman's book, *Engineering Sherman's March.*

We have always been very interested in the Carolinas Campaign, although Wade has the greater interest because of his North Carolina roots. By contrast, Mark's interest developed by accident. Like most people, Mark focused on "Sherman's March to the Sea," but as he read of the Carolinas Campaign, it began to intrigue him more and more. When Mark was stationed at Fort Bragg, North Carolina, in 1993, the Carolinas Campaign came alive for him. The proximity of the Monroe's Crossroads battlefield (which is actually on the grounds of Fort Bragg Military Reservation), Fayetteville, and the Averasboro and Bentonville battlefields attracted his attention, and he read a multitude of books and battle reports on the campaign. Mark L. Bradley's book *Last Stand in the Carolinas: The Battle of Bentonville* caused him to focus on the Fayetteville and Averasboro portion of the campaign. Mark Bradley's use of firsthand accounts made the campaign personal and vivid!

In 1995, Mark began writing and drawing maps on the Battle of Averasboro, and he met Walt Smith of the Averasboro Battlefield Commission, whose group has made tremendous strides in preserving the battlefield. They discussed the battle and shared information. In 1999, Walt Smith introduced Mark to Wade, who was also in the early stages of writing about Averasboro.

Wade focused his master's thesis, *The Role of Union Logistics in the Carolinas Campaign of 1865,* on Sherman's logistics during the campaign. While researching, Wade discovered information on a fascinating Confederate unit, the Arsenal Battalion, that seemed to contradict the conventional wisdom that the unit had evacuated Fayetteville in the face of Sherman's advancing army without firing a shot. He found that the unit engaged in actions west of Fayetteville and at Elizabethtown, which offers fresh insight to present day students of the campaign. Wade tabled this newly found information for later. Subsequently, Wade and Mark decided to join forces in telling the story of two critical aspects of the Carolinas Campaign: Fayetteville and Averasboro.

Fayetteville marked the turning point in Confederate strategy—it was now time to stand and fight. Averasboro set the stage for Bentonville, where Gen. Joseph E. Johnston attacked one of Sherman's wings in the hope of defeating the Federals in detail.

There are many people to thank. We are particularly indebted to Eric Wittenberg. Eric's guidance, professionalism, mentoring, and most of all, his friendship, helped us in our quest to tell the story of this portion of the Carolinas Campaign. Eric's tireless efforts and inspiration have made this study a quality product, and words cannot describe our deepest appreciation.

We also would like to extend our utmost appreciation to Mark L. Bradley. We met Mark many years ago, and he has been a true friend.

Mark Smith's first draft on Averasboro dates back many years, and Mark Bradley graciously and probably painfully read that early draft, which we refer to as the "Big-Chief-Tablet-and-Crayon" phase. We hope that we have improved since then. His encouragement over the years and his insightful discussions are greatly treasured and it was only fitting that we asked Mark to write the foreword to this book, which he kindly agreed to do.

To the many folks who helped us collect the resources for this study, thank you. Special thanks go to Bryce Suderow, for his timely and in-depth researching, and Si Harrington of the North Carolina Archives for the help he gave and the time he took to read and provide excellent recommendations that improved the overall quality of this study.

No study of this nature would be complete without the help of local historians and curators. We extend special thanks to Walt Smith of the Averasboro Battlefield and Jim Greathouse of the Museum of the Cape Fear for all their support and research information. Thanks also to the Phillip Byrd family, who graciously opened their doors to us over the years and allowed numerous tours and photograph sessions of "Oak Grove." We also wish to thank the following individuals for allowing us to publish material from family journals, letters and histories: George R. Farr for Maj. Robert M. McDowell's diary, John DeTreville for Col. Robert DeTreville's photograph, Mrs. Vereen H. Coen for Maj. Thomas Huguenin's journal, Charles and Richard Townsend for the Anthony Riecke narrative, and Jim Mayo for the wonderful photos of Press Smith's revolver. We owe a debt of gratitude to our friend Col. Darrell Combs, USMC (retired), for his outstanding illustrations of some of the key events pertaining to Fayetteville and Averasboro. Darrell's interest stems from our long-term friendship and from the fact that his great-great-grandfather fought at Averasboro as a member of the 82nd Ohio and was killed several days later at Bentonville. To all those people who provided excellent support from the numerous libraries, historical societies, and museums too numerous to list—thank you.

We also owe a special thanks to Larry Strayer, and Eric Wittenberg and Bryce Suderow—again—who were all instrumental in gathering information on and providing photos of Capt. Theodore F. Northrop, Kilpatrick's Chief of Scouts. Our thanks, too, go to Howard Alligood, Kenneth Cain, and Curtis Robertson, Jr. for their help with the map of Fayetteville.

None of this would have been possible without the help, love and support of our families. Mark would like to thank his wife, the former Tracey L. Atkison, for her support, even when he forced her to read the many drafts of the manuscript and trek around the battlefields. Mark is also grateful to his sons, Joshua and Benjamin, who helped in preparing the driving tour portion by bravely entering the ravine on the third line where Vandever's troops struggled to negotiate this obstacle so many years ago. They also tolerated Mark's many evenings on the computer working on this study. Mark would like to thank his mother-in-law, Ann W. Atkison, who taught him the basics of research, which greatly helped in this project. Finally, Mark would like to thank his father, Lawrence M. Smith, Sr., whom he blames for his fanatical love of the Civil War. His numerous stories, talks, and trips to Gettysburg inspired Mark to learn more, or as Joshua L. Chamberlain once stated, "to see where and by whom great things were suffered and done."

Wade wishes to thank his wife, the former Traci Lyn Thompson, for her patience and love, which enabled him to carry through with this project. To his children, Wade Jr. and Karmen, thanks for understanding their dad's passion for studying the Civil War. Thanks also to his friend and former instructor, Dr. William G. Robertson of the United States Army's Command and General Staff College, who unknowingly provided him the inspiration to go through with this project. Finally, he wishes to dedicate this book to his father, the late John Sokolosky, who has joined the ranks of so many World War II veterans in heaven. He only wishes that his dad could have seen the book become reality.

List of Illustrations

List of Maps

Foreword

Until recently, there were no book-length studies of the battles fought during Union Major General William T. Sherman's Carolinas Campaign of 1865. Fortunately, this omission is now well on its way to being rectified. In 1996, two books on the Battle of Bentonville appeared, followed eight years later by yet a third study. Even as I write, Eric J. Wittenberg is putting the finishing touches to his monograph on the Battle of Monroe's Crossroads. I am pleased to say that the Battle of Averasboro can now boast a full-length study by Mark A. Smith and Wade Sokolosky, co-authors of *No Such Army since the Days of Julius Caesar: Sherman's Carolinas Campaign from Fayetteville to Averasboro.*

No Such Army is the result of a decade of battlefield exploration, library research, and painstaking writing and revision on the part of Smith and Sokolosky, two professional soldiers whose expertise, hard work, and determination enabled them to bring this project to fruition. As the title indicates, the authors are not content to recount the Battle of Averasboro; rather, they begin with Sherman's planning for the Carolinas Campaign at Savannah, Georgia, then trace his progress through South Carolina to Fayetteville, North Carolina. From this point, they provide a detailed narrative of the fighting in and around Fayetteville, Sherman's destruction of the Confederate arsenal there, and the events that culminated in the March 15–16, 1865, Battle of Averasboro.

Students of Civil War and general military history will be impressed with the authors' technical knowledge and understanding, and will find themselves swept up in the captivating story of Confederate Lieutenant General William J. Hardee as he fights his tactical masterpiece against Sherman, the relentless practitioner of hard war. The authors continually shift from the commanders' perspective to those of lower-ranking officers and enlisted men, providing a wide-ranging and graphic portrayal of Civil War combat. Their account is by far the most thorough and detailed of the Battle of Averasboro, and it is complemented by a set of excellent tactical maps.

Smith and Sokolosky also include supplemental essays that further elucidate their subject. In "Sherman's Concept of Logistics for the Carolinas Campaign," the authors reveal that Sherman's foraging system was only part of a vast logistical apparatus that supported his army, and they explain how that supply system functioned. A second essay on "Averasboro Field Hospitals" tell the often neglected story of the sick and wounded, reminding us of the grim consequences of warfare.

In *No Such Army* the Battle of Averasboro has at last received is definitive treatment. It has been well worth the wait.

Mark L. Bradley
Graham, North Carolina
September 28, 2004

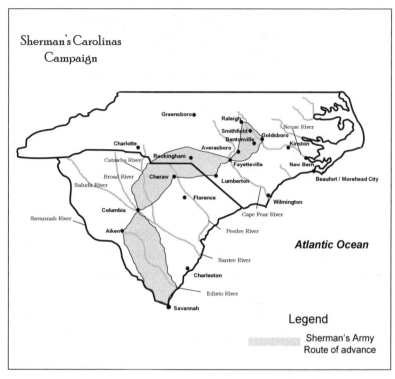

Campaign Map
Wade Sokolosky

Chapter 1 | *"Where other people live we can, even if they have to starve or move away."*

Maj. Gen. William T. Sherman

M aj. Gen. William T. Sherman's Carolinas Campaign spanned the final months of the Civil War, when the Confederacy faced a dire military situation. In Virginia, Gen. Robert E. Lee's Army of Northern Virginia fought desperately to defend the Confederate capitol of Richmond and the vital rail junction at Petersburg. In December 1864, Gen. John Bell Hood's Army of Tennessee was shattered at Nashville by Union Maj. Gen. George H. Thomas's Army of the Cumberland, leaving it a shell of its former self. More recently, Sherman had presented the captured city of Savannah, Georgia, to President Abraham Lincoln as a "Christmas gift."

The fall of Savannah was a tremendous blow to Southern morale, but it was Sherman's drive to the coast from Atlanta that had proved more damaging to the Confederacy's economic war effort. Sherman's march had

Maj. Gen. William T. Sherman
Library of Congress

1

sliced through the Confederate heartland and disrupted the flow of vital logistical resources that Georgia provided to the Southern cause.[1]

Sherman was already deep in discussion with the Union army's general-in-chief, Lt. Gen. Ulysses S. Grant as to his next move. Grant's first thought was to transfer Sherman's army north to Virginia to join him in confronting Lee's Army of Northern Virginia. Grant wrote, "I had no idea originally of having Sherman march from Savannah to Richmond, or even to North Carolina."[2]

Grant was concerned, too, about the weather. The winter of 1864 had been one of the rainiest in memory. Grant knew that the torrential rains had rendered most roads impassable and that the terrible weather would cause Sherman's army much trouble in maneuvering.[3]

Sherman, however, had other ideas. "Sherman realized that by marching his army through the Carolinas," commented historian Mark L. Bradley, "he would inevitably cut Lee's supply lines to the Deep South and induce hundreds—if not thousands—of Lee's troops from that region to desert." His march through Georgia had demonstrated the devastating effect an army could have on an enemy's transportation and supply networks. If Sherman marched his army through the Carolinas, it would eviscerate what remained of the Confederacy.[4]

This argument convinced Grant and, on December 27, 1864, he instructed his trusted lieutenant to "make your preparations to start on your expedition without delay." Grant directed Sherman to "break up the railroads in South and North Carolina, and join the armies operating against Richmond as soon as you can."[5]

Such an undertaking was fraught with risk but Grant had great confidence in Sherman's abilities as a military commander. This confidence stemmed from their close personal relationship, forged through several successful campaigns earlier in the War. Sherman had served under Grant in some of the most significant battles of the Western Theater, including Shiloh, Vicksburg, and Chattanooga and had emerged from these battles as a trusted subordinate who had demonstrated the skills needed to conduct independent operations.

Success had not always come easily to Sherman. Following his graduation from West Point in 1840, he served 13 uneventful years before resigning his commission to pursue civilian job opportunities. For the next six years, he tried his hand, unsuccessfully, at banking and law. In 1859, with the help of two former Army comrades, Braxton Bragg and P. G. T. Beauregard, Sherman secured a position as the superintendent of the Louisiana State Seminary of Learning and Military Academy.[6] From this time in Louisiana and his military tours in South Carolina and Florida earlier in his military career, Sherman came to know, like, and understand Southerners. His insight into the southern psyche would serve him well in the coming campaigns.

Following Louisiana's secession in January 1861, Sherman resigned his superintendent position and returned to Federal service, accepting a commission as colonel of the 13th U.S. Infantry Regiment. His tenure with the regiment was short-lived, and he soon found himself in command of a volunteer brigade at the July 1861 Battle of Bull Run. Following the Union defeat, Sherman was transferred to the Western Theater, where he eventually came to serve under Grant. Over two years of hard-won Union victories, the two generals emerged as the Union's most successful command partnership.

Following Grant's overwhelming victory at Chattanooga in November 1863, Congress reinstated the rank of lieutenant general, and the quiet Grant was promoted to that rank. President Lincoln summoned him to Washington, where Grant designed a grand strategy that was ultimately to win the war for the Union. The new general-in-chief intended to exert constant, unremitting pressure on the limited resources of the Confederacy by campaigning on all fronts, thereby preventing the Confederate army from shifting forces to offset its numerical inferiority. Grant would maintain his headquarters with the Army of the Potomac, leaving Sherman to command all Union forces in the Western Theater.

Sherman proved up to the challenge. From Chattanooga to Savannah, his ability to wage war became more and more evident.

Sherman's reputation and popularity grew. More importantly, the love and admiration of the men who served under him grew steadfast.[7]

Sherman set forth two key strategic goals in the Carolinas, both of which would have serious consequences for Lee's Army of Northern Virginia. First, a march through the Carolinas would break the back of the Confederate logistics system, depriving the Confederacy of its ability to sustain Lee's army in Virginia. Second, Sherman's imposition of "hard war" would have a devastating psychological effect on those Carolinians serving in the Army of Northern Virginia. Some units nearly dissolved overnight as anxious men deserted in hopes of reaching their families and homes, which lay in the path of Sherman's army.[8]

In designing his expedition through the Carolinas, Sherman drew upon invaluable experience gained during the March to the Sea. He would cut loose from his army's logistical base at Savannah and subsist his army off the land as it moved. His concept for supplying his army was simple: "where other people live we can, even if they have to starve or move away." As his army drove north, eviscerating the Carolinas, Sherman planned to link up with other Union forces, which would advance from the coast of North Carolina. These forces would merge at Goldsboro, a key railroad junction in the Tar Heel State. These combined armies would then be linked to the Union-occupied coast by rail.[9]

In January of 1865, Grant ordered an expedition against the Confederate bastion at Fort Fisher to support his trusted lieutenant's planned movement into North Carolina. Located at the mouth of the Cape Fear River, Fort Fisher protected Confederate blockade-runners attempting to penetrate the Union naval blockade and reach the critical port city of Wilmington, North Carolina. The defenders of Fort Fisher had already held out against a Federal amphibious force in December 1864.[10] Grant chose Bvt. Maj. Gen. Alfred H. Terry's Provisional Corps to make the expedition against Fort Fisher. Terry's command consisted of elements from his former XXIV Corps and units from the XXV Corps. Rear Adm. David D. Porter's North Atlantic Squadron, stationed offshore, would support Terry's expedition.[11] If Terry could reduce Fort Fisher and close the Confederacy's last major remaining seaport at Wilmington, Sherman would have a safe haven on the coast halfway between Petersburg and Savannah should he require one. More importantly, occupying Wilmington would enable Sherman to move reinforcements and supplies via the Cape Fear River as far north as Fayetteville. Fayetteville thus became an intermediate objective for Sherman's invasion of North Carolina.[12]

In addition to force and logistics, Sherman's plan also involved deception. When he invaded the Palmetto State, Sherman planned to feint simultaneously toward Augusta, Georgia, and Charleston, South Carolina. In so doing, Sherman would compel the Confederate high command—which included his old comrades P. G. T. Beauregard and Braxton Bragg—to divide their already outnumbered forces to defend both cities. After he reached the interior of South Carolina, Sherman would turn his columns toward Columbia, the state capital and, after capturing Columbia, he would then move north. Upon departing South Carolina, Sherman's next objective would either be Raleigh, the Tar Heel state capital, or the important railroad town of Weldon. He would then be within a week's march of Grant's forces at Petersburg. Sherman wanted his army to cooperate with Grant's final push in Virginia in the spring.[13]

Sherman executed a combination of land- and sea-based movements designed to concentrate both wings of his army and his cavalry at strategic points on the South Carolina side of the Savannah River.[14] During the March to the Sea, his army had moved as two separate wings, and that arrangement had worked well. Sherman intended to retain this organizational scheme for the Carolinas Campaign.

"Wings" were used by large military forces for ease of maneuver during the years leading up to the American Civil War. They permitted a field commander to divide a large force into two separate wings, both focused on a single objective. The wings facilitated movement by relieving congestion along routes of march and, in the case of large armies such as Sherman's, they expanded the foraging over a wider area. The wings formation required ample terrain to maneuver, which is why both the Union Army of the Potomac and the Confederate Army of Northern Virginia had discontinued use of the formation early in the conflict. Another problem that would concern Sherman later in the Carolinas Campaign was the fact that a wings formation is vulnerable to a concentrated enemy. Therefore, it was imperative that the wings remain within a mutually supportive distance in the event that contact was made with a large enemy force.

In order to make certain that neither wing would outpace the other, Sherman imposed control measures on his commanders. Each wing commander adhered to a strict movement table that was adjusted daily based upon that commander's reported progress. In this fashion, Sherman retained positive control of his wings and ensured ease of concentration of his army if necessary.

Maj. Gen. Henry W. Slocum
Library of Congress

Use of the wings formation required excellent communications, a highly trained army, and competent leaders. Interestingly, all of Sherman's major subordinates were rejects from the Army of the Potomac. The Right Wing, commanded by Maj. Gen. Oliver O. Howard, consisted of the XV and XVII Corps, while the Left Wing, commanded by Maj. Gen. Henry W. Slocum, consisted of the XIV and XX Corps. The cavalry, led by Bvt. Maj. Gen. Judson Kilpatrick, operated independently under Sherman's direct guidance. All told, Sherman had a combined force of over 60,000 campaign-hardened veterans "burning with an insatiable desire to wreak vengeance" upon South Carolina, which they blamed for bringing about the hated Rebellion.[15]

During the early weeks of January, the army's subordinate commanders made their designated movements under the most difficult conditions. Shortages of supplies and trans-

Bvt. Maj. Gen. Judson Kilpatrick
Library of Congress

portation assets combined with poor weather delayed Sherman's departure from Savannah. January's winter rains had flooded most of the low-country regions, raising the water levels of rivers and local tributaries, creating natural obstacles that either slowed operations or halted them altogether. The terrible weather conditions, and the havoc they wreaked on his logistics, delayed Sherman's departure by several weeks.[16]

Because of the delays Sherman encountered at Savannah, Terry captured Fort Fisher on January 15, 1865, prior to Sherman's departure. Terry's success pleased Sherman, who understood its value to his logistical plans for the campaign. "The capture of Fort Fisher has a most important bearing on my campaign," Sherman wrote to Grant, "and I rejoice in it for many reasons, because of its intrinsic importance, and because it gives me another point of security on the seaboard." Sherman's ability to resupply his army either from the coast or by utilizing the Cape Fear River increased his confidence and also expanded the possibilities for his coming campaign in North Carolina.[17]

Grant had transferred Schofield's XXIII Corps to the North Carolina coast from Nashville, Tennessee, to support the upcoming operation to capture Wilmington. By appointing Schofield as overall commander for the Wilmington expedition, Grant intended to reinforce Terry's upcoming assault on Wilmington and to support Sherman's movement into North Carolina. Elements of Schofield's corps reinforced Terry at Wilmington, while other elements reinforced the Union garrison occupying New Bern farther up the North Carolina coast. The combination of Schofield's operations and Sherman's advance through the Carolinas would complicate the defensive options available to the Confederate forces operating in North Carolina.[18]

As his subordinate commanders prepared for the upcoming campaign, Sherman focused on the logistical problem of supporting a large army operating far from a major supply depot. Sherman expected his army to reach Goldsboro, North Carolina, by early March, where he hoped to refit his army before marching north into Virginia. However, he would have to establish a logistics infrastructure in eastern North Carolina capable of supporting the flow and buildup of supplies and war matériel at Goldsboro. In early January, the limited infrastructure available in the coastal towns of New Bern and Morehead City hindered any large-scale logistical buildup. Accordingly, Sherman placed a high priority on the planning and execution of the crucial logistical aspects of the forthcoming operation. He deemed logistics so critical to the success of his upcoming campaign that he ordered his chief quartermaster, Bvt. Brig. Gen. Langdon Easton, and his chief of commissary, Col. Amos Beckwith, to travel up the coast and provide the necessary supervision for the massive logistical buildup in North Carolina.[19]

Sherman also recognized the strategic importance of New Bern as a rail link to Goldsboro. The Atlantic and North Carolina Railroad, partially controlled by the Federals since Maj. Gen. Ambrose E. Burnside's 1862 New Bern expedition, required significant repair and upgrading before large quantities of men and matériel could be moved in support of Sherman's army. At the start of the Carolinas Campaign, this railroad connected the seaport at Morehead City to the outskirts of New Bern. Realizing the importance of this rail line, Sherman directed Col. W. W. Wright, Chief Engineer of Military Railroads, to supervise repairs from New Bern to Goldsboro.[20]

On February 1, with most of his infantry divisions and Kilpatrick's cavalry across the Savannah River, Sherman ordered his commanders to initiate the campaign the following day. Despite all the difficulties posed by weather and logistics, Sherman's grand army was once again on the move. As he had done during the Savannah Campaign, Sherman sent Slocum's and Howard's wings off on simultaneous movements that deceived the Confederates as to his real objective. The two wings moved along a front measuring roughly 40 miles across, creating the illusion that Sherman was simultaneously threatening Augusta, Georgia, and Charleston, South Carolina.[21]

Gen. P. G. T. Beauregard, commander of the Military Division of the West, was responsible for organizing an effective Confederate response to Sherman's drive north. Under him were the forces of Lt. Gen. William J. Hardee, commander of the Department of South Carolina, Georgia and Florida, elements of Lt. Gen. Stephen D. Lee's corps from the Army of Tennessee, Maj. Gen. Joseph Wheeler's cavalry corps, and the Georgia state militia, commanded by Maj. Gen. Gustavus W. Smith. Beauregard faced a determined enemy of over 60,000 men with but 15,000 of his own.[22]

Maj. Gen. Joseph Wheeler
Alabama Dept. of Archives and History

On February 2, Beauregard convened a council of war near Augusta, Georgia, to evaluate his options. The council discussed the possibility of concentrating their forces at Branchville, South Carolina, where they might muster enough force to pose a reasonable threat to Sherman. Beauregard, however, had high hopes for an upcoming peace conference in Virginia, and he therefore believed that he should defend the cities of Augusta and Charleston rather than venture forth to give battle. His decision to divide his forces instead of concentrating them, observed historian Mark L. Bradley, "played directly into Sherman's hands, and the Federal advance through South Carolina was virtually unopposed."[23]

As Sherman's army moved into South Carolina, the Confederates made no significant attempt to hinder the Federal advance other than an occasional skirmish or harassing action by Wheeler's cavalry. Union foragers, or "bummers," as they were called, enjoyed the fruits of the countryside, stripping away all resources that lay in the path of the armies. As they rampaged across South Carolina, Sherman's men gleefully implemented his idea of taking the war to the demoralized Southern public. The bummers helped themselves to anything that they wanted, a punishment all the sweeter because they held South Carolina responsible for the long and dreadful war.

As Kilpatrick's Union horsemen neared Aiken, South Carolina, on February 11, the Confederate cavalry reminded the Federals that it remained a potent and effective adversary that could not be taken for granted. Kilpatrick's cavalry was to implement Sherman's plan of deception by demonstrating strongly toward Augusta. Wheeler identified Kilpatrick's objective early enough to concentrate a large force of cavalry at Aiken, where he planned a surprise attack on Kilpatrick's flanks while the Union troopers advanced into the town. With nearly three thousand veteran horse soldiers under his command, Wheeler prepared his trap and then waited patiently to spring it on the unsuspecting Northerners.[24]

Kilpatrick approached Aiken during the early morning hours of February 11. Disregarding reports of Confederate cavalry in the area, Kilpatrick rode blindly into Wheeler's trap. When his lead regiment, the 92nd Illinois Mounted Infantry, met no opposition as it entered the town, Kilpatrick dashed ahead, personally leading the remainder of his force forward. At that moment, Wheeler's troopers struck the flanks of the unsuspecting Federal cavalry, and a desperate hand-to-hand struggle ensued. The Confederates, who enjoyed the element of surprise, quickly gained the upper hand, causing Kilpatrick to beat a hasty retreat with Wheeler's troopers in hot pursuit.[25]

Such recklessness on the part of Kilpatrick lent credence to the unflattering nickname he had carried since early in the war—"Kill Cavalry." No single personality trait marked Judson Kilpatrick more than all-consuming ambition, and he saw the war as an opportunity to advance himself. Kilpatrick's dreams of political power included the White House, and he believed that a distinguished war record would launch his political career. His ambition often caused him to be aggressive to the point of recklessness.

Kilpatrick was an experienced cavalryman, however. A graduate of West Point (class of 1861), Kilpatrick had risen through the ranks of the Army of the Potomac, participating in most of its major cavalry engagements. Prior to his transfer to Sherman's army in 1864, he had commanded a division in the Army of the Potomac's cavalry corps. He had led a raid to the gates of Richmond intending to free Union prisoners of war and, despite its failure, Sherman looked favorably upon his daring. "I know that Kilpatrick is a hell of a damned fool," declared Sherman, "but I want just that sort of man to command my cavalry." Kilpatrick had "a fondness for the fairer sex" which he exhibited throughout the Carolinas Campaign. He was also a martinet who demanded much from his men, who shared a respect for his courage and boldness and his concern for their well-being.[26]

The man confronting Kilpatrick at Aiken was Maj. Gen. Joseph Wheeler, one of the Confederacy's most experienced cavalry commanders. A Georgian by birth and a graduate of West Point (class of 1859), Wheeler served two years in the Regular Army before resigning his commission in 1861. He immediately offered his services to the Confederacy and, because he possessed military experience and a West Point education, Wheeler received a commission as colonel of the 19th Alabama Infantry.[27]

Immediately after the battle of Shiloh, Wheeler transferred to the cavalry, where he commanded all Confederate horse soldiers serving under Braxton Bragg. In October 1862, he assumed command of the Army of Tennessee's cavalry, a position he retained until the fall of Atlanta. His "tenacity and grit, and above all, his strict adherence to orders," earned him the respect of his superiors. His nicknames complemented his tenacity on the battlefield. Wheeler was known as "Fighting Joe" or, due to his youthfulness and diminutive size, the "War Child." His personal courage was widely known—he was wounded three times and had 16 horses shot out from under him during the war. Wheeler's men trusted and respected him.[28]

During the Atlanta campaign, Wheeler "proved himself superior to the Federal cavalry commanders in Sherman's army," including Judson Kilpatrick. Success proved harder to come by when Hood assigned Wheeler the task of confronting Sherman's army during the March to the Sea. Wheeler's command of 3,000 horsemen was the only veteran force other than the local Georgia Militia available to contend with Sherman's large Union army. Facing impossible odds, he confined himself to harassing Kilpatrick's cavalry and the wide-ranging foragers.[29]

If Wheeler had a weakness as a commander, it was his inability to maintain discipline within his ranks. His cavalrymen earned a reputation for being little more than "a band of highway robbers." Citizens whose homes and businesses lay in the path of his cavalry often feared "Wheeler's men" more than they did Sherman's bummers. Still, Wheeler was a fighter, and the Confederacy needed such men to try to halt Sherman's juggernaut.[30]

While Wheeler chased Kilpatrick out of Aiken, the rest of Sherman's army continued unmolested toward Columbia. As Howard's Right Wing neared Columbia, Confederate cavalry under the command of Lt. Gen. Wade Hampton unsuccessfully opposed the Federals at Congaree Creek, near Columbia. Hampton, accompanied by Maj. Gen. Matthew C. Butler's cavalry division from Lee's army, had recently returned to his home state of South Carolina in an effort to bolster the Confederate forces defending the Palmetto State.[31]

Unlike most Confederate corps commanders, Wade Hampton lacked any formal military training. He was a "slave-holding aristocrat" and reputedly the wealthiest man in the South before the war. Although he opposed secession, Hampton threw his entire support behind his beloved state once it seceded from the Union. With his own finances, he raised and equipped the famed "Hampton's Legion," which he commanded at the Battle of Bull Run on July 21, 1861. Hampton was slightly wounded on Henry House Hill that day.[32]

Hampton commanded an infantry brigade during the Seven Days Campaign and then assumed command of a cavalry brigade in July 1862. He served gallantly under the legendary Confederate cavalry chieftain, James Ewell Brown "Jeb" Stuart, and earned a reputation for bravery on the battlefield, suffering serious wounds in the Battle of Gettysburg on July 3, 1863. When he returned to duty in September 1863, Hampton was promoted to major general and given command of a fine division of veteran horsemen. Although Robert E. Lee was reluctant to place a non-West Pointer at the head of the Army of Northern Virginia's cavalry corps after Stuart's death in May 1864, Hampton nevertheless assumed command of Lee's horsemen. His tenure lasted but eight months. Hampton distinguished himself during that time, most notably defeating the Federal cavalry at Trevilian Station in June 1864. The likelihood of Sherman's invasion of South Carolina prompted Hampton to seek a transfer there to defend his native state. In January 1865, a reluctant Lee granted Hampton's request in hopes of "arousing the spirit and strength of the State."[33]

Few had sacrificed more for the Confederacy than Hampton, who had lost a son, a brother, and his home near Columbia. In recognition of his faithful service, (and because Hampton refused to serve under Wheeler) the Confederate Senate confirmed his promotion to lieutenant general on February 15, 1865. In spite of Hampton's personal sacrifices and his efforts to resist Sherman's advance, he could do nothing to prevent the capture of his hometown of Columbia.[34]

Once Sherman's army occupied the capital of South Carolina. they destroyed everything of value to the Confederate war effort. They razed the arsenal and government warehouses containing military supplies and filled their supply wagons with captured bags of corn meal and other staples.[35] They meted out a punishment to Columbia more severe than to any other city, for this was the "cradle of secession." A fire started by the burning of cotton bales spread into a conflagration throughout the city, with widespread destruction of homes and property. In its aftermath, Sherman and Hampton exchanged accusations, while both held themselves blameless for the carnage.[36]

Lt. Gen. William J. Hardee
Library of Congress

When Sherman left the smoldering capital of South Carolina on February 20, thousands of freed Union prisoners and civilian refugees followed his columns. The number of refugees grew with each passing day, as noncombatants sought security and support from the Federals. During the march from Atlanta contraband slaves had joined his columns, but now the refugee train included elite whites who could not be abandoned. These refugees soon hindered Sherman's progress.[37]

On February 11, in the hope of blocking Sherman's route, Beauregard had ordered Lt. Gen. William J. Hardee's Corps to evacuate Charleston and move by rail to Chester, South Carolina. Because of a week-long delay in evacuating Charleston, Hardee was unable to reach Chester ahead of Sherman. Forced to modify his plan, Hardee instead headed for Cheraw. Fortunately, the recent heavy rains had swollen the region's creeks and rivers, halting Sherman's advance while his engineers grappled with these natural obstacles.[38] The delays caused by heavy rains permitted Hardee to consolidate his command at Cheraw, although his stay there would be all too brief.

A West Point graduate (class of 1838), Hardee was a veteran of the Seminole and Mexican Wars and a 23-year veteran of the Regular Army when war came in 1861. In the late 1850's, he had written the U.S. Army's standard infantry manual, *Rifle and Light Infantry Tactics*. Although weapons technology had rendered the infantry formations specified by Hardee in the manual outdated by the time of the Civil War, it remained an important handbook for both the Union and Confederate armies.

After resigning from the Federal service in 1861, Hardee accepted a commission as brigadier general in the Confederate army. In the Battle of Shiloh, he commanded an Arkansas brigade that he had helped organize. By October 1862, Hardee had been promoted to lieutenant general and commanded a corps in the Army of Tennessee. In September 1864, after the disastrous Confederate defeat at Jonesboro, Hardee tendered his resignation, having clashed with the Army of Tennessee's new commander, Gen. John Bell Hood. Confederate President Jefferson Davis approved Hardee's request and transferred the general to Savannah, where he assumed command of the Department of South Carolina, Georgia and Florida. Once ensconced in Savannah, Hardee faced the approach of Sherman's army from Atlanta.

Hardee had earned a reputation as one of the Confederacy's most capable corps commanders and from his men the affectionate nickname, "Old Reliable." On several occasions, he had had the misfortune to achieve early success on the battlefield, only to see it slip away due to Union numerical superiority or tactical mistakes on the part of the Confederate leadership. Old Reliable would need to call on all of his considerable skill if he hoped to stop Sherman's army.

On the night of March 2, Hardee held a council of war at Cheraw. Butler reported that his troopers had skirmished with Sherman's forces earlier in the day and that he was certain the Federals were only a day's march from Cheraw. Butler therefore recommended that Hardee evacuate at once. Hardee agreed and his troops began withdrawing immediately. Hardee ordered Butler to deploy cavalry on the outskirts of town and Butler established his defensive positions south of the Pee Dee River, hoping to use the river to delay Sherman's attacks on the town. Infantrymen of the 1st Georgia Regulars deployed in line on the other side of the river, reinforcing Butler's division.[39] While the rest of Hardee's Corps withdrew and headed north, Butler and the Georgians waited for Sherman's army to arrive. Butler used the time wisely, and had his men coat the bridge over the Pee Dee with rosin so that it could be quickly and easily burned. Its destruction would deprive Sherman of a good crossing and would further hinder the Federal advance.

On the morning of March 3, after a brief stand by Butler's troopers, elements of Howard's Right Wing drove the Confederate horse soldiers through the town. As the Confederates retired, they torched the bridge, which was quickly engulfed in flames. The Federal infantry, supported by artillery, advanced to the bridge and opened fire on the Confederate forces massed on the opposite bank. Unable to extinguish the flaming bridge, the frustrated Federals watched it collapse into the rain-swollen river. The Confederate rear guard tarried to enjoy the spectacle for a moment, then withdrew and caught up to the rest of Hardee's Corps as it made its way toward the North Carolina state line.[40] Butler's well-executed delaying action had accomplished its goal—it had bought sufficient time for Hardee to escape and had deprived Sherman of a bridge across the unfordable Pee Dee. His engineers would have to build a pontoon bridge. As Hardee moved north, he now faced internal enemies: demoralization and desertion. With each passing day, disheartened men abandoned the ranks and headed home. Most of the men in Hardee's Corps were former coastal artillerymen, unused to the hardships of campaigning. With an unreliable command that had contin-

Gen. Joseph E. Johnston
USAMHI

ually retreated before Sherman's advance, Hardee now had to decide where and when his untested command should confront Sherman's veterans.[41]

Frustrated by Beauregard's performance, the Confederate army's newly appointed general-in-chief, Robert E. Lee, restored Gen. Joseph E. Johnston to field command. Lee placed Johnston in command of the Department of South Carolina, Georgia and Florida, and the remnant of the Army of Tennessee, which had been shattered at Nashville in December 1864.[42]

Johnston, a native Virginian, was a West Point classmate of Robert E. Lee and a veteran of both the Seminole and Mexican Wars. Prior to his resignation in 1861, Johnston had risen to the position of Quartermaster General of the Army, which carried the rank of brigadier general. Upon entering the Confederate service, Johnston was commissioned a brigadier general. In combination with Beauregard, Johnston defeated Brig. Gen. Irwin McDowell's Union forces at First Manassas and later assumed command of what was to become the Army of Northern Virginia. Severely wounded while lead-ing his troops in the May 31, 1862 Battle of Seven Pines, Johnston relinquished command to Maj. Gen. Gustavus W. Smith, who was quickly replaced by Gen. Robert E. Lee.

After recovering from his wounds, Johnston found himself with-out a command, largely the result of his inability to get along with the prickly Davis. In 1863, when Grant's army crossed the Mississippi River and began moving on the critical bastion at Vicksburg, Davis put Johnston in command of the Confederate forces at Jackson, Mississippi. Johnston's small force was unable to combine with Lt. Gen. John C. Pemberton in Vicksburg and he eventually retreated to Jackson. Vicksburg fell in July 1863 and Johnston was once again a supernumerary. Following the disastrous rout of the Army of Tennessee at Chattanooga in late November, Braxton Bragg resigned his command and Davis replaced him with Johnston, who quickly restored the army to fighting trim, earning the respect and the affec-tion of his men in the process. In the Atlanta Campaign that ensued, Johnston adopted a purely defensive strategy against Sherman, which soon caused President Davis to question his fitness for command. On July 17, 1864, Davis replaced him with John Bell Hood and Johnston found himself in virtual retirement.[43]

Lee's decision to restore "Ole Joe" to field command came from the knowledge that many political and military leaders of the South, as well as the general populace, believed that only Johnston possessed the necessary qualities to build an army and defeat Sherman. Among Johnston's first acts was to retain Beauregard as his second in com-mand.[44] He faced a daunting task—he would have to forge an army from diverse and in many cases inexperienced forces unaccustomed to working together. Johnston knew that the odds were heavily against him.

Sherman paused in Cheraw long enough for his columns to close up. As he waited, he learned that Johnston now led most of the Confederate forces opposing him. Sherman respected his old adversary, later writing, "I then knew that my special antagonist General Joseph Johnston, was back, with part of his old army; that he would not be misled by feints and false reports, and somehow compel me to exercise more caution than I had hitherto done." To his horror, Sherman found a copy of a New York newspaper in Hardee's former headquarters that identified Goldsboro as the ultimate objective of the Federals. Sherman was confident that Hardee had read the newspaper,

Lt. Gen. Wade Hampton, Jr.
Library of Congress

and that Hardee had reported this intelligence to Johnston, suggesting that his elaborate feints had gone for naught. Nevertheless, Johnston and Lee were already of the belief that Sherman was focusing his movement more to the east than the disposition of his troops might otherwise have suggested.[45]

In keeping with Lee's order to "concentrate all available forces and drive back General Sherman," Johnston began concentrating the widely-scattered Confederate forces already in the Carolinas with the remnants of the Army of Tennessee. Johnston instructed Beauregard to coordinate the necessary troop movements for integrating the Confederate units entering North Carolina. This relieved Johnston of much burdensome staff work and freed him to focus his efforts on developing a plan for attacking Sherman's approaching army.[46]

The Confederate forces in the Carolinas consisted of elements from all corners of the Confederacy. Gen. Braxton Bragg's Department of North Carolina consisted primarily of Maj. Gen.

Robert F. Hoke's veteran infantry division from the Army of Northern Virginia, as well as local militia and the North Carolina Junior Reserves. President Davis had appointed General Bragg as the departmental commander following Chattanooga and a brief stint as his military adviser. Hardee's Corps consisted of Brig. Gen. William B. Taliaferro's division of former coastal artillery and infantry units from Charleston, as well as Maj. Gen. Lafayette McLaws's division, with its mixture of frontline and reserve brigades. Lt. Gen. Wade Hampton's cavalry supported Hardee's infantry. Hampton's force consisted of Wheeler's cavalry corps and Butler's cavalry division. Finally, Lt. Gen. A. P. Stewart's contingent of the Army of Tennessee had orders to concentrate at Charlotte, North Carolina.[47]

While Sherman halted at Cheraw, Hardee continued moving toward Rockingham, North Carolina, in obedience to Beauregard's previous order. Upon reaching Rockingham on March 4, Hardee began a correspondence with Johnston, Beauregard, and Bragg that left "Old Reliable" confused as to where the high command expected him to march. Conflicting reports regarding the movement of Federal forces from Wilmington toward Fayetteville caused Johnston to question the wisdom of his decision to move Hardee toward Fayetteville. Hardee had already begun moving in that direction, making his compliance with the contradictory orders that followed virtually impossible. Hardee informed Johnston that he was well on his way to Fayetteville and that he expected to reach the town by March 9 or 10.[48]

Sherman remained at Cheraw until March 6, permitting his army to complete the crossing of the Pee Dee.[49] His army then began its advance on Fayetteville. Howard's Right Wing followed two direct roads well to the east. Upon reaching Fayetteville, he was to enter the town from the south. To the west there was only a single road, which Slocum's Left Wing would follow, entering Fayetteville from the west. With the cavalry of Hampton and Wheeler operating to Slocum's left rear, Kilpatrick was assigned to screen that area and protect the army's trains.[50]

By March 8, the first elements of Sherman's army had entered the Old North State. The terrible force of total war had come to North Carolina. Its citizens were about to feel the full weight of Sherman's army.[51]

Chapter 2 | *"[T]he enemy will overrun this country"*

Raleigh *North Carolina Standard,*
March 1, 1865

The citizens of North Carolina welcomed 1865 with feelings of apprehension. Except for the Federal occupation of portions of the state's coastal regions, North Carolina had remained relatively unscathed by the horrors of war. During the first months of 1865, however, prominent North Carolina newspapers began predicting doom and destruction. Sherman's veteran army of more than 60,000 was rapidly approaching the North Carolina border. The Yankees had cut a swath across Georgia and South Carolina, spreading terror throughout the Southeast. Sherman's successes in South Carolina fueled growing feelings of uneasiness in the Tar Heel population, prompting the editor of the *Raleigh Progress* to complain, "South Carolina was whipped and would not check Sherman." The (Raleigh) *North Carolina Standard* was similarly pessimistic: "We hope for the best, but we confess that Sherman will not be routed, or even checked...Goldsborough, Fayetteville, and even Raleigh are in danger. We fear that what has been will be; in other words, that the enemy will overrun this country."[1] The *Standard* editorial demonstrated the psychological impact of Sherman's "hard war" concept on the Confederate leadership and public. As the people of North Carolina wrestled with their uncertainty, the Confederate civil and military authorities did so as well. As Sherman's army approached the state line, panic spread across North Carolina.

Few felt this trepidation more than the residents of Fayetteville, North Carolina. Theirs was an obvious target. In addition to being the northernmost navigable port on the Cape Fear River, Fayetteville was also the site of one of the few functional armories left in the South.

The Fayetteville Arsenal and Armory had been the property of the United States Army from 1838 until it was seized in the spring of 1861.[2] The state initially used the newly acquired arsenal to manufacture infantry ammunition and accoutrements, and to repair small arms. With the transfer of captured machinery from the Federal arsenal at Harpers Ferry, the Fayetteville Arsenal began producing rifles. The Arsenal's capacity grew throughout the war, and by 1865, it consisted of several foundries, machine shops and other facilities necessary to sustain the Confederate war effort. By January 1865, the Arsenal was fully manned and operational, but the combination of a shortage of raw materials and Fayetteville's isolation from any of the state's key rail lines limited the Arsenal's productivity.[3]

In addition to Sherman's advancing army, two additional Federal corps positioned on the North Carolina coast also threatened Fayetteville. Maj. Gen. Alfred Terry's Provisional Corps had captured the stout Confederate bastion at Fort Fisher, opening the Cape Fear River to Federal traffic and thereby threatening Wilmington. Maj. Gen. John M. Schofield's XXIII Corps had arrived from Tennessee to aid Terry's effort to capture Wilmington as well as Brig. Gen. Innis N. Palmer's planned advance on Goldsboro from New Bern. Terry and Schofield intended to unite with Sherman's army as it passed through the state en route to a link-up with Grant's armies in Virginia. Since mid-February, the buildup of Union forces and supplies at Morehead City and New Bern had increased significantly.[4]

As Johnston studied the growing Federal threat, questions arose as to whether he possessed the authority to command Bragg's Department of North Carolina troops, which consisted mostly of Maj. Gen. Robert F. Hoke's veteran division. On March 4, Lee therefore gave Johnston the necessary authority.[5]

Unlike his predecessor Beauregard, Johnston assumed command with some idea of Sherman's ultimate objective. Until now, Sherman's feints had kept the Confederate command off-balance and uncertain as to his destination. However, reports drifted in from South Carolina that suggested Sherman was moving northeast rather than northwest.[6] Johnston concluded that Sherman was headed for either Raleigh, the capital of North Carolina, or Goldsboro, a key rail hub linking Wilmington to Petersburg and Morehead City to Raleigh and Charlotte.[7]

With Terry's and Schofield's forces threatening the eastern part of the state, and Sherman advancing from the south, Johnston faced Federal threats from two directions. He assumed that these forces would combine at some point, probably either at Raleigh or Goldsboro.[8] Regardless of the Federals' next move, Johnston knew that he had to unite Hardee's Corps, the remnant of the Army of Tennessee, Bragg's command, and Hampton's cavalry to have even a faint hope of stopping Sherman's numerically superior army.

Once Bragg evacuated Wilmington on February 21, the threat of a Federal attack on Fayetteville grew dramatically. The loss of Wilmington and the Cape Fear River opened an accessible invasion route into the interior region of North Carolina and exposed Fayetteville and its Arsenal to attack. A member of the Arsenal garrison, Capt. James W. Strange, commander of Co. F, 2nd Battalion North Carolina Local Defense Troops, voiced these concerns. "I have thought until the evacuation of Wilmington that Fayetteville was one of the safest places in the Confederacy," wrote Strange. He realized now that Fayetteville's location on the Cape Fear River exposed it to danger, and understood that an enemy force could "at any time that there is a swell in this river go up to Fayetteville in the gunboats and frigates."[9]

Bragg also recognized the potential threat to Fayetteville. When he evacuated Wilmington on February 21, Bragg notified the Fayetteville authorities that they were now vulnerable to attack from the Cape Fear. He advised the Arsenal's commanding officer to evacuate "his most valuable stores, especially ammunition for small arms," and procure the wagons necessary to transport these supplies to the nearest railroad depot. Future Confederate operations in North Carolina had no hope of success unless these critical supplies were secured.[10]

The Arsenal's commanding officer was Lt. Col. Frederick L. Childs, a former U.S. Army officer who had graduated ninth in the West Point class of 1855 and was the only son of Bvt. Brig. Gen. Thomas Childs, a veteran of both the War of 1812 and the Mexican War. Colonel Childs had served at Wilmington, Charleston, and Augusta before being transferred to the Fayetteville Arsenal in the spring of 1863. His command was a mixture of artisans, laborers, and other servicemen organized into Companies A and B, 2nd Battalion North Carolina Local Defense Troops.[11]

Since assuming command, Childs had pondered how best to defend his post, fearing that Federal cavalry forces stationed at New Bern posed a significant threat to the Arsenal. His initial assessment of the town's defensive posture identified major weaknesses, two above all. First, there were no prepared defensive lines or works along the town's avenues of approach. Second, the Arsenal garrison had no mounted forces, thereby rendering Childs blind to possible enemy activity in the surrounding area.[12]

Childs began strengthening the town's defenses. Recognizing the need for earthworks, he appealed to the residents of Fayetteville to supply a labor force of 50 to 75 slaves.[13] Childs directed the construction of these works along the key roads into Fayetteville and in the vicinity of the Arsenal. While these works would help, Childs knew they were not nearly enough to deter Sherman's 60,000 veterans.

In September 1863, Childs had received authorization to raise Cos. C, D, and E for the purpose of local defense. In 1864, the battalion was further expanded by the authorization of Co. F, a mounted force, and Co. G, consisting of soldiers detailed for light duty. With these additional companies, the 2nd Battalion, or "Arsenal Guards," now consisted of seven companies mustering more than 500 men. Despite Childs's efforts to bolster the Arsenal's defenses, he realized that his motley command could not withstand the twin threats posed by Sherman's and Schofield's forces.[14] Consequently, on February 22, 1865, Childs asked Bragg for guidance regarding the future of Fayetteville and the Arsenal. Childs rightly feared the possibility of an enemy advance on Fayetteville up the Cape Fear.[15]

Bragg's response was less than reassuring: "The enemy's superior force will, I fear, enable him to send a detachment against you, which can only be met by your own resources."[16] Those resources were simply incapable of defending against a large-scale Federal advance. In a February 23 message to Bragg, Childs reported his operative strength at about 250, with the possibility of 100 or 200 last-minute reinforcements. At that time, portions of the battalion were detached to other posts throughout the state.[17]

In December 1864, Childs's battalion was sent to Wilmington to assist in the defense of Fort Fisher. When the Federals' first attempt to reduce Fort Fisher failed, Childs and most of the battalion returned to Fayetteville. Childs left Cos. B and G in Wilmington under the command of Co. B's Capt. Armand L. DeRosset.[18] His meager force was thus further reduced.

The Cape Fear River provided a navigable water route between Fayetteville and Wilmington. Bragg hoped to block any movement along the river by deploying DeRosset's two companies of infantry and Capt. Abner A. Moseley's Sampson Light Artillery. Bragg chose Elizabethtown, just south of Fayetteville, as the position for this small garrison.[19]

Like DeRosset's foot soldiers, Moseley's battery had served in the defenses of Wilmington. The British-manufactured Whitworth breech-loading rifled guns of Moseley's battery were ideal for the blocking mission. The Whitworth's rifled bore was extremely accurate, and it was an ideal weapon for use against the wooden light-draft vessels that could be employed on the Cape Fear River near Fayetteville. During the battery's field service in and around Wilmington, Moseley's men actively engaged both Union army and naval forces. They proved the effectiveness of the Whitworths during the defense of Fort Anderson on February 3, successfully repulsing the Union vessel *Tacony* by scoring three direct hits that passed completely through its hull.[20]

In addition to transferring DeRosset's and Moseley's units to Elizabethtown, Bragg ordered Childs to "place scouts well out, and obstruct the river as much as possible," and he also instructed Childs as to the proper placement of Moseley's field battery in order to prevent river passage. The wording of Bragg's order suggests that he intended for Childs to direct the operations for the defense of the Cape Fear River south of Fayetteville, extending his area of responsibility beyond the town.[21] Childs dispatched Lt. Samuel A. Ashe to supervise efforts to obstruct the river at Elizabethtown. To assist Childs, Bragg granted the Arsenal commander authority to "impress Negroes sufficient to vigorously obstruct the river," and further augmented his efforts with Capt. John C. Winder's Co. A, 2nd Confederate States Engineers.[22]

Childs perceived that the authorities were not adequately concerned about the safety of the Fayetteville Arsenal, and he reminded Brig. Gen. Josiah Gorgas, the Confederate Chief of Ordnance, of the importance of the town and its arsenal. "Do the authorities appreciate the importance of Fayetteville?" inquired Childs. "Eight cotton factories here, machinery of naval ordnance works, coal and iron of Deep River country, besides what we have here." Unfortunately, Gorgas had no reinforcements to send, leaving Childs no choice but to go it alone with the meager forces already at his disposal.[23]

On February 27, having realized that he would get no help from the Ordnance Department in Richmond, Childs asked Bragg for permission to destroy the substantial cotton and naval stores in

Fayetteville. Several days later, Bragg instructed Childs to prepare for destruction "all cotton or naval stores and other stores serviceable to the enemy" to prevent the capture of such items.[24] Shortly thereafter, Bragg changed his mind and countermanded his original order, instead directing Childs to "suspend removal of all subsistence and forage and collect all you possibly can at Fayetteville." Hardee had decided to halt at Fayetteville to refit his force after its escape from South Carolina, and he would need those supplies.[25]

Prior to February 28, Childs had concerned himself principally with the defense of Fayetteville. Bragg, the departmental commander, had operational control over the 2nd Battalion North Carolina Local Defense Troops and he intended to employ these troops as needed, whether at Fayetteville or elsewhere. Accordingly, Bragg maintained constant communication with Childs and ordered him to utilize his small battalion both as infantry and as a mounted force. Once it became obvious that Sherman was about to enter North Carolina, Bragg extended Childs's area of operations west of Fayetteville to the Lumber River and beyond. Bragg ordered Childs to destroy the railroad trestle south of Lumberton, and to prepare to burn the bridge across the Lumber River.[26]

Childs required cavalry to accomplish these tasks over such a large area. He therefore requested the return of Capt. James W. Strange's Co. F, which was the only mounted force assigned to the Arsenal Guards, and which was guarding the Wilmington & Weldon Rail Road in the northeastern part of the state.[27] In a letter to Childs, Captain Strange wrote: "I should think that the time has now arrived when my company might be [more] carefully employed at Fayetteville [than] here."[28] The transfer request was nevertheless denied, leaving Childs without a proper mounted force. Although Bragg declined to reassign Strange's company, he granted Childs authority to impress horses for mounted videttes. Once again, Childs asked the citizens of Fayetteville to assist his efforts by picketing the approaches to the town.[29]

The approach of Sherman's army prompted Bragg to modify his previous instructions to Childs. Two railroads, the Wilmington & Manchester and the Wilmington, Charlotte, & Rutherford, both originated in Wilmington and linked the geographical interiors of the Carolinas to the coast. These rail lines provided a ready communication link to the Union-occupied coastline. On February 28, Childs informed Bragg that Federal troops were repairing the Brunswick Railroad Bridge on the Wilmington & Manchester. A week earlier, during Bragg's unsuccessful defense of Wilmington, members of the 2nd South Carolina Cavalry had destroyed the bridge. When Wilmington fell, Bragg believed that Sherman would use these railroads, and Childs's report only reinforced his belief.[30] As a result, Bragg ordered Childs to destroy all bridges and railroads leading to the town of Lumberton, including any on the Wilmington & Manchester from the Pee Dee River north. This further extended Childs's lines below geographic area of operations, stretching his limited resources to the breaking point.[31]

Maj. Matthew P. Taylor, Childs's second-in-command, led the 2nd Battalion Scouts, which consisted of the officers and men of the remaining Arsenal companies. Taylor faced the daunting task of disrupting Sherman's approaching columns with his meager force.[32]

Fortunately for Childs, Johnston decided to relocate his headquarters from Charlotte to Fayetteville in order "to obtain quick intelligence of the enemy's movements," and to direct those of the Confederate troops." Childs must have felt great relief when Johnston and his staff arrived at Fayetteville and established their headquarters in the Fayetteville Hotel on Hay Street.[33] In the meantime, Hardee's infantry moved into North Carolina, while Hampton's cavalry shadowed Sherman's advance, harassing the Union army's advance.

Hampton's horsemen had already clashed with Kilpatrick's troopers at Hornsboro and at Phillips' Crossroads, where they had surprised the Federal horse soldiers and nearly routed them. The Southern cavaliers remained full of pluck, and they were determined to resist the

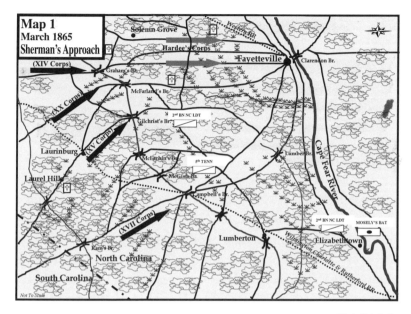

Map 1
March 1865
Sherman's Approach

Wade Sokolosky

advance of the blue-clad horde then pushing into North Carolina. It became a race to see who could reach Fayetteville first: Hardee or Sherman. As Hardee's foot soldiers slogged along the muddy roads, Maj. Gen. Matthew C. Butler's cavalry division operated to the east on the flank of Howard's Right Wing, while Maj. Gen. Joseph Wheeler's Cavalry Corps harassed the flanks of Slocum's Left Wing. A detachment of Wheeler's 5th Tennessee Cavalry, commanded by Lt. Col. John G. W. Montgomery, linked up with Taylor's 2nd Battalion Scouts. The rest of the 5th Tennessee operated with the bulk of Wheeler's command to the northwest.[34]

While Taylor and DeRosset resisted the Federal advance, Childs began evacuating the Arsenal's machinery and supplies. On March 2, Childs ran an advertisement in the *Fayetteville Observer*, ordering all military personnel and contractors to report to the Arsenal immediately to assist in the evacuation operation.[35] Childs intended to use the Western Railroad to relocate the Arsenal's heavy machinery from

Fayetteville to the Egypt Coal Mines in Chatham County. Unfortunately for Childs, he had only two locomotives, two coaches, three boxcars, thirteen flatcars, and twelve dirt cars available to him at Fayetteville. Childs also intended to move the remaining supplies to Greensboro by wagon.[36] Given the importance of this machinery to the Confederate war effort, Childs likely detached part of his under-manned force to escort the materiel to its destination, further depleting his command.

During late February and early March, Childs's battalion provided important intelligence on Federal movements and hindered Sherman's advance by destroying several key bridges. Montgomery and Taylor focused on the Lumber River bridges that would provide Sherman's men with the greatest freedom of movement towards Fayetteville. Recognizing their importance, the two Confederate officers deployed their men so as to provide early warning of the Federals' approach and to make the necessary preparations to destroy the bridges over the Lumber River.[37]

Taylor's 2nd Battalion Scouts and Montgomery's detachment established a picket line along the Lumber River, extending from Gilchrist's bridge in the north to McEachin's, McGist's, and Campbell's bridges to the south. Taylor and Montgomery prepared the bridges for immediate demolition. On March 7, Montgomery reported his location to Childs. "I shall cover the three bridges below Gilchrist's and destroy them if the enemy advance this way," he wrote. "When forced I shall fall back to Antioch Church and thence to Davis' Bridge [on Rockfish Creek], and communicate any information I obtain of importance."[38]

The forces of Taylor and Montgomery successfully destroyed Gilchrist's Bridge, delaying Sherman's XV Corps until a pontoon bridge could be laid. They failed, however, to destroy Campbell's Bridge, which could not be ignited in the heavy rains,[39] and the Confederate forces could only briefly delay the inexorable advance of Sherman's wings. By March 8, most of Sherman's army was closing in on Fayetteville, forcing Taylor and Montgomery to retire to prevent their commands from being cut off.[40] As the Arsenal Guards withdrew, they destroyed Davis's Bridge over Rockfish Creek.[41]

As Hardee approached Fayetteville, he asked Childs to detail scouts on the main routes into town: the McFarland, Bennettsville, and Gilchrist Roads. Sherman's lead elements constantly harassed Hardee's rear guard, and the beleaguered infantry commander called for help.[42] Confederate forces operating to the west of Fayetteville reported that Sherman was heading straight for the town. In addition, Schofield's force was moving into the interior of North Carolina from its bases at New Bern and Wilmington. Terry's northward advance from Wilmington threatened DeRosset's small blocking force on the river at Elizabethtown. On March 7, Bragg therefore directed DeRosset to "march direct to Fayetteville and report to General Johnston."[43]

To the east, Bragg concentrated his force near Kinston and challenged Schofield's column as it advanced out of New Bern. Reinforcing Bragg were units of Lt. Gen. Stephen D. Lee's Corps from the Army of Tennessee, led by a North Carolinian, Maj. Gen. D. H. Hill. Including Hoke's veteran division, Bragg commanded roughly 8,000 men. On March 8, Bragg attacked the advance units of Maj. Gen. Jacob D. Cox's XXIII Corps near Wise's Fork (or Wyse Fork), five miles east of Kinston. Bragg achieved initial success, forcing Cox to assume a defensive position. Over the next two days, Bragg unsuccessfully tried to dislodge Cox's infantryman. The action at Wise's Fork convinced Johnston to send additional units from the Army of Tennessee to reinforce Bragg, meaning that Hardee and Hampton would have to contend with Sherman's army with no reinforcements.[44]

As Bragg and Cox battled at Wise's Fork on March 8, Sherman established his headquarters at Laurel Hill Presbyterian Church, 30 miles from Fayetteville. Sherman decided that Slocum's Left Wing should have the honor of being the first Federal troops to enter

Fayetteville. His decision to give Slocum the honor originated from the latter's hurt feelings that had arisen when Howard had occupied Columbia.[45]

Hoping to establish communications with Terry's corps at Wilmington, Sherman dispatched several scouts from Laurel Hill disguised as Confederates, bearing messages for Terry. Cpl. James Pike of the 4th Ohio Cavalry, who served with Capt. Theodore F. Northrop's scout contingent of Kilpatrick's cavalry division, carried a dispatch for Wilmington. Pike concealed the document inside a plug of tobacco so that he could chew it up if he was captured. Although he was not the first scout from Sherman's army to reach Wilmington, Pike required the assistance of local Negroes to do so. Pike made his way through the Confederate defenses at Elizabethtown, where he observed the engineering efforts to disrupt river traffic to Fayetteville. "At [Elizabethtown] was an immense raft, which the rebels deemed sufficient to check the progress of the boats," Pike recalled. "At some points, they had the river nearly blocked up by trees, which they had chopped into it." After several trying days, Pike completed his mission and delivered Sherman's message to Terry at Wilmington.[46]

On March 9, Hardee's footsore and hungry infantry approached Fayetteville. With Sherman's lead elements following closely behind, the Confederate rear guard came into increased contact with the pursuing Union forces. Capt. Thomas Huguenin of the 1st South Carolina Artillery, a hero of Fort Sumter and the actions around Charleston, recalled his first experience as an infantryman on the outskirts of Fayetteville. "The enemy pressed very closely upon us," he wrote, "We had hardly halted before I received orders to take a portion of my regiment back, drive off the enemy pickets and take possession of a small stream." Huguenin continued. "I did so and after the exchange of a few shots drove the enemy across the stream and took possession."[47]

Anticipating Hardee's arrival, Capt. J. M. McGowan, the Fayetteville post quartermaster, placed an advertisement in the

Fayetteville Recorder, calling upon local farmers to help out because "the army of Hardee is in want of food. It is the army to which we have to look for protection and safety." The *Fayetteville Recorder* also announced a March 7 meeting of the town ladies to be held at the Fayetteville Hotel to discuss important business regarding the hospitals. Confederate General Hospital No. 6 was operated in the former Young Ladies' Seminary on Hay Street, and the hospital staff received instructions to prepare accommodations for an additional 400 patients.[48]

During the next several days, Fayetteville residents watched Hardee's infantry and Hampton's cavalry arrive. On March 10, Hampton unleashed a savage dawn surprise attack on Kilpatrick's sleeping and unguarded camp at Monroe's Crossroads, fourteen miles from Fayetteville.[49] Hampton's horse soldiers enjoyed initial success, but Kilpatrick's troopers rallied and eventually drove the Southerners from their camp. Hampton then broke off the engagement and retired. The surprise attack on Kilpatrick's camp nevertheless stopped Kilpatrick's command dead in its tracks for an entire day, thus clearing the roads and permitting Hardee's infantry to win the race for Fayetteville. Hardee would now control the critical Clarendon Bridge over the Cape Fear River at Fayetteville, enabling him to withdraw his entire force to safety on the far bank of the river and then burn the bridge behind him.[50]

Hardee's command began moving into Fayetteville on the afternoon of March 9. A formation of "galvanized" Yankees preceded the advance of Hardee's Confederates. These former prisoners of war had opted to serve in the ranks of the Confederate army as a means of escaping the squalor of Southern prisons. Armed with axes, picks, and spades, these men moved in front of the regular formations to repair and build roads for the Army's movement.[51] Hardee's footsore infantry followed just behind, followed by Hampton's horse soldiers, weary from their encounter with Kilpatrick's cavalry.

The townspeople anxiously awaited the arrival of the Confederate defenders. "Only a few detachments and some officers with their staffs came in the first day and the greater part of the night," recalled schoolgirl Josephine Bryan. "The defenders of Charleston poured through the place, making an incessant moving panorama of men, horses, cannons, and wagons."[52] Young Josephine, who was staying in her aunt's home on Haymount Hill, recalled that the columns of infantry looked "so worn and ragged."[53] The ladies of Fayetteville opened their homes to Hardee's tatterdemalion infantry-men, providing cooked meals and sewing jobs. Pvt. Anthony W. Riecke, a South Carolina artilleryman, recorded the warm welcome afforded by the ladies of Fayetteville. "From nearly every house the ladies came out, and offered us something to eat according to what was in their power to give, even if it only was corn bread with salt strewn on it was received as thankfully as something better, our appetites were too good to allow our stomachs to be choosers in those days." Riecke and his comrades in arms regretted "that we could not stay and protect them against Sherman's visit."[54]

H. W. Graber, a member of Terry's Texas Rangers, recalled that the "army passed through Fayetteville very rapidly."[55] Their brief stay in Fayetteville nevertheless afforded some units in Hardee's Corps the opportunity to re-supply themselves with new arms and ammunition from the Arsenal. Arthur Ford of the 18th South Carolina Battalion recalled that many of the men in his unit were issued new Enfield rifles and ammunition to replace some of the ineffective old Belgian rifles they carried out of Charleston. Hardee also received reinforcements during his respite in Fayetteville. After finally being relieved from their hazardous position at Elizabethtown, DeRosset's command arrived and was attached to Brig. Gen. Stephen Elliott's Brigade of South Carolinians in Brig. Gen. William B. Taliaferro's division.[56]

Fayetteville also afforded Hardee his first opportunity to consult with Johnston since the latter had assumed command of the Confederate forces in North Carolina. They met at Johnston's headquarters in the

Fayetteville Hotel on Hay Street. Johnston informed Hardee that he did not intend to defend Fayetteville from Sherman's converging wings. The earlier commitment of Army of Tennessee forces to Bragg at Kinston did not leave him sufficient strength to challenge Sherman's advance. If Hardee tried to defend Fayetteville against a numerically superior enemy force capable of maneuvering along a wide front, he would place the Confederate forces in the precarious situation of fighting with their backs against the Cape Fear River. Johnston realized that his best chance to hinder Sherman's advance was to attack an isolated element of his army without the possibility of support from the remainder. In short, Johnston would have to defeat Sherman in detail if he hoped to have any chance of success. The first weeks of March presented no such opportunity. Instead, the opportunity would have to materialize somewhere east of the Cape Fear River.

Before Sherman reached Fayetteville, Johnston decided to withdraw Hardee's infantry and Hampton's cavalry to the east bank of the Cape Fear River and to burn the bridge. Sherman would have to bring up pontoons to cross the Cape Fear, which ran fast and deep at Fayetteville. The resulting delay in Sherman's advance would buy precious time for the Confederates to locate and defend a stronger position. Before departing for Raleigh, Johnston instructed Hardee to hold Fayetteville for as long as possible to permit the arrival of additional reinforcements from the Army of Tennessee.[57]

By March 10, Hardee could no longer remain at Fayetteville. Lead elements of Sherman's army were rapidly approaching from multiple directions, and Sherman's foragers were pressing Hardee's skirmishers on the outskirts of town. Early that morning, Johnston informed Lee that Sherman's lead elements were within seven miles of Fayetteville and that Hardee would begin evacuating the city and crossing the Cape Fear that evening. Johnston also advised Hardee to keep his reserve artillery within supporting distance, so that he could bring it into action if necessary, and also to do what he could "to impede the enemy, with Hampton's help."[58]

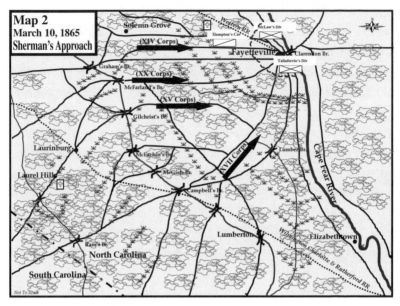

Wade Sokolosky

Hardee complied with Johnston's orders, directed the evacuation of Fayetteville, and began crossing the Cape Fear that evening. His artillery and wagon trains went first, followed by McLaws's and Taliaferro's divisions, which moved out at 8:00. The Confederates proceeded north along the Fayetteville-Raleigh Road, heading for Averasboro. In order to cover the evacuation of the infantry and the military hardware from the Arsenal, Hardee ordered Hampton's cavalry to remain at Fayetteville until they were compelled to retire. Once pressed by the Federals, Hampton would withdraw his command across the Cape Fear River and destroy the Clarendon Bridge.

In spite of Hardee's efforts to evacuate the town, H. W. Graber of Terry's Texas Rangers found time to visit a local shopkeeper near the Market House. Graber wanted to trade a $10 gold piece for some Confederate money. As the Texan and the storeowner haggled, shots rang out in a nearby street. The Federals had arrived, and the wise store keeper quickly counted out fifteen hundreds dollars of Confederate money, considerably more than Graber's asking price of two hundred. The Texan agreed to the trade, quickly mounted his horse, and galloped across the Clarendon Bridge before it was set ablaze.[59]

Hardee had formulated a sound plan for the evacuation of Fayetteville. But as Clausewitz had noted, military plans have a way of unraveling once they are implemented and this case was no exception. In the early hours of March 11, Childs's last trainload of Arsenal machinery departed for the Egypt Coal Mine. The remaining members of the Arsenal garrison joined Hardee's force as it withdrew across the river.[60] After Childs bade farewell to his family, he secured the Arsenal's flag, which had been fashioned from the old Stars and Stripes by a group of Fayetteville ladies, in order to prevent it from falling into Federal hands.[61]

With Hardee's departure, only Hampton's cavalry and a few infantry stragglers remained at Fayetteville. As the cavalrymen picketed the primary routes into the town, Hampton and his subordinate commanders and staff awoke from a much-needed night's rest in the

General Johnston and General Hardee Meet
Drawing by Col. Darrell L. Combs, USMC (Ret.)

Arsenal Battalion Departing the Post
Drawing by Col. Darrell L. Combs, USMC (Ret.)

Fayetteville Hotel and the residences of generous locals. Hampton and his trusted scout, Hugh H. Scott, had just finished eating their breakfast at the hotel, and had stepped unto the front porch when several shots rang out. They spotted Confederate cavalry dashing through the streets, closely pursued by Union horsemen. The Federals had arrived.[62]

Sherman had ordered his Left Wing commander, Maj. Gen. Henry W. Slocum, "to do all that is possible to secure the [Clarendon] bridge across the Cape Fear River."[63] On March 11, Bvt. Maj. Gen. Absalom Baird's XIV Corps division led Slocum's advance. Baird had bivouacked about ten miles from Fayetteville, and he began the march before sunrise. Almost immediately, his lead regiment encountered Confederate skirmishers, who were determined to contest his advance. As the morning hours passed, Baird's division slowly pushed on to the outskirts of Fayetteville, where a "battle line appeared across the road, their color flaunting in the breeze." The scene reminded George W.

Pepper, an Ohio chaplain in Baird's division, of an incident in the Battle of Atlanta, when Gen. John B. Hood launched a fierce attack against unsuspecting Federals. Fortunately for Baird's men, the Confederate battle line defending Fayetteville chose to withdraw rather than attack. Still, the delay of Baird's division created an opportunity for elements of the Right Wing to reach Fayetteville first.[64]

Capt. William H. Duncan of the 15th Illinois Cavalry rode at the head of Howard's scout company, which consisted of fifty mounted infantrymen. They were joined by foragers eager for plunder.[65] As Duncan approached Fayetteville, he divided his small force and sent it on two parallel roads. Duncan, and a dozen of his men approached to within three miles of Fayetteville, where they surprised the Confederate picket line, which was posted behind light earthworks. The startled Confederates offered no resistance and permitted Duncan and his men to proceed unmolested toward Fayetteville, where one half would attempt to seize the Clarendon Bridge, while the other half reconnoitered the town.[66]

Alerted to the Federals' arrival, Hampton rallied several cavalrymen, some scouts, and members of his staff, and attacked Duncan's advance. During the fight, Duncan's scout element soon became disorganized and scattered in the streets and alleys of Fayetteville. Hampton's aggressive leadership bought time for the startled Confederates to rally, and they compelled Duncan's force to beat a hasty retreat. The Federals left behind several killed and wounded, as well as a number of prisoners, including Captain Duncan. Duncan escaped several days later with the aid of some local slaves, who guided him safely back to Federal lines.[67]

Duncan's detachment hastily withdrew to the protection of the advancing Federal infantry, consisting of Bvt. Maj. Gen. Giles A. Smith's division of the XVII Corps. After hearing reports from Duncan's men, Smith immediately dispatched an additional force of 200 men under the command of Lt. Col. Jeff J. Hibbets. Smith instructed Hibbets "to take the city if possible, and guard it" until the

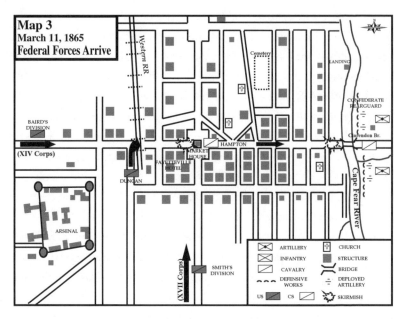

Wade Sokolosky

rest of the Right Wing could arrive. As the blue-clad infantryman poured into the town, Hibbets learned that the Clarendon Bridge had not yet been destroyed. Hoping to seize it intact, he led his mounted infantry toward the river. On the way they met Hampton's rear guard, supported by artillery near the Market House. General Wheeler had also deployed artillery and dismounted horse soldiers on the far bank of the Cape Fear to cover the withdrawal of Hampton's rear guard. Hibbets skirmished with Hampton's rear guard while the Confederate horsemen withdrew across the river under the cover of friendly artillery and small arms fire.[68] Hampton then set fire to the Clarendon Bridge, denying it to the Federals.

Captain Huguenin and a portion of his company of the 1st South Carolina Artillery participated in the final actions in Fayetteville. As his unit crossed the bridge, Huguenin was "ordered to take four companies and hold the bridge until all the infantry and artillery had passed," and until they were relieved by the cavalry's rear guard. With flames licking at the bridge, Hampton's last remaining horsemen safely withdrew. Hampton then gave Huguenin permission to withdraw his small command, and the last Confederate troops evacuated Fayetteville.[69]

The Left Wing was denied the honor of occupying Fayetteville first, as Sherman had ordered. The unexpected entry of the Right Wing's advance units enabled one of Howard's staff officers, Lt. Col. William E. Strong, to receive the formal surrender of Fayetteville from Mayor Archibald McLean. Just a few minutes after the ceremony, Baird's men reached the center of town. Obeying Sherman's original order, Howard quickly relinquished the town to Slocum.[70]

While the Clarendon Bridge blazed, several of Slocum's staff officers ordered a group of foragers to save the bridge. The group "struggled manfully, with washtubs full of water" to extinguish the fire, but the bridge could not be saved. The opposing forces traded pot-shots from across the river until Hampton withdrew his rear guard from the river bank.[71]

Baird's division assumed the duty of provost guard and immediately cleared the streets of Union stragglers in an effort to restore order. The remaining elements of Sherman's army established their camp sites on the outskirts of Fayetteville while they awaited the construction of pontoon bridges across the Cape Fear River. The day so long dreaded by the citizens of Fayetteville had finally arrived. They had been left to the tender mercies of William T. Sherman and his army.[72]

44

Painting of the Fayetteville Arsenal for the Destruction by Sherman's Troops
Painted by Miss Nena Morrow. Courtesy of North Carolina Museum of History

Chapter 3

"[W]e have just stopped here to take breath and destroy a fine arsenal"

Maj. Henry Hitchcock to his wife
March 14, 1865

Amid the excitement caused by the arrival of the Federals, a group of Fayetteville women cared for the wounded and dying brought in from both the earlier fighting at Wilmington and the more recent combat at Monroe's Crossroads. These casualties overwhelmed Confederate General Hospital No. 6 and required the establishment of temporary hospitals in several locations around the town.[1]

Anne K. Kyle, the assistant matron at General Hospital No. 6, volunteered her time to help deal with her personal anguish: her husband, a Confederate officer, was a prisoner of war at Fort Pulaski. Though a frail woman who needed crutches to walk, she possessed the "indomitable spirit of a lion." The night before Sherman captured Fayetteville, the surgeon sent for her to assist with the large number of wounded men. She described the scene at the hospital as "horrible" and one she "shall never forget."[2]

As Mrs. Kyle and other local ladies tended to the wounded, Sherman's men announced their arrival by displaying the United States flag at several prominent locations in town, including the Old Market House and in front of the Fayetteville Hotel.[3] The reappearance of the Stars and Stripes brought feelings of joy to those loyal Unionists who had patiently awaited Sherman's arrival. At the same time, horror gripped the town's secessionists, to whom Fayetteville looked like it was being "overrun with blue coats." The fate of the town's residents lay in the hands of one man—Sherman.

Sherman arrived in Fayetteville about noon on March 11 and established his headquarters on the grounds of the former United States Arsenal. Fayetteville residents immediately visited Sherman to proclaim their loyalty to the Union or to seek protection for their personal property. In a twist of fate, a former Regular Army friend, Sgt. Thomas Stevens, who had served in Childs's Battalion, greeted Sherman upon his arrival at the Arsenal. Sherman smiled briefly when he first spotted his old comrade, but his expression quickly turned to disgust. Sherman dismissed Stevens as a traitor to the United States, but he also assured his former friend that his home would be spared. Sherman proved true to his word—Stevens's home on the Arsenal grounds was the only structure left standing.[4]

Childs's mother, accompanied by his sister, Mrs. W. W. Anderson, whose husband was a Confederate surgeon serving in Virginia, also called upon Sherman. Childs's family hoped to play on Sherman's sympathy because he had served under Childs's father, Bvt. Brig. Gen. Thomas Childs, early in his army career. Sherman showed no pity, but instead mortified the women by expressing his displeasure at not capturing the traitorous Arsenal commander.[5]

Sherman intended to accomplish four tasks during his occupation of Fayetteville. First, the Arsenal had to be destroyed. Second, because of the burning of the Clarendon Bridge his engineers had to lay pontoon bridges across the Cape Fear River. Third, his army required refitting, many of his men needed new uniforms and shoes, and there were widespread shortages of coffee and hard bread. Fourth, the evacuation of the Federal wounded and the thousands of displaced civilians who had joined his force during the preceding weeks had to be completed before the army could move again. The many extra mouths to feed had become a burden on an army that had difficulty feeding itself.

While Sherman and his headquarters staff busied themselves with a backlog of paperwork, the army's veterans enjoyed a well-deserved rest. The previous weeks of difficult campaigning had been worsened by rain, mud, and cold weather. Lt. Col. Alexander McClurg described the army's condition upon its arrival at Fayetteville as shabby, ragged and tattered: "Here a Confederate coat, and there a Confederate hat, did duty on a Federal back or head."[6] Despite the army's ragged appearance, morale remained high, and the soldiers' confidence in Sherman had only increased.

The next morning, a shrill whistle shattered the stillness of "the Sabbath morning and sent a thrill of gladness through the army which knew well its meaning." It was the tug *Davidson*, announcing its arrival from Wilmington. The *Davidson* carried the first news from the North since the army had departed Savannah. During the next few days, other vessels made round trips between Fayetteville and Wilmington, carrying newspapers, dispatches, and critical supplies to the army. To the men in the ranks, opening this line of communication with the coast enabled them to send mail to loved ones back home for the first time in more than a month.[7]

Maj. Henry Hitchcock, a member of Sherman's staff, wrote to his wife, "I continue in perfect health and my usual good spirits—only anxious when I think of you." Major Hitchcock told his wife that the army was about "to begin the last stage of this march" and that his time in Fayetteville would be brief. "We have just stopped here to take breath and destroy a fine arsenal which Uncle Sam built and the rebels stole but will never steal nor use again." [8]

Lt. Samuel Storrow, a XX Corps staff officer, penned a few words to his parents. His letter captured the difficulties encountered by the army since the start of the campaign. Lieutenant Storrow wrote, "this campaign has been harder in every respect than the last…this Army is a cheap thing for the Government; it boards itself. We haven't had 5 days rations issued, since we started. Bumming has been reduced to a science." Sadly, this letter proved to be Storrow's last. He fell mortally wounded four days later at the Battle of Averasboro.[9]

Tug "Davidson"
Harper's Pictorial History of the Civil War

For some Union soldiers, this was their first opportunity to write loved ones since their release from Confederate prisons. Since the capture of Columbia, the Federal columns had included many former prisoners of war. One of those former prisoners, Capt. Joseph Fiske, wrote his parents that he was "free and well" and "will come home soon as possible." At Fayetteville, Fiske and many of his fellow ex-prisoners boarded river vessels bound for Wilmington.[10]

Sherman's chief engineer, Col. Orlando M. Poe, supervised the destruction of the Confederate Arsenal, situated on Haymount, which overlooked the rest of Fayetteville and the Cape Fear River to the east. Many Southerners and visitors to the area during the time considered the Arsenal "one of the loveliest spots anywhere in the South." The Arsenal grounds were enclosed by a large wall with iron railings. "Conspicuous octagonal high brick and stone towers" stood at each corner of the Arsenal. Inside the grounds stood neat rows of quarters for the officers and enlisted men, administrative offices, storehouses for arms and ammunition, and gun and carriage shops. The rifle factory, equipped with machinery captured at Harpers Ferry, stood near the rear of the Arsenal, and the two brick powder magazines were located about 100 yards outside the Arsenal walls. Most of the Arsenal's structures were constructed of stone and presented a formidable challenge to the destructive talents of the 1st Michigan Engineers and Mechanics.[11]

The demolition work began early on the morning of March 12 and continued for two days, leaving the Arsenal little more than a rubble pile. To knock down the walls, the engineers built several battering rams by suspending bars of railroad iron from 20 foot-long timbers joined in the shape of an "X." Once the walls were sufficiently weakened, the roof collapsed. The Federals had a festive time smashing the walls, a band saluted each crash, and the men cheered every act of demolition. Once the wrecking operations were complete, the rubble was fired to complete the destruction.[12]

Despite the festive atmosphere, the demolition work proved hazardous to the men involved: several were killed or severely injured. Capt. John B. Van Vliet, a topographical engineer in the XX Corps, was critically injured when a building doorway collapsed on him. His injuries required that he be evacuated to Wilmington.[13]

The residents who witnessed the Arsenal's destruction were awestruck. Mrs. John B. Anderson vividly recalled the sight of the "angry flames, leaping from the numerous piles of debris, roared and crackled, creating terrific heat; great billows of black smoke darkened the heavens." Another observer thought the whole affair resembled an artillery duel, with screaming shells exploding in the air.[14]

As the Michigan men destroyed the Arsenal, Baird's division destroyed everything else of use to the Confederate war effort. Baird's men destroyed two iron foundries, four cotton mills, and the offices of the town's three newspapers, the *Observer,* the *North Carolina Presbyterian,* and the *Daily Telegraph.*[15] E. J. Hale, Jr., the son of the editor of the *Fayetteville Observer,* recalled how the burning mills pro-

Union Engineers' Ram Destroying the Arsenal
Drawing by Col. Darrell L. Combs, USMC (Ret.)

vided a pleasant spectacle for Slocum and his officers, who watched the dancing flames from the veranda of the hotel and "hobnobbed over wines" stolen from the local cellars.[16]

The private residences of Fayetteville were not spared from acts of vandalism and theft. Many citizens remained behind locked doors, hoping for the best. Samuel Merrill of the 70th Indiana Volunteer Infantry remembered that several soldiers from his regiment entered a private residence where the lady of the house had prepared a fine meal of turkey, sweet potatoes, and biscuits, supposedly for Confederate Maj. Gen. Joseph Wheeler and his staff. The reluctant hostess met them with cries of "get out of here or I'll scald you." The tip of a bayonet dissuaded her from using the hot water as a weapon, but it did not stem her torrent of abuse. The soldiers quickly "scooped up the meal into a dishpan, wrapped it in a tablecloth to keep it warm and disappeared."[17]

Such acts of thievery occurred throughout Fayetteville, but the "plundering of private property was done, for the most part," noted historian John G. Barrett, "before Baird took command of the city."[18] Once order was restored, Union soldiers performed acts of kindness and compassion. Although guards were posted at many residences, they were seldom received with gratitude. According to one soldier, "Union inhabitants were a minority, compared to the arch-traitors of the town, where faces showed the rebel spirit within."[19]

Meanwhile, the 58th Indiana Pontoniers of the Left Wing, and the 1st Missouri Engineers of the Right Wing, laid two pontoon bridges across the Cape Fear River.[20] By mid-afternoon on March 12, the 58th Indiana had constructed a pontoon bridge of seventeen boats, spanning 400 feet across the Cape Fear, just below the ruins of the Clarendon Bridge. The Right Wing's crossing site stood opposite the Cade Plantation, several miles downstream from the Clarendon Bridge. In his post-campaign report, Howard described the difficulties encountered by the 1st Missouri Engineers, observing that "[t]he banks of the river are very high and exceedingly abrupt." After the bridge's completion, the water level of the river dropped 5 or 6 feet, "so that it was with the greatest of difficulty that wagons could be gotten over."[21]

Despite these difficulties, both bridges were ready by March 13, demonstrating the extraordinary ability of Sherman's engineers to overcome enormous obstacles in a timely and efficient manner. Confederate Maj. Gen. Lafayette McLaws received reports of the rapid crossing by the Federals and considered it

Maj. Gen. Lafayette McLaws
Library of Congress

impossible, prompting him to note in his daily journal that "the enemy were reported as crossing the river at various points during the day, but the accounts were surely much exaggerated."[22]

Before crossing the Cape Fear River, Sherman reviewed his troops, watching as they passed through Fayetteville en route to the pontoon bridges. Sgt. Rice C. Bull of the 123rd New York Infantry remembered the comical notion of a review, considering the ragged condition of their uniforms. "Orders were issued to clean up as well we could," Bull wrote in his diary, "but about all we could do was to scrape the mud off our uniforms."[23]

The river crossings commenced on the morning of March 13, and continued throughout the night and into the next day. Lt. J. M. Branum of the 98th Ohio Infantry remembered that they "marched through the streets in style, bands playing, and in the moonlight the spectacle was fine." Soaring rocket flares seized from the Arsenal only made the scene even more spectacular. Slocum's Left Wing crossed the river and marched several miles north along the Fayetteville-Raleigh Road before camping, while Howard's Right Wing crossed and then camped near the Cade Plantation.[24]

The Federals crossed unmolested and established a toehold on the far bank of the Cape Fear River. However, the apparent inactivity on the part of Southerners soon changed. The Federals encountered Hampton's cavalry soon after crossing the river. The commander of the 129th Illinois Infantry, Lt. Col. T. H. Flynn, reported that upon crossing the Cape Fear River, his foragers advanced two miles and made contact with the enemy. A running skirmish continued for another two more miles before the foragers captured a mill.[25]

In accordance with Johnston's wishes, Hampton's cavalry watched the Federals closely in order to determine Sherman's next move. Wheeler positioned his force on the Fayetteville-Raleigh Road and several other northbound roads, then established his headquarters near the Widow Denning's house. In addition to posting pickets, Wheeler deployed scouts at several ferry sites along the Cape Fear River to warn of any major Federal crossings. To the east, Butler deployed his cavalry division at the main crossings of the South River, thus covering the routes to Clinton and Goldsboro.[26]

On March 11, Johnston instructed Bragg to remain at Goldsboro, still unsure whether Sherman would move on Goldsboro or Raleigh. As previously noted, Bragg had engaged Cox's Federal troops at Kinston on March 8–10. Johnston wrote Hardee that "it may be Sherman's design to unite with that force [Cox] and for that object to move toward Goldsborough instead of Raleigh."[27] Johnston therefore wanted to position his infantry so that it could cover either Raleigh or Goldsboro. He instructed Hardee to "keep as near the river as you can without compromising yourself until Sherman's course is developed." Johnston stressed the need to remain flexible in reacting to Sherman's movement. He determined that Sherman "will either move toward Raleigh or Goldsborough...If he takes the first course, General Bragg's troops will be brought to yours; if the second, yours to his."[28]

Hardee led his command north along the Fayetteville-Raleigh Road toward Averasboro, thus staying close to the Cape Fear River as ordered. Hampton's cavalry covered Hardee's retreat by maintaining contact with Sherman's army along the routes north of Fayetteville. Captain Huguenin of the 1st South Carolina Regulars remembered the march toward Averasboro as difficult, noting that his "men were very tired and a long way behind." They had covered only a few miles when he decided to rest them for the night. "It was a cheerless place, the low ground was partly covered with rainwater, and we had to pick out spots to lie down," he recalled. "With nothing to eat we threw ourselves upon the wet ground and exhausted as we were fell asleep almost instantly."[29]

Poor roads hindered Hardee's progress for the next few days. His objective was Smithville, named after the 8,000 acre plantation of the Smith families who dotted the area, on the Fayetteville-Raleigh Road about twenty miles north of Fayetteville. The nearest town was Averasboro, four miles to the north. Smithville provided

Washington Artillery Departing Fayetteville
Anthony Riecke, Courtesy of Charles and Richard Townsend

an excellent location for Hardee to establish his defensive line, because the South and Cape Fear Rivers close near this natural choke point, thus mitigating Sherman's numerical advantage. Furthermore, regardless of whether Sherman's objective was Raleigh or Goldsboro, the Left Wing would have to pass through Smithville. By placing his corps at Smithville, Hardee blocked the critical Goldsboro road junction.[30]

Sherman delayed his advance for a few more days, hoping to receive badly needed supplies from Wilmington. Meanwhile, Slocum ordered a reconnaissance in force along both the Raleigh and Goldsboro roads for March 14.[31] Before dawn, Bvt. Brig. Gen. William Cogswell's XX Corps brigade moved out along the Fayetteville-Raleigh Road to a point where it split, one road continuing north to Raleigh and the other east toward the Black River.

When he arrived at the split, Cogswell divided his brigade and advanced up both roads. Cogswell had specific instructions to drive the enemy, but only if he could do so without becoming heavily engaged. Three regiments of Federal infantry commanded by Lt. Col. Philo B. Buckingham of the 20th Connecticut Infantry moved north along the Fayetteville-Raleigh Road and skirmished with elements of Wheeler's cavalry until they reached Silver Run Creek, where the Federals found a brigade of dismounted cavalry behind works bristling with artillery. Earlier in the day, Hampton had relieved a brigade of Confederate infantry at this position, and he now stood ready to oppose the advancing Federals. For several hours, the two forces skirmished before Buckingham broke off the engagement and withdrew.[32]

To the east, a second Federal reconnaissance force, consisting of four regiments commanded by Lt. Col. Samuel H. Hurst of the 73rd Ohio Infantry, found Butler's cavalry division picketing the road leading to the South River. The Federals drove Butler's troopers across the river but soon encountered stiff resistance, including an artillery battery. After suffering several casualties, the Federals broke off the fight and withdrew.[33] As daylight waned, the Federals retired toward Fayetteville, having accomplished their mission. The determined resistance of Wheeler's and Butler's men fueled Federal apprehension that rough work lay ahead.

On March 14, while Cogswell conducted his reconnaissance, Sherman transferred his headquarters from the Arsenal grounds. "I am across the Cape Fear River with nearly all my Army," Sherman wrote to Grant. "I shall...draw out ten miles and begin my maneuvers for the possession of Goldsboro."[34] Sherman's plan called for Kilpatrick's cavalry, followed by Slocum's infantry, to move north along the Fayetteville-Raleigh Road to deceive Johnston into thinking that Raleigh was the Federals' objective. Howard's Right Wing would move directly toward Goldsboro and would support Slocum if necessary.[35]

That same day, the vessel *Howard* arrived from Wilmington laden with supplies. The army's desperate need for clothing, shoes, and coffee had prompted Sherman to order Terry in Wilmington "to send me all the shoes, stockings, drawers, sugar, coffee, and flour you can spare." To the despair of Sherman's quartermasters, the *Howard's* cargo contained only sugar, coffee and oats. During the next several days, vessels from Wilmington brought 3,800 pairs of shoes and 2,400 pairs of pants–hardly enough to refit an army of more than 60,000.[36]

If the quartermasters at Wilmington failed to meet Sherman's needs, his soldiers once again demonstrated their mastery of making do, turning up enough food and clothing to suffice. Sgt. Rice Bull of the 123rd New York fondly remembered the bounty of hams and bacon brought in by the regiment's foragers. A brigade of the XIV Corps seized a wagonload of Richmond tobacco and a sizeable amount of corn meal and meat. Because their uniforms were in such a wretched state, many men wore articles of civilian clothing or Confederate uniforms. Though the officers were, by and large, well dressed, the men "looked more like Falstaff's ragged regiment than soldiers of the United States."[37]

One task remained for Sherman to ensure his army freedom of movement. He had to disencumber his army of the thousands of refugees who had joined his columns since leaving Savannah. Most of these were former slaves, but there were also many white civilians.[38] In addition, wounded or unfit men (including many former prisoners of war) were sent to Wilmington. Captain Van Vliet, who had been injured at the Arsenal several days earlier, was transported down river.

Van Vliet's assistant, Pvt. William F. Goodhue, remained at the captain's side throughout his journey aboard the steamer *Lady Lang*. Private Goodhue described the journey and the conditions aboard the *Lady Lang* in his journal. He also noted the frustration of Sherman's quartermasters over the shipment of oats to the army. "On the lower deck had been stored with oats, the floor six inches deep with them, the sick were laid out in rows on this deck."[39] He was annoyed that the *Lady Lang* transported only one hundred wounded, while refugees filled the remaining space. In his mind, the load of oats meant that one hundred wounded would have to make the overland trip to Wilmington. On the *Lady Lang*, Captain Van Vliet and the other wounded had to lie in the damp, smelly lower deck of the vessel while the refugees enjoyed far more pleasant quarters. "This is an instance where our uniform is a disgrace to us," Goodhue wrote. "I felt my uniform was my bondage of serfdom."[40]

Most refugees traveled overland in a column commanded by Maj. John S. Windsor of the 116th Illinois Infantry. The escort consisted of men eligible for discharge from the army, including the 56th Illinois Infantry, which had 205 officers and men.[41] Their joy at the prospect of returning home soon turned to tragedy. Upon reaching Wilmington, the men boarded the army steamer *General Lyons*, which was bound for New York with 550 liberated prisoners, discharged soldiers, and civilian refugees. On April 12, in a tragic twist of fate, the vessel caught fire in rough seas and sank off Cape Hatteras, the Graveyard of the Atlantic. Only five men of the 56th Illinois survived. The impact of this loss no doubt fell hard on several Illinois communities, for Civil War-era companies typically consisted of men from the same town or county.[42]

The tragedy of the *General Lyons* affected not only the Federals, it also saddened a Confederate officer serving in Childs's Arsenal Battalion: the wife, daughter, and sister of Lt. Charles Banks were among those who went down with the *General Lyons*. Banks's family had been traveling north to stay with relatives in New York.[43] His family had survived the vicissitudes of the long, cruel war, only to meet their fate at sea.

Nearly 10,000 refugees traveled from Fayetteville to Wilmington during March 1865. The largest column consisted of 6,000 refugees, and it arrived on March 21. Sherman had eliminated his refugee problem by passing it on to the Union occupation forces at Wilmington. The thousands of additional mouths to feed and care for severely strained an already over-taxed Union commissary and medical system.[44]

With the army finally across the Cape Fear and free of the refugees, Sherman gave the order to move forward on March 15. The army retained its two-wing formation but traveled in a manner that afforded mutual support. Kilpatrick's cavalry marched before dawn, preceding Slocum's wing, which had four unencumbered divisions prepared for battle. Slocum's remaining two divisions escorted his nonessential wagons along a direct route to Goldsboro behind Howard's wing. In accordance with Sherman's plan, Howard kept five divisions in light marching order to support Slocum, if necessary. Sherman's caution resulted from his respect for Johnston's ability to strike an isolated column of the Union army.[45]

The day was stormy, with bright lightning and loud claps of thunder, the heavy rains rendering the roads almost impassable. A lightning bolt killed one man and severely injured two others of the 73rd Ohio Infantry—an ominous sign of things to come. The Union soldiers would soon have far more to deal with than terrible weather: to the north lay Hardee's infantry, stoutly entrenched astride the Fayetteville-Raleigh Road.[46]

Chapter 4 | *"We must not lose time for Joe Johnston to concentrate ..."*

Maj. Gen. William T. Sherman

THE DEPLOYMENT OF HARDEE'S CORPS; MARCH 15, 1865

On March 15, Sherman again set his army in motion, with Goldsboro as its next objective. To date, Sherman had enjoyed a relatively uneventful campaign. The Confederates had offered minimal resistance to his advance. However, Sherman anticipated a fight in the near future; he assumed that Johnston would contest his advance to prevent a link-up with Schofield. Sherman correctly expected the attack to fall upon Slocum's wing, since it was nearer to Johnston's army than Howard's wing.

Kilpatrick's cavalry moved north on the Fayetteville-Raleigh Road, also known as the Stage Road, leading Slocum's wing. Slocum would feint north toward Raleigh as far as Averasboro before turning east toward Goldsboro. Meanwhile, Howard's wing would march north on the Goldsboro Road. The two wings would ultimately converge on Goldsboro from two directions. Sherman planned to unite the two wings of his army at Goldsboro, where his command would also merge with Schofield's army before continuing on to Virginia.

As the Federals marched north on the Fayetteville-Raleigh Road, they passed the abandoned barricades and entrenchments used by Hampton's cavalry and Rhett's infantry on the north side of Silver

59

Run Creek. For Pvt. William Grunert of the 129th Illinois, passing the scene of the previous day's fights convinced him "that the enemy was close in our front, and did not feel like giving way."[1]

On the morning of March 15, the XX Corps paused and permitted Kilpatrick's cavalry to take the lead. Maj. Robert Morris McDowell, Slocum's chief engineer and cartographer, remembered that the rains set in once again, adding to the misery of the marching soldiers. By noon, the rear of Kilpatrick's cavalry had passed the lead elements of the XX Corps near Silver Run Creek.[2]

Before his departure from Fayetteville, Johnston gave Hardee discretionary orders, "Do what you can to impede enemy, with Hampton's help." To oppose Sherman's advance Old Reliable decided to make a stand.[3] In a postwar memorandum, Hardee claimed that he fought at Averasboro to "ascertain the strength and destination of the forces in his front," in compliance with Johnston's orders of March 10. At some point in their conversation (whether documented or not), Johnston and Hardee agreed that Hardee's Corps would stand and fight at Averasboro. This would accomplish two vital goals: Hardee would delay Sherman's advance, thereby permitting Johnston to concentrate his forces; the selection of Averasboro would create an opportunity for Hardee to fight one of Sherman's isolated wings.[4] Maj. Gen. Lafayette McLaws, who commanded one of Hardee's divisions, was surprised by Hardee's decision to fight at Averasboro. "I did not select any position for my command, did not know the status of affairs," asserted McLaws. "Never thought about making a stand at Averasboro."[5] With Confederate options rapidly diminishing, Hardee's decision to stand and fight at Averasboro was a good one, and his subordinates did their part by constructing a strong defensive position to resist Sherman's advance.

The fragile state of Hardee's command is often overlooked. Hardee was deeply concerned with the condition of his little army; desertions and low morale were taking their toll and sapping the strength of his corps.[6] General Johnston also had concerns about Hardee's command. In a dispatch to Gen. Robert E. Lee, Johnston

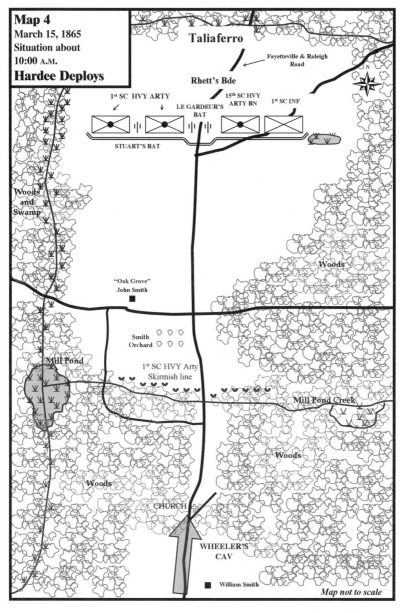

Map 4
March 15, 1865
Situation about
10:00 A.M.
Hardee Deploys

Taliaferro

Fayetteville & Raleigh
Road

N

Rhett's Bde

1st SC HVY ARTY

15th SC HVY
ARTY BN

1st SC INF

LE GARDEUR'S
BAT

STUART'S BAT

Woods
and
Swamp

Woods

"Oak Grove"
John Smith

Smith
Orchard

Mill Pond

1st SC HVY Arty
Skirmish line

Mill Pond Creek

Woods

Woods

Woods

CHURCH

WHEELER'S
CAV

William Smith

Map not to scale

Mark Smith

professed, "Hardee's troops have seen little service, and I have among the superior officers few who have shown themselves competent in their grades."[7] Hardee's Corps numbered 10,000 when it arrived at Cheraw, South Carolina on March 1, 1865. On the eve of the Battle of Averasboro, March 15, he mustered only 6,455 effectives.[8]

Realizing that he had only a small force available to resist Sherman's advance, Hardee selected a defensive position that had far-reaching implications: it presented the Confederates with a chance to stop running, to bleed the enemy, to employ a defensive position that neutralized the enemy's significant manpower advantage, and more importantly, to instill confidence in Hardee's men. A good performance by these men could have great benefits for the continued viability of Hardee's Corps as a fighting force.

By March 15, Hardee had concentrated his corps south of Averasboro and was busily constructing fortifications. He planned to oppose Sherman's advance by preparing and implementing a classic defense in depth, relying upon what modern army doctrine defines as "successive defensive lines designed to absorb and disorganize an attack and prevent observation of successive lines of resistance."[9] Hardee's defense in depth consisted of three consecutive lines of prepared positions. Brig. Gen. William B. Taliaferro's division, consisting of about 2,800 volunteer and garrison troops, manned the first two lines. Rhett's brigade held the first line, and Elliott's brigade held the second. The third and final line consisted of McLaws's division of 3,655 mostly veteran troops.[10]

Brig. Gen. William B. Taliaferro
Generals in Gray

Hardee's defensive scheme closely resembled the formation employed by American commander Brig. Gen. Daniel Morgan during the Revolutionary War Battle of Cowpens.[11] Morgan also designed a defense in depth, deploying his troops in three successive defensive lines. His first two lines consisted of inexperienced militia, while the third line was made up of veteran Continental Army regulars. Faced with the probability that the militia would break, Morgan told his men: "three fires, and you are free." Morgan wanted his green militia to stand and fight long enough for the British to deploy, and for his militia to disrupt their formations. They would then fall back behind the main line held by the regulars.[12] Hardee's defensive scheme at Averasboro was virtually a carbon copy of Morgan's plan, but there is no evidence to suggest that Hardee used the Battle of Cowpens as a template.

Just as Morgan had no illusions about his militia, Hardee probably considered Taliaferro's division to be unreliable. The majority of Taliaferro's men had limited field combat experience. While most of them were veterans of siege warfare, few had fought as infantry in a major open-field engagement. Hardee had every reason to worry about how these men would fare against Sherman's seasoned veterans. Rhett's brigade consisted of Confederate "regulars," a designation normally associated with long-term professional soldiers. Even so, while they were highly skilled at defending Charleston's fixed defenses, they lacked field combat experience. Elliott's brigade consisted mainly of heavy artillerymen with limited combat experience. Elliott's brigade was also a "melting pot" that consisted of several hastily consolidated units whose cohesion was questionable.

Col. Alfred M. Rhett's brigade occupied Hardee's first line. Alfred Moore Rhett was born in Beaufort, South Carolina, on October 18, 1829, the son of Robert Barnwell Rhett, a staunch secessionist, a one-time editor of the Charleston *Mercury* newspaper, and a former U.S. congressman from South Carolina. Alfred Rhett attended Harvard University and then returned home to assist his father in pub-

Col. Alfred M. Rhett
Time/Life Civil War Series

lishing the *Mercury;* like most young South Carolina men of the time, Rhett strongly supported secession and longed to prove his bravery in battle.

On December 31, 1860, Rhett received a commission as a first lieutenant in Company B, 1st South Carolina Heavy Artillery. Rhett commanded one of the batteries at Fort Moultrie on the day South Carolina troops fired on Fort Sumter in April 1861. After the fall of Fort Sumter, Rhett rose to the rank of lieutenant colonel and was second-in-command of the fort's garrison. Rhett soon proved extremely difficult to get along with, for he was arrogant, impetuous, argumentative, hot-headed, and sharp-tongued. His hot temper and exaggerated sense of honor led to an unfortunate duel between Rhett and his commander, Col. William Ransom Calhoun, a nephew of Senator John C. Calhoun. The incident resulted from an argument between Rhett and Arnoldus Vanderhorst as to whether West Pointers or volunteers made better officers. The argument grew heated, with Vanderhorst reminding Rhett that their commander was both an excellent officer and a West Pointer. Rhett also carried a grudge against Calhoun because he believed that the colonel had robbed him of command of the Sumter garrison. He referred to Calhoun as a "puppy,"–a euphemism for "son of a bitch." The offended Vanderhorst thereupon demanded satisfaction. The two men fought a duel in which Vanderhorst missed and Rhett fired his pistol in the air. Rhett nonetheless still refused to apologize for his comments about Calhoun, who "threatened to horsewhip Rhett after the war." On August 31, 1862,

Calhoun challenged Rhett to a duel. The two met at the Charleston Oaks Club on September 5 and exchanged shots with smoothbore pistols at ten yards. Calhoun fell with a mortal wound and died an hour later. Rhett thus achieved what he coveted—command of the 1st South Carolina Heavy Artillery.[13]

Rhett proved himself competent in command, enduring numerous bombardments and thwarting several sea-borne assaults against Sumter, earning

Maj. James J. Lucas
Courtesy of the Darlington County Historical Society

himself several commendations. When Charleston finally fell in February of 1865, Rhett took command of a brigade in Hardee's Corps.[14]

A few miles south of Averasboro, Rhett's brigade dug in on a slight rise just north of the large "Oak Grove," the John C. Smith plantation house. Rhett's 1,051-man brigade covered a 600-yard front that left both of its flanks dangerously exposed. Serving as infantry, the 1st South Carolina Regular (Heavy) Artillery held the right side of the road, with two twelve-pound howitzers of LeGardeur's Battery in the road, Maj. Gen. James J. Lucas's Battalion (15th South Carolina Heavy Artillery Battalion) to the left of the guns, and the 1st South Carolina Regular Infantry on Lucas's left.[15] (See Huguenin's sketch). One twelve-pound Napoleon of Stuart's Battery was deployed in the middle of the 1st South Carolina Artillery.[16]

Rhett's position made good use of natural obstacles. A small creek bed, thick woods and a pond offered some protection for Rhett's left flank, while a dense swamp protected Rhett's right. Heavy woods also concealed the Confederate second line from the prying eyes of Federal soldiers. Furthermore, Rhett's position offered excellent fields of fire. While his first-line force was undermanned, Taliaferro had chosen his position well and made his dispositions wisely. Rhett moved "some three companies" of skirmishers about two or three hundred yards to the front of the main line to "hold the ravine," as Taliaferro later explained.[17] In addition, Rhett deployed a strong skirmish line on his left flank to prevent the Federals from turning it. On the other hand, only a few pickets held Rhett's right flank. It is unclear why neither Hardee, Taliaferro, nor Rhett rectified this oversight. Quite possibly, they believed that Federal troops would be unable to penetrate the swamp while under fire. In any event, Taliaferro approved the dispositions of Rhett's troops and made no further adjustments. Despite their open right flank, Rhett's South Carolinians confidently awaited the arrival of Sherman's infantry.

"My object in this was to check the enemy," reported Taliaferro, who intended to slow the Federal advance by increasing the level of resistance at each successive line. "I designed to retire Rhett's upon Elliott's brigade, or to take such positions as should be directed."[18]

About three hundred yards north of Rhett's line, Brig. Gen. Stephen Elliott's brigade constructed a second defensive line on the high ground on the north side of a creek bank. Several hundred yards farther north stretched a slight ridge that ran perpendicular to the road and extended from the Cape Fear River to the Black River. A thick swamp lay in front of that position, and a deep ravine dominated the right front of the ridge. Hardee selected this ridge for his third and strongest line. Because of the terrain, the third line could not be easily flanked. According to Hardee's plan, the defenders of the first and second lines would eventually retire to the third line, where they would make their stand.

FIRST CONTACT - MARCH 15, 1865

Before first light on the morning of March 15, Kilpatrick's cavalry moved north on the Fayetteville-Raleigh Road. They led the advance

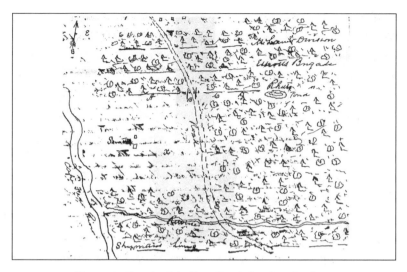

Huguenin Sketch of the First South Carolina Artillery,
First Confederate Defensive Position
Courtesy of Mrs. Richard E. Coen

of the Left Wing, with scouts and foragers fanning out ahead of their line of march. Following Kilpatrick, Bvt. Maj. Gen. William T. Ward's division of the XX Corps corduroyed the muddy roads as they advanced north. Brig. Gen. Nathaniel J. Jackson's division brought up the rear of the XX Corps. The XIV Corps came next, led by Brig. Gen. James D. Morgan's division, followed by Brig. Gen. William P. Carlin's division.

The weather was miserable and wet. An abnormally rainy winter had turned the dirt roads into quagmires. Sherman recalled, "Almost every foot of it had to be corduroyed, to admit the passage of wheeled vehicles."[19] Ward's men worked incessantly to make the roads passable. While the infantry corduroyed the roads, the cavalry pressed forward. The Federal horse soldiers found plenty of action from the outset, with Wheeler's dogged troopers contesting Kilpatrick's advance at every creek crossing.

On the morning of March 15, Hardee's troops prepared their defensive positions while reports on the advance of the Union army flowed in from Hampton's vigilant cavalry. In response, Rhett's brigade hastily constructed earthworks. After spending a dismal night in the cold rain, daylight brought little relief to the bedraggled Southerners. To make matters worse, Rhett decided to teach his command an unpleasant lesson. That morning, he formed the 1st South Carolina Heavy Artillery to witness the execution of a deserter from Company C.[20] Desertion had reached epidemic proportions in Rhett's brigade, and Rhett believed that drastic measures were required if he had any hope of retaining enough strength to resist Sherman's advance. Thus, after witnessing the spectacle of a comrade's execution, the South Carolinians silently returned to their positions along the defensive line.

At 8:00 A.M., Hardee received a dispatch from Hampton's cavalry, reporting that "the infantry of the enemy were pressing our cavalry back," and that Kilpatrick's horsemen would arrive at Smithville the next day.[21] With a growing sense of urgency, Hardee inspected Taliaferro's lines. Dissatisfied with the positioning of Rhett's skirmishers, Hardee ordered them to deploy further to the south to provide ample warning of Sherman's approach. Rhett immediately complied, but heavy firing along Rhett's entire skirmish line brought his advance to a sudden halt. Union scouts and foragers, deployed at a fork in the road near the church, opened fire on Rhett's skirmishers. The two lines blazed away at each other until superior Union firepower drove Rhett's skirmishers back to their starting point just south of Mill Creek. The Federals now threatened Rhett's main line of battle.

An alarmed Rhett sent an urgent message to Col. William Butler, the commander of the 1st South Carolina Regulars, directing him to rush three companies forward to reinforce the skirmishers. Butler directed Capt. Thomas Huguenin to assume command of the three companies. Captain Huguenin advanced his three companies at the double quick. "Colonel Rhett explained the situation and ordered me to retake the ravine," recalled Huguenin. Recognizing the developing Federal threat, Huguenin quickly deployed his companies on either side of the Fayetteville-Raleigh Road and moved out. Rhett watched as Huguenin and his men disappeared into the woods. As he listened anxiously, the small arms fire suddenly intensified, indicating that the two opposing forces had collided. After 30 minutes of heavy skirmishing, Huguenin recaptured the Confederates' lost ground, shoving the Union skirmishers as far back as the William Smith house, where

Capt. Thomas Abram Huguenin
Courtesy of Julius Huguenin

they rallied on Kilpatrick's lead regiment, the 9th Michigan Cavalry. The skirmish lines swayed back and forth, with neither side gaining a clear advantage. Huguenin managed to stabilize his line along the ravine, though hard-pressed by skirmishers of the 9th Michigan Cavalry. "I rode back to where Colonel Rhett was in the road," recounted Huguenin, "and reported that I had possession of the ravine." Satisfied with the results, Rhett left Huguenin in charge of the skirmish line, with instructions to "keep me informed of events." Rhett informed Huguenin that there was cavalry to his right, and that he was heading back to the main line to find additional support for Huguenin's left. While en route, Rhett spotted a group of mounted troops to the right rear of Huguenin's line, "in the direction of the (John) Smith house," recalled Huguenin.[22]

* * *

At about 3 P.M., the commander of the 9th Michigan Cavalry, Col. George S. Acker, arrived near Smithville. Acker reported heavy skirmishing in his front. Union skirmishers and Confederate prisoners confirmed Acker's suspicion that he was fighting Confederate

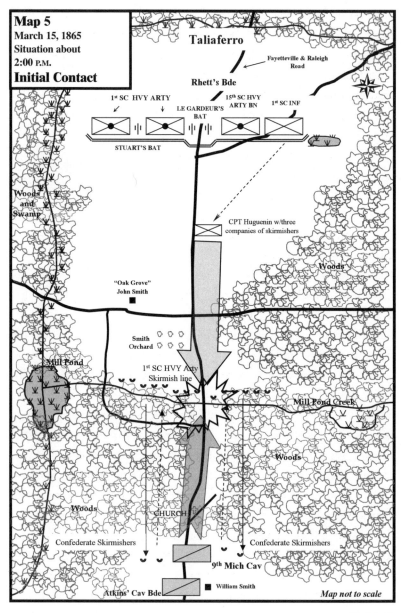

Map 5
March 15, 1865
Situation about 2:00 P.M.
Initial Contact

Taliaferro

Fayetteville & Raleigh Road

Rhett's Bde

1st SC HVY ARTY

LE GARDEUR'S BAT

15th SC HVY ARTY BN

1st SC INF

STUART'S BAT

Woods and Swamp

CPT Huguenin w/three companies of skirmishers

Woods

"Oak Grove" John Smith

Smith Orchard

Mill Pond

1st SC HVY Arty Skirmish line

Mill Pond Creek

Woods

Woods

CHURCH

Confederate Skirmishers

Confederate Skirmishers

9th Mich Cav

Atkins' Cav Bde

William Smith

Map not to scale

Mark Smith

infantry, rather than dismounted cavalry. Acker dismounted his regiment and advanced on foot.[23] Bringing the firepower of their seven-shot Spencer carbines to bear, the Wolverines slowly drove the skirmishers of the 1st South Carolina Heavy Artillery back across a creek about a quarter mile from the first Confederate defensive line. The Wolverines' advance soon bogged down, however, as heavy artillery and small arms fire from the Confederate first line prevented them from crossing the creek bed.[24] Huguenin's timely arrival bolstered the beleaguered skirmishers of the 1st South Carolina Artillery and together, they resisted every attempt by the Michiganders to drive them back.

Meanwhile, Bvt. Brig. Gen. Smith D. Atkins, commander of Kilpatrick's Second Brigade, arrived at the front with his troopers following closely behind. When prisoners of the 1st South Carolina Artillery reported that "Johnston's army was in our front and entrenched," Atkins grew concerned for the safety of his command. He ordered the 9th Michigan to continue skirmishing with the enemy while he deployed the remainder of his command, which he "barricaded strongly" on each side of the Fayetteville-Raleigh Road. Atkins immediately reported his findings to Kilpatrick and awaited further instructions.[25] Kilpatrick was at the rear of the column when he learned that his troops were skirmishing with the enemy, and he quickly trotted forward to take personal command. If the reports of Confederate prisoners were true, Kilpatrick thought he would need infantry support to drive the Rebels from their field works. Kilpatrick sent "Aide after Aide with dispatches" for General Sherman, urgently requesting reinforcements. In the meantime, Kilpatrick ordered the remainder of his division to advance to the front as quickly as possible.[26] What had begun as scattered skirmishing was rapidly evolving into a large-scale engagement.

As the 9th Michigan drew heavy small arms and artillery fire from Rhett's troops, a section of Capt. Yates V. Beebe's 10th Wisconsin

Battery, Kilpatrick's horse artillery, unlimbered to support the hard-pressed Michiganders. The Wisconsin gunners opened fire and brought the power of their 3-inch ordnance rifles to bear against Rhett's position. While his brigade deployed, Atkins ordered the men to build field works. The 9th Michigan then retired to Atkins's main defensive position. Meanwhile, Kilpatrick's couriers had reached Sherman and much-needed infantry support was now on its way.[27]

RHETT'S CAPTURE

At about noon, Capt. Theodore F. Northrop, Kilpatrick's chief of scouts, arrived at Smithville with a small group of his scouts and some foragers, who were the vanguard of the approaching Union Left Wing. Arriving at a branch in the road about 900 yards northwest of the William Smith house, Northrop decided to reconnoiter the approaches with a few of his men. "We turned to our left, going up the main road by the church," recalled Northrop. "I left the scouts, perhaps 30, and 50 bummers at the old church." Northrop then rode

Theodore Northrop
Larry Strayer

ahead with three of his best scouts, Charles F. Grey, of the 5th Iowa Cavalry; a man named Fry of the 10th Ohio Cavalry; and a third, unidentified man.[28]

Northrop's band cautiously moved north, crossed a small creek, and passed through some piney woods before entering an open field. Fog and light drizzle limited visibility, permitting Northrop and his men to approach unwittingly to within a few hundred yards of the Confederate first line. Northrop soon realized that he and his

scouts had ventured closer to the enemy fortifications than he intended. "We came immediately in sight of Colonel Rhett's main line,"
Northrop recalled, "we were also within less than a hundred yards of
quite a body of mounted men." So close, in fact, that Northrop recognized them as "some generals with staffs, and couriers," he wrote. "We
had reason to believe afterwards that they were Generals Hardee,
Taliaferro, and Hampton." One of Northrop's scouts found the group
of officers a tempting target and raised his Spencer to his shoulder.
"Remembering about 'the boy and the hornets' nest,' I held him up,"
the captain recalled.[29] Northrop realized that he would have to withdraw toward the church, where he would collect his remaining men
and report his findings to Kilpatrick.

Hoping to avoid contact with the enemy, Northrop and his band
worked their way south. They had not traveled far when Northrop
spotted two mounted soldiers riding toward them. The Federals immediately identified the two riders as Confederate officers, but they did
not realize that they had a brigade commander within their grasp.

Colonel Rhett had left his skirmishers and made his way towards
a group of mounted soldiers he spotted riding behind Huguenin's line.
Rhett and his aide assumed that they were Confederate cavalry; Union
scouts often dressed in Confederate uniforms or civilian clothes to
enable them to move undetected behind enemy lines (see photograph
on p. 98 for Scout dress). They even mimicked "the dialect of the poor
people of the South," recalled Union Capt. George W. Pepper. Posing
as Rebel stragglers, Union scouts often fooled the locals, who willingly
offered a wealth of information on Hardee's movements. Pepper
claimed that some of the scouts had the "audacity to visit the headquarters of the rebel Generals, and in one instance, we remember one of
them carried off the officer's monthly return of the strength and equipment of his command."[30] In Rhett's case, poor visibility and muddied,
non-regulation clothing concealed the identity of Northrop and his
men. Rhett therefore blithely rode up to Northrop and asked, "Where
are Generals Hampton and Taliaferro?"

Rhett's Capture
Drawing by Col. Darrell L. Combs, USMC (Ret.)

Northrop replied, "They are right back here a short distance on the road." Concerned that Rhett would soon realize that they were Yankees, Northrop decided to capture the Rebel colonel and then beat a hasty retreat while fortune still smiled on him. "You will have to come with us," ordered Northrop.

A stunned Rhett snapped, "Do you know who you are talking to?" Suddenly realizing that Northrop and his band were the enemy, Rhett reached for his revolver. Grey "trained the point of his Spencer so close to Rhett's ear that when he discovered we were Yankees he had nothing to do except surrender," Northrop recalled many years later.[31]

Hugenin saw the brigade commander approach Northrop and his scouts in the open field. (See Map 6, Rhett's capture location annotated by ✠ symbol.) Huguenin watched while Rhett briefly conversed with the mounted party and then saw Rhett and the group ride off to his right and disappear. Assuming that the horsemen were some of the

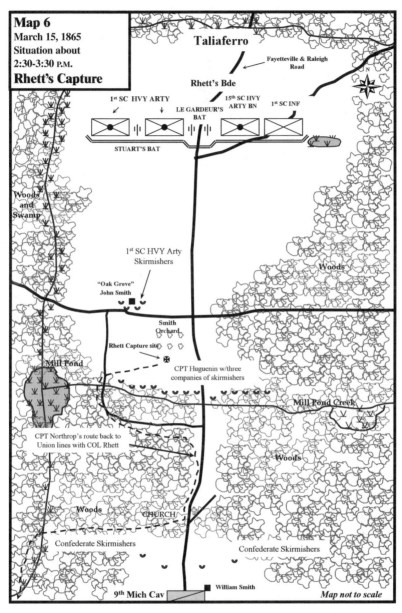

Map 6
March 15, 1865
Situation about
2:30-3:30 P.M.

Rhett's Capture

Taliaferro

Fayetteville & Raleigh
Road

Rhett's Bde

1st SC HVY ARTY

15th SC HVY
ARTY BN

1st SC INF

LE GARDEUR'S
BAT

STUART'S BAT

Woods
and
Swamp

1st SC HVY Arty
Skirmishers

Woods

"Oak Grove"
John Smith

Smith
Orchard

Rhett Capture site

CPT Huguenin w/three
companies of skirmishers

Mill Pond

Mill Pond Creek

CPT Northrop's route back to
Union lines with COL Rhett

Woods

Woods

CHURCH

Confederate Skirmishers

Confederate Skirmishers

9th Mich Cav

William Smith

Map not to scale

Mark Smith

cavalry Rhett promised to send to protect his exposed flank, Huguenin concluded that Rhett must have led them into position himself, and he therefore gave it no more thought, sealing Rhett's fate.

Northrop and his scouts returned to the church with their prisoners. Upon arriving, Northrop was surprised to find the churchyard deserted, his scouts and the foragers evidently having retreated in the face of a strong Confederate skirmish. Northrop now realized that he stood between the Confederate main line and the Confederate skirmish line. He decided that the best route to safety was to skirt the Confederate right flank via a deep ravine west of the church. He backtracked a short distance and then headed west, successfully passing through the ravine. Northrop thus maneuvered his command through the Confederate skirmish line and passed through the Union picket line to safety.

Northrop delivered Rhett to Kilpatrick's headquarters for questioning. Kilpatrick watched Northrop ride up and called out, "Hello Northrop, what troops are these we are fighting?"

"Taliaferro's Division of Heavy Artillery from Charleston," responded Northrop. "I have one of their brigade commanders with me."

"The h— you have!" answered Kilpatrick. Nevertheless, Kilpatrick soon realized that Northrop spoke the truth. To his amazement, Colonel Rhett stood in front of him.[32] Rhett and Kilpatrick soon exchanged insults. "I was taken through a mistake of my own and you have the advantage of me now, but you damned Yankees will not have it your own way for long," declared a still-defiant Rhett. In South Carolina, he declared, "there are 50,000 fresh men ready and waiting for you."

"Yes," replied Kilpatrick, "and if that is true we will have to hunt every swamp to find the damned cowards." This stinging insult silenced Rhett.[33]

Rhett received undue criticism for years after his capture. His critics claimed that he was careless, for a brigade commander had no business deploying skirmishers. Given the threat to his exposed flank, his concern with this portion of his line is entirely understandable. In any event, Rhett did what he felt was necessary. His only mistake was being in the wrong place at the wrong time.

Rhett's capture occurred between 2:30 and 3:30 P.M. on March 15. The colonel's capture proved to be an ironic development for both Northrop and Kilpatrick. Northrop recalled a conversation with Kilpatrick in which the two men discussed the capture of a Union general in the Shenandoah Valley. Kilpatrick jokingly challenged his chief scout, declaring, "Northrop, you must capture some rebel General in his own camp."[34] Although Rhett was not a general officer, a brigade commander captured behind enemy lines was not a bad second choice, Northrop undoubtedly concluded.

After he wearied of bantering with his prisoner, Kilpatrick sent Rhett to Sherman's headquarters. A Lieutenant Mann and two guards first escorted Rhett to Bvt. Maj. Gen. Alpheus Williams's XX Corps headquarters, and then Williams transferred the South Carolinian to Sherman's custody. While escorting Rhett to Williams's headquarters, Rhett asked Mann if he and his men would shoot should he try to escape. Mann replied, "If he (Rhett) wanted to make the experiment he might try it."[35] Rhett wisely declined the invitation.

Sherman invited the South Carolinian to dinner that evening, and lacking any other invitations, Rhett graciously accepted. The dinner conversation touched on a myriad of topics, ranging from politics to Rhett's conduct of the war. Sherman's aide, Maj. Henry Hitchcock, recalled that Rhett boasted of his reputation as a strict disciplinarian. "I've shot twelve men myself in the past six weeks," he bragged, much to the amusement of Sherman and several other generals. However, Hitchcock did not find Rhett as amusing as the generals did. Instead, he described the South Carolinian as "a devil in human shape, whose polished manners and easy assurance made only more hideous to me the utter heartlessness and selfish ambition and pride of class."[36]

Later that evening, Rhett was returned to Kilpatrick's headquarters. His treatment there was not as accommodating as Sherman's had been.

Rhett was tossed into the "bullpen," where he languished among other Confederate prisoners captured that day. He was evidently not welcome among his own men. Pvt. Morris Holt of the 10th Wisconsin Battery decided to get a good look at a captured rebel colonel. Holt spotted Rhett sitting on a rail, surrounded by his men, who "were abusing him with their tongues in the worst way." The South Carolinians wanted the guards "to turn their backs and give them a chance to kill Rhett." One of the guards asked why they wanted to kill him, prompting a Johnny to speak up: "He killed my brother that is why." The man told the guard that his brother was a boy of 18, that they had camped near the family home while marching, and that the boy wanted to pay a quick visit to his mother. When Rhett refused the boy's request, he went anyway. The following morning Rhett called the youth out and had him shot for desertion, gaining the eternal enmity of the older brother. [37]

Rhett closely followed the progress of the fighting at Averasboro on March 16. Col. William D. Hamilton, the commander of the 9th Ohio Cavalry, observed Rhett and the other Confederate prisoners that day. Word quickly spread that "a regiment had been taken." Rhett assumed that his troops had captured a Yankee regiment, recalled Hamilton, and "a bright look of joy came over his face, and [he] raised [himself up] on his elbows to look." Out of the smoke came a column of gray "between two columns of blue with muskets at right shoulder shift." Realizing that the regiment taken was actually a Confederate unit, Rhett lay back down, wearing a look of utter despair.[38]

After the Battle of Averasboro, Rhett and many other Confederate prisoners were marched to New Bern and then shipped north to Hart's Island Prison in New York. Rhett was soon transferred to Fort Delaware for the remainder of the war. Command of Rhett's brigade devolved upon Col. William Butler, the commander of the 1st South Carolina Regulars.

Years later, Northrop nominated himself for the Medal of Honor for his "actions in capturing Colonel Rhett (who commanded a brigade of heavy artillery) within his own lines by myself and three scouts the evening before the Battle of Averasboro, N.C." Northrop's application was rejected, because "the action was not mentioned in the Official Records as the law requires." Northrop believed that his exploit never was mentioned in the Official Records because he personally delivered his report and prisoner directly to Sherman's headquarters by order of General Kilpatrick, instead of submitting a written report that could be included in the Official Records.[39] Thus, Northrop's feat of daring went unrewarded.

HAWLEY'S BRIGADE TO THE FRONT

At dusk on March 15, the XX Corps camped between Silver Run and Taylor's Hole Creek, about fifteen miles northeast of Fayetteville. Col. William Hawley's First Division brigade arrived at Bluff Church and camped for the night. His foot-weary soldiers had endured a day of hard marching and corduroying roads under terrible conditions. "The day had been stormy, with fierce lighting and thunder," making the roads all but impassable.[40] Hawley's men regarded the opportunity to rest as a welcome relief, and, like all veteran campaigners, they quickly took advantage of the respite.

Slocum's chief engineer, Maj. Robert Morris McDowell, recalled a humorous incident that occurred late on the afternoon of March 15. While searching for a dry place to sleep, he entered a cooper's shop near the Confederate earthworks along the banks of Silver Run Creek. He found a note carved on a barrel stave addressed to Sherman and

Col. William Hawley
USAMHI

referring to Kilpatrick. Making an obvious reference to the plundering of the Union cavalry camps at Monroe's Crossroads a few days earlier, the Confederate jokester had addressed his note to "Mr. Corporal Kilpatricko," stated that their men were not "regularly armed with Spencer repeating rifles" and that they also needed a fresh supply of "rubber blankets and coffee for the summer campaign." The cheeky rebel further requested that General Sherman "trot out Mr. Corporal Kilpatrick in order that they might procure the articles." The barrel stave was signed, "The Rebels." An amused Major McDowell gleefully forwarded the message to Sherman. "We considered it quite an animadversion on Kilpatrick whose command is alike and held in contempt by ourselves and the enemy," declared McDowell. [41]

Despite the terrible weather, Hawley's troops prepared for a welcome night's rest and a hot meal, making fires and pitching tents around on the grounds of Bluff Church. At 7:30 P.M., Samuel Toombs of the 13th New Jersey spotted a rider galloping toward brigade headquarters. The unwelcome arrival of the staff officer

Capt. Daniel Oakey
USAMHI

meant that the brief respite of Hawley's weary command was about to end. Edwin Bryant of the 3rd Wisconsin heard the dreaded command, "Fall in," which caused an uncharacteristic uprising in the church cemetery.[42] "In a few minutes orders were issued to pack up and move immediately," Bryant recalled. Despite the day's labors, there was evidently more work ahead, recalled Toombs.[43] Capt. Daniel Oakey of the 2nd Massachusetts was not surprised that his brigade received the call to support the cavalry, as "it was the turn of our brigade to do special duty."[44]

The brigade was to move north to assist Kilpatrick, who had been engaged in a lively skirmish with Hardee's troops since 3:00 P.M. Hawley's troops reluctantly extinguished their fires, fell into line, and trudged north through the rain and darkness to reinforce Kilpatrick's beleaguered troopers.

Toombs recalled that the road was a perfect "sea of mud" that made slogging through it sheer misery. "We hugged the margins of the woods on either side, marching in single file." Men had their "shoes sucked off by the mud," while others stumbled, lost their guns, and were thankful that they "were not trampled under by the moving column and buried alive."[45] During a halt, Captain Oakey remembered seeing a sergeant with "one arm in the mud up to his elbow...trying to find his shoe."[46]

Hawley's brigade arrived at the front a little after midnight, and immediately deployed into line of battle. The drenched foot soldiers briefly huddled around the cavalry's campfires before deploying in the center of Kilpatrick's defensive line. Relieved by the arrival of the infantrymen, the cavalry took up new positions on either side of Hawley's brigade. The 13th New Jersey wasted no time resuming what had been interrupted at Bluff Church. "We built fires, cooked coffee and retired for the night," noted Toombs.[47]

The actions of Hawley's brigade exhibit the rough professionalism of Sherman's men. Footsore, tired, and hungry, the men fell into formation and marched within minutes of receiving the order to move out. Once again, Sherman's infantry advanced to the sound of the guns. The enemy lay in wait a few miles to the north, uncharacteristically ready and eager to make a stand against Sherman's veterans.

On the Confederate side of the creek, Generals Hardee and Taliaferro rode out to make one last inspection of the Confederate lines before nightfall. They fully expected the Union cavalry to resume their attack the next morning, and they also realized that the Union

82

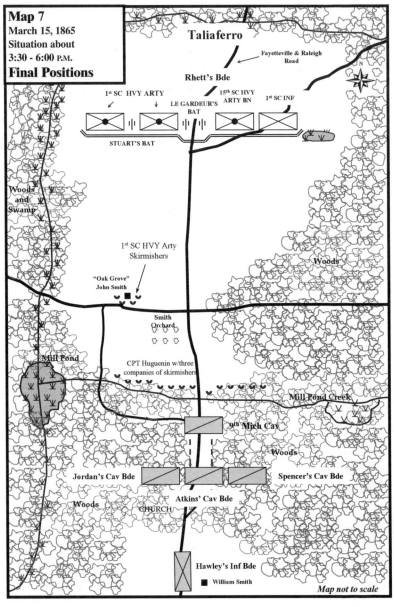

Map 7
March 15, 1865
Situation about
3:30 - 6:00 P.M.
Final Positions

Taliaferro

Fayetteville & Raleigh
Road

N

Rhett's Bde

1st SC HVY ARTY   15th SC HVY   1st SC INF
                       ARTY BN
         LE GARDEUR'S
              BAT

STUART'S BAT

Woods
and
Swamp

Woods

1st SC HVY Arty
Skirmishers

"Oak Grove"
John Smith

Smith
Orchard

Mill Pond

CPT Huguenin w/three
companies of skirmishers

Mill Pond Creek

9th Mich Cav

Woods

Jordan's Cav Bde   Spencer's Cav Bde

Atkins' Cav Bde

Woods   CHURCH

Hawley's Inf Bde

■ William Smith

Map not to scale

Mark Smith

infantry would be close behind. The two generals made their way to the forward skirmish line, where they met with Captain Huguenin. They explained the situation to the young South Carolinian. "I was informed that I would be attacked early in the morning, and must hold my position as long as possible," recalled Huguenin. If necessary, he was to "fall back slowly onto the main line contending every foot of ground."[48]

Earlier, Huguenin had posted Lt. Edward Middleton and twelve men of the 1st South Carolina Artillery on picket duty in advance of the main skirmish line. Middleton's men were so near the main Federal line that they could not light fires, despite being cold, wet, and miserable. Nevertheless, they tried to sleep as best they could. The band of the 2nd Massachusetts played a medley of popular tunes, and Middleton and his men tried to forget their misery as they thought of home and loved ones while enjoying the soothing strains of the music.[49]

Later that evening Huguenin, "having ridden up and down the line to see that all was right," returned to his position in the road. "My orderly came up and brought me a tin can containing some corn bread and bacon," recalled Huguenin. "As the can had no top the contents were saturated with rainwater, and tho' very hungry I was unable to eat." By now, the captain was exhausted and desperately needed sleep. "I coiled myself up on a wagon trough which was by the side of the road," he recounted. "I ordered my orderly to arouse me upon the slightest disturbance."[50] Before long, quiet fell over the field as the men of both sides did their best to ignore the rain, waiting for the coming of the dawn and the fighting that would inevitably follow.

Chapter 5 | *"The Rebels have shown*
more pluck than we have
seen since Atlanta."

Major George W. Nichols, one of
Sherman's staff officers

THE BATTLE BEGINS: UNION
ASSAULT ON THE FIRST LINE
MARCH 16, 1865

At 3:00 A.M. on March 16, the officers of
Hawley's brigade began waking their sleeping
soldiers. Capt. Daniel Oakey of the 2nd Massachusetts remembered
the sight of a "long line of blue coats spread over the ground in
motionless groups" just before he called them into formation. Soon,
cries of "Fall-in" shattered the morning calm, and "gruff tones broke
upon the chilly air," bringing everyone "shivering to our feet," recalled
Oakey. All along the Fayetteville-Raleigh Road, troops awoke and
prepared breakfast. The Union Left Wing was about to begin another day's march north, with Ward's division taking the lead and corduroying the road as it advanced.[1]

At 6:30 A.M., Kilpatrick gave the order, "Boots and saddles!" The
men mounted to the sounds of creaking leather, clinking metal, and
commanders barking orders. Quickly and methodically they formed
lines of battle. Before long, the command "Forward!" broke the
silence. With Kilpatrick's horsemen covering each flank, Hawley's
brigade stepped forward and then halted when it approached the edge

85

Capt. James I. Grafton
USAMHI

of the woods lining the ravine. The soldiers whispered among themselves, searching for explanations for the delay. Riding together, Kilpatrick and Hawley passed through the ranks of their commands, heading for the front. The aggressive Kilpatrick urged Hawley to order the attack, but Hawley was a veteran and understood the importance of reconnoitering and determining the dispositions of the enemy before attacking. Upon reaching the 2nd Massachusetts, Hawley remarked to Kilpatrick, "No, Sir, I shall not charge until I find out what is on my flanks." Determined to discover what lay in front of his brigade, Hawley advanced two companies of skirmishers under the command of Capt. James I. Grafton of the 2nd Massachusetts.[2]

On the Confederate side of the ravine, an equally concerned Lt. Ravenel Macbeth awoke Capt. Thomas Huguenin just before dawn, having learned that Lieutenant Middleton and his skirmishers had spotted a body of Union cavalry moving in their direction. Middleton promptly called in his pickets and ordered his skirmishers to engage the enemy. He did not have long to wait.[3] At first light, a picket reported to Huguenin that he had noticed movement to his front, and that "he could see men coming around the bend in the road moving towards our lines." Huguenin knew that he had no men in that direction and therefore ordered his pickets "to fire upon the body of troops."[4]

In response to the picket fire, Captain Grafton deployed his skirmishers and entered the woods. Kilpatrick also dismounted a portion of his command and deployed them as skirmishers alongside Grafton's men. Gunfire erupted along the entire line as soon as the Federal skirmishers entered the woods. About a quarter-mile in front of the

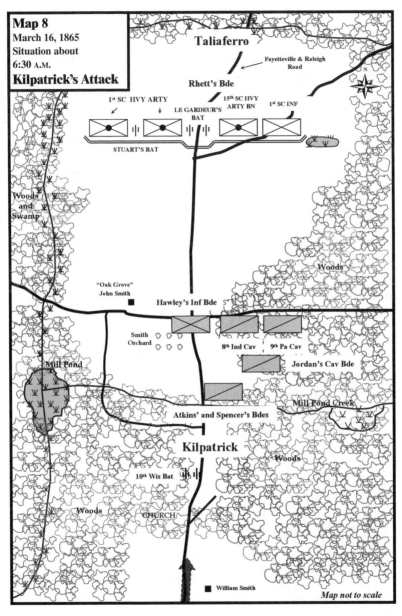

Map 8
March 16, 1865
Situation about
6:30 A.M.
Kilpatrick's Attack

Taliaferro

Fayetteville & Raleigh
Road

Rhett's Bde

1st SC HVY ARTY   15th SC HVY   1st SC INF
                    ARTY BN

LE GARDEUR'S
BAT

STUART'S BAT

**Woods
and
Swamp**

Woods

"Oak Grove"
John Smith

Hawley's Inf Bde

Smith
Orchard

8th Ind Cav   9th Pa Cav

Mill Pond

Jordan's Cav Bde

Mill Pond Creek

Atkins' and Spencer's Bdes

Kilpatrick

Woods

10th Wis Bat

Woods   CHURCH

William Smith

Map not to scale

Mark Smith

Confederate first line, the Union skirmishers encountered Southern pickets near the creek bed. After waiting patiently, Middleton's and Huguenin's men unleashed a devastating sheet of fire on the advancing Union troops, halting the Federal advance. After the repulse of Grafton's skirmishers, Hawley's and Kilpatrick's men anxiously waited to see how the situation would develop.

Retreating Union skirmishers reported that Captain Grafton had suffered a severe leg wound, but that he had refused to leave his command. Moments later, Grafton staggered out of the thick smoke and fog, "his face buried in his hands," his sword hanging limply from his wrist by its sword knot. A horrified Daniel Oakey watched Grafton struggle to reach the safety of the Union lines. Grafton bound his leg with a handkerchief, and with "his uniform covered in blood," dropped his hands from his face, gazed towards the Union line, wavered slightly, and then fell, mortally wounded.[5]

Advancing once again, Hawley's brigade continued pressing Huguenin's skirmishers. Hoping to support the infantry's attack,

Bvt. Maj. Gen. Alpheus S. Williams
Library of Congress

Kilpatrick deployed additional cavalry on Hawley's right. At 7:30 A.M., Kilpatrick reported to Bvt. Maj. Gen. Alpheus S. Williams, the commander of the XX Corps, that he had "found the enemy in his front in force and entrenched."[6] Seeing the stout Confederate works looming in their front, Hawley and Kilpatrick realized that additional infantry would be required to dislodge the defenders. Williams ordered Ward to double-quick to Kilpatrick's support. In the meantime, the cavalry commander bolstered his line with additional regiments from his division. The Battle of Averasboro had begun in earnest.

Alpheus Williams was a competent and reliable officer who had been acting as a corps commander since the March to the Sea. Born in Saybrook, Connecticut, on September 20, 1810, "Old Pap," was at 54 the oldest corps commander in Sherman's army. He had never received formal military training. Williams had graduated from Yale University, studied law in New York, then established his own practice in Detroit in 1836, serving briefly as a probate judge. Williams also joined the local militia, and during the Mexican War, served as lieutenant colonel of the 1st Michigan Volunteer Infantry, gaining invaluable experience as an officer.[7]

After the Mexican War, Williams served as the president of the Michigan state military board and received a commission as brigadier general in the state militia. In August 1861, he was commissioned as a brigadier general in the U.S. Army and commanded a division for most of the war. Although he had performed capably at Chancellorsville and Gettysburg, he was not promoted to major general. During the Atlanta Campaign and the March to the Sea, Williams commanded the XX Corps, a testament to his competence. Unfortunately for him, he was demoted to division commander soon after the Battle of Averasboro. On April 5, 1865, Williams wrote to his daughter, "This is about the fortieth time that I have been foisted up by seniority to be let down by rank! But no matter."[8] Despite this blow to his pride, Williams faithfully resumed his duties as division commander. After Sherman's army reached Goldsboro, Williams lost his position as corps commander to the younger and more aggressive Maj. Gen. Joseph A. Mower. However, Williams performed solidly throughout the campaign, and probably deserved better treatment.

Coming up to support the dismounted cavalrymen, Lt. Elbert W. Fowler unlimbered his section of two 3-inch ordnance rifles of the 10th Wisconsin Artillery on an elevated plain to the left of the Fayetteville-Raleigh Road, about 1,500 yards south of the Confederate first line.

Although a slightly wooded area in the creek bed along his front partially concealed his cannon, Confederate smoothbore guns on the first line immediately opened fire on the horse artillery. Fortunately for Fowler's section, the Confederate artillery fire had no effect, their shells falling harmlessly in front of the Union guns. The Confederate artillery therefore shifted its fire to the Union right, where Hawley's infantry and Kilpatrick's cavalry presented more tempting targets.

Safely beyond range, Fowler's two-gun section opened an accurate counter-battery fire that wreaked havoc among the Confederate gunners. As the battle developed and the first Southern prisoners glumly made their way into captivity, Fowler eagerly interrogated captured Confederates from the first line as to the effect of his fire. He was told that his "first five rounds fired (Fuse and Shell) took effect, each killing a man and horse. The third shot fired exploded a limber." Fowler also learned that he had "dismounted one of their guns—hitting it on the face." [9]

The accurate fire of the Wisconsin gunners took a heavy toll on both Southern artillery and infantry. In his after-action report, General Taliaferro recounted, "the enemy established a battery on a rising ground beyond the swamps in our front to their left of the main road and shelled our lines with great determination and vigor."[10] Until the XX Corps artillery relieved his gunners, Fowler's section provided effective, continuous artillery support, discharging 150 rounds of shell and case into the Confederate first line.

Col. Thomas J. Jordan immediately deployed his First Cavalry Brigade. His lead regiment, Lt. Col. Fielder Jones's 8th Indiana Cavalry, soon found itself in a spirited engagement on the Union right. Jones requested additional support, prompting Jordan to feed in troops to reinforce the heavily engaged Union right flank. However, Jordan's ammunition supply was running low, forcing the colonel to bring up his supply trains. The resulting lull in the Federals' fire enabled Huguenin's gray clad skirmishers to delay the Union advance for more than an hour. Still, the reinforced Union cavalry eventually overlapped Huguenin's left flank, compelling the Southern skirmishers to retire. Taliaferro sent two companies of the 1st South Carolina Artillery to support and reinforce Huguenin's skirmishers near the John Smith house. The soldiers holding the left flank reported to Huguenin that "the enemy had overlapped the left and turned the flank," forcing them to break off and withdraw. Huguenin immediately ordered his men "to retire as skirmishers, keeping up a heavy fire."[11] Their disciplined fighting withdrawal greatly pleased Taliaferro, who praised the coolness and professionalism of Huguenin's troops: "Captain Huguenin, First South Carolina Infantry," wrote the general, "received [the enemy's] advance very handsomely and fell back when forced by greatly superior numbers."[12]

The severe fire of the combined Union infantry and cavalry drove Captain Huguenin and his skirmishers back to the safety of the first line. Rejoining the 1st South Carolina Regulars, Huguenin realized that it had suffered many killed and wounded at the hands of Fowler's deadly horse artillerists. Lt. Col. Robert Detreville had assumed command of the regiment only a day earlier, replacing Col. William Butler, who was now in command of Rhett's brigade. Detreville's tenure as regimental commander was brief, for an exploding shell killed him early in the battle.[13]

As Hawley's infantry and Jordan's cavalry skirmished with the Confederate main line, Colonel Butler realized that the Union force was not strong enough to carry his line. Butler therefore launched a series of savage counterattacks to drive back the Federals. David Miller

Lt. Col. Robert Detreville
Courtesy of John Detreville

of the 9th Pennsylvania Cavalry remembered the desperate fighting near the first line. "We would drive the enemy back at one time and they would rally and drive us back and so on," recalled Miller. "I do not remember how many times we crossed and were driven back through the swamp, but one thing I do know, we never let them get on our side of the swamp."[14] Jordan's men fought hard, and the fire grew so hot that his brigade expended nearly all of its ammunition in repulsing Butler's determined counterattacks.

In response, Kilpatrick ordered Bvt. Brig. Gen. Smith D. Atkins's brigade to support Jordan's hard-pressed troopers, but it took Atkins and his men some time to make their way to the front lines. The boldness of the desperate Confederate counterattacks concerned Hawley, who held his position and waited for infantry support to come up.

Hearing the heavy fire from the front, Sherman and Slocum rode up to assess the situation. Sherman decided to probe the Confederate flank: "Kilpatrick, I want you to move your cavalry around the left and develop the enemy's line."

Pvt. Arthur Ford
Southern Historical Collection, UNC-Chapel Hill

A confused Kilpatrick asked, "How do you propose that I shall do it?"

Visibly annoyed, Sherman responded, "Move your men to the left and charge the enemy. Develop their line-make a d—d big time. You know how. You know how."[15] Kilpatrick rode off to comply with the army commander's instructions.

Sherman was stunned that a veteran commander like Kilpatrick needed guidance in conducting such an elementary maneuver. Coming on the heels of "Little Kil's" near-disaster at Monroe's Crossroads less than a week earlier, this caused Sherman to lose whatever remaining faith he still had in Kilpatrick. In his correspondence with other officers, Sherman began to express the hope that Maj. Gen. Philip H. Sheridan's 10,000 veteran cavalrymen would march from Virginia to join his army.[16] Fearing that Kilpatrick was incapable of performing the service required of him, Sherman relegated his cavalry chieftain to a supporting role for the rest of the war.

Brig. Gen. Stephen Elliott, Jr.
Generals in Gray

Having enjoyed early success against the Union forces, Taliaferro reinforced his first line with troops from his second line. The reinforcements joined in the counterattacks against the hard-pressed Federal cavalrymen. Pvt. Arthur Ford and nineteen comrades from Brig. Gen. Stephen Elliott's 18th South Carolina Battalion took position on the left of the 1st South Carolina Regular Infantry and anxiously awaited the next Union assault. They would not have long to wait.

Col. Daniel Dustin
Library of Congress

To the rear, the men of Sherman's Left Wing could hear the familiar sounds of battle in the distance, prompting some units to "hurry to the sound of the guns." Despite the abysmal road conditions, Ward's division made good time. Col. Daniel Dustin's brigade led the way, reaching the battlefield at about 9:00 A.M. Dustin was ordered to support Hawley's brigade, which had been fighting since dawn. The arrival of reinforcements relieved Hawley's battle-weary men, who maintained their skirmish fire. By 9:30 A.M., the remainder of Ward's division (the brigades of Bvt. Brig. Gen. William Cogswell and Col. Henry Case) had arrived on the battlefield and quickly formed into battle lines. Many of Cogswell's men, including Pvt. Israel Spencer of the 136th New York, left camp in such a hurry that they did not have time to finish breakfast. As Cogswell's brigade deployed, the New Yorkers formed into "lines of battle still carrying a five-quart pail of cooked beans from breakfast."[17] Dustin's brigade moved into position with its right resting on the main road, with Cogswell's brigade on Dustin's right, while Case's brigade anchored the right flank. (See Map 9.)

Brig. Gen. Nathaniel J. Jackson's XX Corps division arrived on the battlefield shortly after Ward's division and took up a position on Ward's right. Jackson deployed his brigades into lines of battle, freeing Hawley's hard-pressed command to rejoin the rest of the division while it formed on Ward's immediate right. Brig. Gen. James S. Robinson's brigade then followed Hawley, while Col. James L. Selfridge's brigade relieved Jordan's cavalry brigade on the right flank. (See Map 10.) Relieved of front-line duty, Jordan's horsemen moved to the extreme right of the Union line, where they protected the Federal right flank. As Selfridge's brigade moved into position, Jordan's cavalry tumbled back in the face of a sudden Confederate counterattack.

The 123rd New York assumed the position just vacated by Jordan's horsemen. One of the New Yorkers, Sgt. Rice C. Bull, watched while "from our right and front a body of Kilpatrick's cavalry came down on us in retreat," with the determined Rebels in close pursuit. Selfridge's

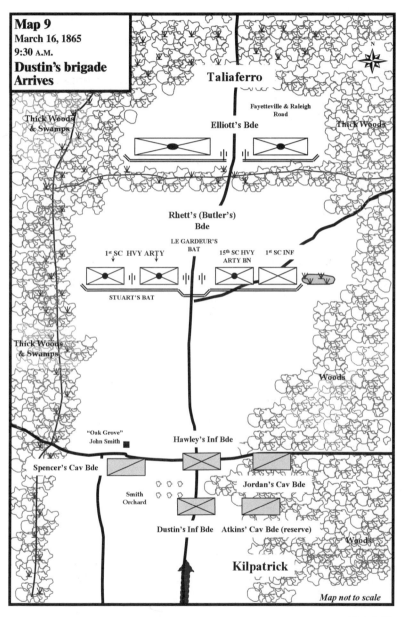

Map 9
March 16, 1865
9:30 A.M.
Dustin's brigade Arrives

Taliaferro

Fayetteville & Raleigh Road

Elliott's Bde

Thick Woods & Swamps

Thick Woods

Rhett's (Butler's) Bde

LE GARDEUR'S BAT

1st SC HVY ARTY

15th SC HVY ARTY BN

1st SC INF

STUART'S BAT

Thick Woods & Swamps

Woods

"Oak Grove" John Smith

Hawley's Inf Bde

Spencer's Cav Bde

Smith Orchard

Jordan's Cav Bde

Dustin's Inf Bde   Atkins' Cav Bde (reserve)

Woods

Kilpatrick

Map not to scale

Mark Smith

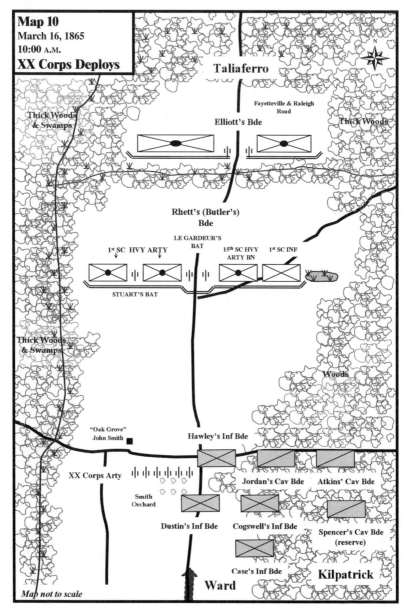

Map 10
March 16, 1865
10:00 A.M.
XX Corps Deploys

Taliaferro

Fayetteville & Raleigh Road

Elliott's Bde

Thick Woods & Swamps

Thick Woods

Rhett's (Butler's) Bde

LE GARDEUR'S BAT

1st SC HVY ARTY

15th SC HVY ARTY BN

1st SC INF

STUART'S BAT

Thick Woods & Swamps

Woods

"Oak Grove" John Smith

Hawley's Inf Bde

XX Corps Arty

Jordan's Cav Bde

Atkins' Cav Bde

Smith Orchard

Dustin's Inf Bde

Cogswell's Inf Bde

Spencer's Cav Bde (reserve)

Case's Inf Bde

Kilpatrick

Ward

Map not to scale

Mark Smith

men held their fire until the withdrawing cavalry had cleared the front. Once the fleeing cavalry had passed through the infantry's line, Selfridge's men unleashed a volley that stopped the Confederates dead in their tracks. Realizing that they now faced infantry rather than dismounted cavalry, Butler's South Carolinians quickly "lost their vim."[18] Jordan's troopers soon rallied and pursued them back toward the first line.

At 10:00 A.M., Atkins's cavalry brigade finally reached the battlefield, reinforcing Jordan's hard-pressed brigade. A relieved Kilpatrick ordered Atkins to move his brigade to the right flank, and to assume overall command of the troops in that sector.

Jackson's and Ward's divisions advanced in unison to within striking distance of Butler's defensive line. Once in position, the two lines blazed away at each other. On Butler's right flank, Private Ford and nineteen other members of the 18th South Carolina Battalion drew intense fire from Jackson's division. "The fighting took place in a piece of pine forest, and there were many trees that afforded protection to the men on both sides," recalled Ford. The Federal bullets made a distinctive "thwack" as they struck Ford's protective pine tree and rustled the dry leaves in a nearby stump hole. The racket so annoyed Ford that he sought the safety of another tree. As he did so, a Federal bullet struck Ford, "full in the middle of my body and knocked me down to a sitting posture." Luckily, the bullet passed through the blanket roll across his chest and struck one of his buttons, leaving only a large bruise in the center of his chest.[19]

So far, the performance of Rhett's inexperienced infantrymen had pleased Hardee and Taliaferro. "[The Federals] made several attacks with their infantry upon our lines, chiefly upon the left, in all of which they were repulsed," reported a satisfied Taliaferro.[20] Despite the stout defense of the South Carolinians, however, the weight of the Federals' numerical superiority was beginning to tell. As more Union troops filed onto the battlefield, the fighting along the first line intensified.

Scouts of the Army of the Potomac
(John Landigan is seated at far right)
Library of Congress

THE UNION FINDS AN UNGUARDED FLANK: CASE
ATTACKS THE CONFEDERATE RIGHT

While Ward and Jackson were deploying their divisions,
Kilpatrick ordered Captain Northrop to "investigate the enemy's right
flank" and report his findings. Northrop and his scouts moved out to
search for a weak spot in the Confederate line of battle.

Accompanying Northrop that morning was John Landigan, one
of the best scouts in the Union army. Before the start of the Carolinas
Campaign, Kilpatrick and Northrop had convinced Landigan to leave
the Army of the Potomac and serve in Northrop's elite scout company. Landigan agreed, and received orders to join the army at
Savannah. For these scouts, this was their great opportunity.

The Federal scouts moved around the Union left and into the
swamps. After slogging through the thick bog, Northrop and his
scouts found a spot where they could observe the Confederate right

flank, which surprisingly, was only lightly picketed. Northrop recalled, "I found it to be only a thin line with a battery posted only a little way from its end." Seeing an opportunity, Northrop and his scouts discussed a plan of action. "We concluded that we could guide a brigade of infantry close to the enemy's line without their discovering it." Northrop left some of his men to monitor the Confederate line and rode off. "Landegon [sic] and the few scouts I had with me remained to watch and notify me if the situation had changed while I went back and reported to Kilpatrick," recounted Northrop.[21]

Kilpatrick listened intently while Northrop related his findings and recommendations. Kilpatrick forwarded Northrop's intelligence to XX Corps commander Williams, who was then conferring with Major General Slocum, commander of the Left Wing. After hearing Kilpatrick's report, Williams recognized the opportunity identified by Northrop's scouts and ordered Ward to attack the Confederate right flank with a brigade.

It is important to note that none of these commanders—Sherman, Williams, Kilpatrick, and Case—mentions Northrop's actions in finding the open Confederate flank in their reports. Nevertheless, it is unlikely that any of the commanders had the means to find the unprotected Confederate flank on their own, and that they received this information from another source—the active and diligent Union scouts. It is possible that each thought Northrop's actions were not noteworthy enough to mention him by name. Northrop's account is a likely scenario, and we can conclude that it was Union scouts, not Case's infantrymen, that found the weak Confederate flank, as later reported by Northrop.

Meanwhile, Maj. John A. Reynolds, chief of the XX Corps artillery, arrived on the field and quickly deployed his three batteries: Battery I, 1st New York Artillery, armed with four 3-inch Ordinance rifles; Battery M, 1st New York Artillery, armed with four 12-pound Napoleon smoothbores; and Battery C, 1st Ohio Artillery, also armed with four 12-pound Napoleons. At about 10:00 A.M., Reynolds

Sergeant of LeGardeur's Battery and General Taliaferro
Drawing by Col. Darrell L. Combs, USMC (Ret.)

deployed his twelve guns into line about 500 yards from the Confederate works, with Battery M closest to the road, followed by Battery I, and then by the Ohio battery. Reynolds's guns went to work on the overmatched Confederate artillery, quickly silencing the pesky Southern guns. A direct hit blew "up one limber, killing all the horses, and driving the cannoneers from their pieces," reported Reynolds, "one wheel horse on another piece was killed as they were attempting to withdraw it."[22] The intense Union artillery barrage also inflicted great damage on Hardee's first defensive line. Capt. Hartwell Osborn of the 55th Ohio of Cogswell's brigade closely watched the effect of the artillery bombardment on Butler's men. "From this point in the line the enemy was in plain view," wrote Osborn, "the effect of the shells from our guns was plainly visible," with each round causing both confusion and casualties.[23]

During the Federal bombardment, Taliaferro and his staff rode up to LeGardeur's battery to ascertain why the Southern guns were not returning the enemy's fire. Taliaferro spotted a sergeant of the piece standing beside his gun, his elbow resting on the muzzle. A furious Taliaferro demanded, "What is the matter?" The Sergeant pointed to "the carriage and caisson, with every mule lying dead. A shell had burst on the cannon, killing everyone but him." In a more sympathetic tone, Taliaferro "complimented him, furnished him a horse and gave him the headquarters flag to carry."[24] In just a few hours of shelling, the XX Corps artillery expended an estimated 170 rounds. Given this heavy fire, it was no wonder that the Union artillerists inflicted such a heavy toll on the Confederate position.

Table 1. Ammunition Expenditure for the XX Corps artillery at Averasboro

Battery M, First NY Artillery fired 45 rounds of artillery shells (first line)
Battery I, First NY Artillery fired 172 rounds of artillery shells (total engagement)
Battery C, First Ohio Artillery fired 60 rounds of artillery shells (first line)

Source: *The War of the Rebellion*, ser. 1, vol. 47, pt. 1, p. 850, 852, 854.

As the XX Corps artillery blasted away at the Confederate first line, Ward assigned Case's brigade the task of attacking Hardee's right flank. Case immediately set his brigade in motion, marching it diagonally to the left of the Union line, where it passed behind the first and third brigades and the "Oak Grove" plantation house. Northrop and his scouts guided Case's brigade to a position where it could deploy and attack the exposed Confederate flank. Case formed his brigade into a line of battle under cover of the woods. His battle report offered a detailed account of his actions and also gave a rare explanation of a textbook deployment of an infantry brigade into battle formation (See Map 11):

> I formed the 102nd Illinois and the 79th Ohio in a line of battle, the 102nd on the right, and the 79th on the left, and placed the 120th and 105th Illinois in close column by division, respectively, behind the right of the 102nd Illinois and the 79th Ohio, at the same time throwing forward one wing of each of the regiments in the second line as skirmishers, and also one company on each of my flanks as flankers, at least 150 yards from the right and left of my line of battle. This disposition being made, I ordered my brigade forward.[25]

Case's men negotiated a thick swamp and then emerged from the woods. Peering into the open field, Case quickly realized that he had not moved his brigade far enough to the left. He ordered his men to realign farther to the north, placing his troops squarely on the Confederate flank.

After dressing his lines, Case advanced again, his men slogging through the thick swamp, heading toward the edge of the open field. They quickly overwhelmed the few Confederate pickets in the area before they could alert the first line of Case's presence on its flank. Case kept his troops hidden in the swamp, advancing to the edge of the wood line. The brigade commander realized that he was now positioned squarely on the right flank of the Confederate line, with "my line of battle, being perpendicular to their works, about 300 yards from the right of their line."[26] Inexplicably, Case's movements remained undetected by the Confederate troops on the first line. Nevertheless, some Federals could not tell whether the men before them were friends or foes. Sgt. Thomas Simpson of the 102nd Illinois was confused by "the blue clothes which they wore." The sight froze some of the Federals in their tracks. "Some of us thought them to be our own

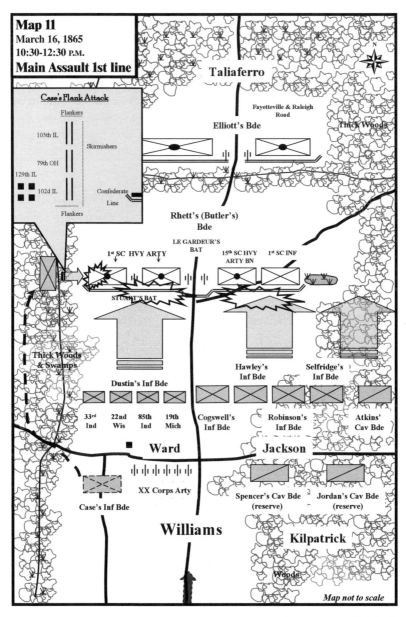

Map 11
March 16, 1865
10:30-12:30 P.M.
Main Assault 1st line

Case's Flank Attack

Flankers

105th IL

79th OH   Skirmishers

129th IL

102d IL   Confederate
                        Line
Flankers

Taliaferro

Fayetteville & Raleigh
Road

Elliott's Bde   Thick Woods

Rhett's (Butler's)
Bde

LE GARDEUR'S
BAT

1ˢᵗ SC HVY ARTY   15ᵗʰ SC HVY   1ˢᵗ SC INF
                                ARTY BN

STUART'S BAT

Thick Woods
& Swamps   Hawley's   Selfridge's
                                        Inf Bde   Inf Bde

Dustin's Inf Bde

33ʳᵈ   22nd   85th   19th   Cogswell's   Robinson's   Atkins'
Ind   Wis   Ind   Mich   Inf Bde   Inf Bde   Cav Bde

                        Ward   Jackson

                    XX Corps Arty

Case's Inf Bde   Spencer's Cav Bde   Jordan's Cav Bde
                         (reserve)   (reserve)

Williams   **Kilpatrick**

                        Woods

                                        Map not to scale

Mark Smith

men. Even some of [our] officers were deceived." The artillerymen of the 1st South Carolina Heavy Artillery wore blue uniforms that closely resembled those worn by the Northern infantry. When the "heavies" served in the defenses of Fort Sumter, the color of their uniforms had not mattered; however, now that they were in the field acting as infantrymen, and their blue uniforms caused confusion on both sides. Once Case's men had seen these "blue clothed soldiers" unleash a deadly volley into Dustin's advancing column, any lingering doubt about the identity of the men in their front vanished.[27]

While Case's brigade took position on the right flank, Ward's and Jackson's divisions continued pressing the Confederate line. After allowing Case's brigade sufficient time to get into position, General Williams ordered the remainder of his command to unleash a general assault on the first line, hoping to distract Butler's troops while Case concentrated his superior numbers against the Confederate right flank. In order for William's plan to succeed, Dustin's brigade had to be positioned on the far left of the Union line of battle, where it would join Case's brigade in rolling up Butler's flank. Preoccupied with the threat in their front, Butler's men never realized that their fortunes were about to change drastically.

As the bugles sounded the advance, Dustin's men stepped off, passing through the orchards and outbuildings of the nearby "Oak Grove" plantation house, advancing steadily toward the Confederate defensive line. Sgt. Charles H. Dickinson of the 22nd Wisconsin recalled the movement. "We fully expected to meet a charge of canister, but nothing came but a volley of musketry," he wrote, "and fortunately for us the bullets nearly all went over us."[28]

The right flank regiments of Dustin's brigade did not enjoy the same good fortune. Butler's men poured a hailstorm of fire into the advancing Federals. "The enemy opened on us with musketry and artillery," recalled Maj. Jefferson E. Brant of the 85th Indiana. "The right wing of the regiment suffered severely and doubled down on the left wing under the cover of a small ravine and some negro huts." The

85th quickly recovered, wrote Brant, and "again moved forward on the double quick and in the charge were soon in the enemy's works." During the charge, Sgt. Maj. William Trice Patton was "shot through his brain," and "fell in the high tide and flush of life. He now sleeps in an unknown grave."[29] Patton's body was later removed from the battlefield and reburied in the National Cemetery in Raleigh.

Peering from his concealed position, Case realized that a general assault against the Confederate defenses was already underway and that there was no time to waste. Two of his regiments carried seven-shot Spencer repeating rifles and would not have to stop to reload after each shot, meaning that they could bring to bear tremendous firepower. With his units in position and at the ready, Case ordered his men to emerge from the woods and quickly form into lines of battle. They assembled in the open field, about 150 yards from the Confederate flank, forming and dressing their lines. Within seconds, they were ready to make the assault. Still preoccupied with the attack in their front, Butler's men did not notice the blue mass forming on their flank. Once his men were in line and ready to move out, Case cried, "Charge at the double quick!" His men sprang forward, yelling and firing as they charged. "We broke for the Johnnies on the run," recorded Pvt. Thomas Finley of the 102nd Illinois in his diary, "and with a demoniac yell we rushed in on their flank pouring volley after volley from our Spencers."[30]

Case's charge fortuitously coincided with Dustin's frontal attack, which crashed into the exposed Confederate right flank simultaneously. The combined onslaught overwhelmed Butler's men, who broke and fled for the second line in total confusion. "The Johnnies showed us their heels as fast as God would let them," crowed Finley. General Hardee was on the first line encouraging his troops when Case's brigade fell upon his flank. U. H. Farr of the 70th Indiana observed General Hardee's reaction when the Federals entered the works. "General Hardee came near capture while he was watching the troops in the front," reported Farr. "Suddenly, he saw the flank line, put spurs to his horse and dashed from the field."[31]

Case's Brigade Entering the First Confederate Line
Drawing by Col. Darrell L. Combs, USMC (Ret.)

On the other end of the Confederate line, Capt. Daniel Oakey of Hawley's 2nd Massachusetts entered the Confederate works near the position held by the 1st South Carolina Regulars. Oakey moved "past the dead and wounded of Rhett's brigade" as his battle line passed through the Confederate position. "I remember seeing the body of a very young officer, whose handsome, refined face attracted my attention." Oakey stopped and "knelt at his side for a moment," and gazed upon the lifeless officer. He immediately noticed the dead officer's buttons, which "bore the arms of South Carolina." Oakey realized that "evidently we were fighting the Charleston chivalry."[32]

Not surprisingly, the Confederates did not remember their abandonment of the first line as a panicked rout. Rather, they contended that the retreat was an organized withdrawal that occurred only after "a general charge upon our whole front was made, the right was out flanked and my left was soon turned," as Captain Huguenin recounted. "We then were ordered to fall back upon the second line and help

Second South Carolina Infantry Rear Guard Action
Drawing by Col. Darrell L. Combs, USMC (Ret.)

Elliott's Brigade hold it." However, the impact of the crushing flank attack probably meant that the Confederates made a less than orderly retreat. Pvt. Presley Boylston of the 2nd South Carolina Heavy Artillery, who was among those sent forward to support the first line, had a different perspective. Boylston found himself firing at the advancing Federals from the trenches. "I noticed the shots of the enemy getting closer at hand, recalled Boylston, and looking around found I was the only man left in the trench." He quickly joined his panicked comrades in their disorganized flight back to the second line. As he fell back to the safety of the second line, a terrifying thought ran through his mind. He remembered that he was carrying his tin pan "hanging on his back"; worse yet, the tin pan quickly "became a target upon which the enemy concentrated their fire."[33]

The victorious Union troops could see the large number of Confederate dead and wounded left behind by the routed South Carolinians. "It was the terriblest slaughter of men that I ever witnessed," observed Private Finley. The XX Corps artillery had devastated Butler's line, wreaking havoc on the defending artillery and infantry, making it all too obvious as to why Dustin's brigade did not receive canister fire from the Confederate gunners. "In the mud in the bottom of the ditch he [a Confederate artilleryman] had been hit by a cannon ball from one of our guns," wrote Sergeant Dickinson. An artillery shell had penetrated six feet of earth works, tearing "off the whole right side of his body." Remarkably, the man was still alive, and begged the Federals to shoot him. The poor soul only wanted to be "put out of his misery and pain; but he only lived a few minutes," recalled Dickinson. Sgt. Franklin Rice of the 19th Michigan Infantry saw a similarly horrific sight when he entered the Confederate works. "I saw one man Confederate at least, with a hole made through his breast as slick as you could have bored it with an auger."[34]

Lyman Widney of the 34th Illinois recalled another sad moment. "One of the wounded artillerymen lay on the ground with his back to [illegible] with ashen face, pale [illegible] look in his eyes. To our boys who stopped to [offer] sympathy and assistance he only replied in weak voice, 'Boys, let me see a doctor,' and when one of our Surgeons rode ahead, he was hailed and came over to investigate. When the Surgeon opened his clothing a small blue circle in the white undershirt marked the spot where the fatal bullet had entered his stomach.

"During this examination, his keen eyes searched the face of the Surgeon for an answer to the question that trembled on his lips, 'Doctor, am I hurt bad?'

"The Surgeon quickly turned away without a reply, cleared his throat several times, and noticing an approaching ambulance, ordered it to be stopped for the boy, who now knew as well as we did that there was no hope. A faint sigh, a quiver of the lip, and then a look of quiet, uncomplaining resignation rested on that boyish face, when we turned away and saw it no more."[35]

Fearing a counterattack, Case immediately wheeled his brigade to the left and faced it to the north, where it linked up with the remainder of the XX Corps. Union artillerymen followed the victorious infantry, turning a captured gun on the retreating Confederates. Lt. Edward P. Newkirk, commander of Battery M, 1st New York Artillery, reported that three of his men fired twenty rounds of the Confederates' own ammunition into the backs of the retreating Rebels.[36]

Ward's and Jackson's divisions quickly left the Confederate first line behind them, pausing to reform their ranks for a determined push on the Confederate second line, which lay some 300 yards to the north. A lull fell over the battlefield. The XX Corps artillery also deployed on the captured first line and, by 11:30 A.M., the XX Corps had consolidated its new position. Casualties were evacuated to the Union field hospital at "Oak Grove," where overworked surgeons cared for the wounded of both sides.

The Confederates had suffered terrible losses. The 1st South Carolina Heavy Artillery had borne the brunt of Case's and Dustin's assaults and suffered heavily, losing 215 killed, wounded, or captured out of 458 officers and men engaged. Lucas's battalion had also suffered severely. "Captain Richardson's company went into the fight that morning ninety strong," reported Samuel Ravenel. "At roll call the next morning only nineteen answered," a staggering loss of 80% in just a few hours' fighting. Case reported that his brigade captured 2 pieces of artillery and 56 prisoners. He could not recall the exact numbers of killed and wounded, but "judging from what I saw upon the field their losses in killed and wounded could not have been less than 80 killed and 450 wounded."[37] General Williams reported that he captured 175 prisoners, and buried another 128 on the field, including seven officers. Williams also reported that he lost 438 killed, wounded, and missing during the morning's action, a heavy loss.[38] Later that day, Butler's (Rhett's) brigade reported to McLaws with only 400 combat-ready men in the ranks.[39] Butler had gone into battle with 1,051 men that morning and therefore lost an astounding 62% of those engaged. His brigade's officer corps suffered especially heavy losses.

The 1st South Carolina Regulars lost 3 officers killed, 6 wounded, and 2 missing, while the 1st South Carolina Artillery lost 4 killed, 6 wounded, and 2 missing.[40]

THE FEDERAL ASSAULT ON HARDEE'S SECOND LINE

The remnant of Butler's shattered brigade withdrew to Elliott's second line of defense. In order to reorganize his battle lines, General Williams ordered a temporary halt to the Union advance. Furthermore, elements of the XIV Corps were now arriving on the battlefield, and Williams wanted to utilize them as well.

While the Federals dressed their ranks, interesting events unfolded on the Confederate second line. Strong evidence suggests that the performance of elements of Elliott's brigade on the second line was less than stellar. At least some of Elliott's men had abandoned their positions during the route of Rhett's brigade. Captain Huguenin returned to the second line and was shocked to find it empty. "To our surprise when we got there Elliott's Brigade was gone," he recalled. With no other alternative, "we took possession of the line." Maj. Gen. Lafayette McLaws, who commanded the troops holding the third line, watched Taliaferro's troops melt away, noting that they had "deserted or retired from their lines and came into mine."[41]

Hardee was displeased with the performance of Elliott's brigade, which he displayed in an encounter with Pvt. Arthur Ford of Elliott's 18th South Carolina Battalion a few days after the Battle of Averasboro. Ford, along with some of the other men of his command, paused to wash his feet in a cool stream. Hardee spotted the South Carolinian and called out, "You there, Sir! What are you doing straggling from your command? I suppose you are one of those men who behaved so badly at Averysboro."[42] Clearly, the Confederate commander held a low opinion of the combat worthiness of his men, but he had no choice but to do the best he could with what he had available to him.

Although badly mauled on the first line, Butler's brigade soon recovered and rallied on the second line, while many of Elliott's troops stood their ground and fought with the same tenacity displayed by Butler's men on the first line. One of Elliott's units, Bonaud's (28th Georgia) Battalion, reported that it lost one man killed, 17 wounded, and 15 missing at Averasboro, suggesting that the Georgians fiercely defended the second line.[43] One of Elliott's veterans, Pvt. Robert W. Sanders of the 2nd South Carolina Heavy Artillery, recalled an intense firefight with Union sharpshooters on the second and third lines. "Many of our men were killed and wounded on both lines," lamented Sanders.[44]

Capt. Armand L. DeRosset's Fayetteville Arsenal Battalion, about 179 strong, held that portion of the second line to the left of the Fayetteville-Raleigh Road. When the Federals attacked the second line and drove the Arsenal Battalion from its initial position, the situation grew desperate. DeRosset knew that his line could not hold for long, and he also knew that General Elliott was too far away to provide quick guidance in this emergency, so he turned to the commander of Rhett's Brigade, Col. William Butler, for orders. Butler was reluctant to give orders to units that were not under his command and replied, "I have no orders to give you." DeRosset then turned to the commander of the unit to his right, the 22nd Georgia Battalion, and recommended that both commands counterattack and drive the Yankees back. The commander of the 22nd Georgia Battalion concurred. While he was barking out orders for the counterattack, DeRosset took a bullet that passed through both lungs. He was too severely wounded to be moved, and was left on the battlefield to die. Union troops later found DeRosset and evacuated him to the field hospital.[45]

Hardee recognized the gravity of the situation and knew he had to act quickly to prevent disaster. He knew that Taliaferro's division was in no condition to repulse a determined attack by overwhelming Union forces. Heavy skirmishing continued while Hardee contemplated his options and the Union army prepared for another assault on the second defensive line. Williams fed still more troops into the battle, extending his lines to the left and to the right until they overlapped both Confederate flanks. Williams then shifted Ward's division to the left of Jackson's division on the left side of the Fayetteville-Raleigh Road, while Kilpatrick's cavalry covered the right flank to guard against a possible flank attack. Williams also sent the lead elements of Brig. Gen. James D. Morgan's XIV Corps division to deploy on the left flank, connecting with Ward's division and extending the main Union line of battle.

With Union troops overlapping both of Taliaferro's flanks, Hardee's only viable option was to cover those flanks with veteran troops from McLaws's division, permitting Taliaferro's men to disengage and withdraw to prepared positions on the third line. McLaws's troops would then retire to the third line. Accordingly, Hardee ordered three regiments of McLaws's division to reinforce Taliaferro. This ran contrary to Hardee's original tactical scheme, which was for Taliaferro's division to conduct a fighting withdrawal to the third and main line. However, the gravity of the situation dictated an immediate change of plans, prompting Hardee to do whatever was necessary to protect his command. Captain Huguenin also realized that the situation on the second line had grown desperate. "In our weakened condition we had not enough men to hold the front and could not guard the flanks," he noted, unaware that help was on the way.[46]

Lt. Col. William Wallace commanded the 2nd South Carolina Infantry of Conner's brigade of McLaws's division. Wallace received orders to move out of his entrenchments and take up a position on Taliaferro's right flank. The 2nd South Carolina was also to serve as the rear guard when the second line was ordered to withdraw. As the 2nd South Carolina approached the second line, it easily drove back a few Union skirmishers. The South Carolinians watched as other troops dressed in blue uniforms jumped over the reverse slope of the breast works. "On the impulse of the movement my regiment took this front line to be the enemy," recounted W. F. Johnson of the 2nd South Carolina. "We were in the act of opening fire." But Johnson noticed something odd about the blue-clad soldiers in his front, and ordered his men not to fire. A concerned Colonel Wallace sent Johnson forward to investigate. As Johnson approached the blue-clad soldiers, a voice called out, "Who are you?"

Johnson responded. "Who are you?"

The soldier replied, "I belong to the 2nd South Carolina Heavy Artillery."

A relieved Johnson declared, "I belong to the 2nd South

Earnest J. Bachoven, 82nd Ohio Infantry
Collection of Col. Darrell L. Combs, USMC (Ret.)

Carolina Infantry." Johnson then rejoined his troops, and Wallace resumed his advance toward the second line.

Like the 1st South Carolina Heavy Artillery of Rhett's brigade, the 2nd South Carolina Artillery also wore blue uniforms, which caused the same confusion among Wallace's men as it had the Federals of Case's brigade. No sooner had the 2nd South Carolina Infantry reached its position than the Union infantry attacked in overwhelming numbers. The 2nd South Carolina could not hold and slowly withdrew to the third line, fighting a rearguard action to cover Taliaferro's retreat.[47]

Meanwhile, Kilpatrick's cavalry was operating on the Union right flank. Northrop's diligent scouts had found an unguarded road that passed directly behind the enemy's fortifications. Prisoner reports persuaded Kilpatrick that the Confederate troops on the second line were falling back. Seeing an opportunity, Kilpatrick ordered the 9th Ohio Cavalry of Atkins's brigade to launch a mounted attack on the Confederate flank and rear. Col. William D. Hamilton, commander

114

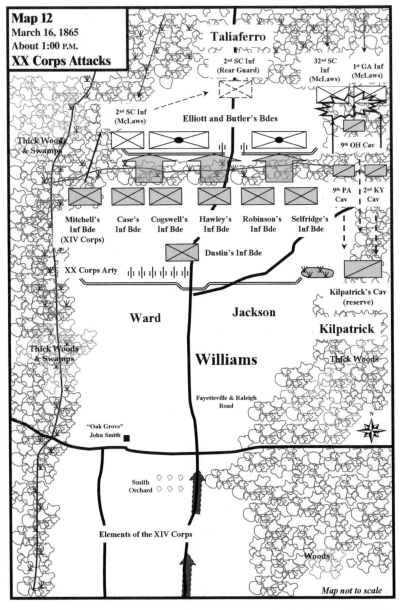

Mark Smith

of the 9th Ohio, informed Kilpatrick that his ammunition supply was exhausted because his regiment had been skirmishing for most of the morning. Kilpatrick nevertheless repeated his order, and a perplexed Hamilton promptly obeyed.[48]

At the same time and in obedience to Hardee's orders, the 32nd Georgia and the 1st Georgia Regulars assumed a position to the left rear of Elliott's brigade, protecting Taliaferro's left flank. Sgt. W. H. Andrews of the 1st Georgia Regulars, received orders to advance from his company commander, Capt. James R. DuBose. "There is a [Confederate] line of battle to your front," DuBose told him. "You will not fire a gun until that line retreats past you." The officer continued. "You will then fight for every inch of ground as you fall back and not...retire on the work unless the enemy goes with you." Andrews quickly acted to implement DuBose's instructions.[49]

At about 1:00 P.M., an all-out Union assault on the second line began. "In obedience to orders my lines pressed steadily forward," reported General Ward, "driving the rebel line before it."[50] As the blue-clad infantry surged ahead, the 9th and 10th Ohio Cavalries trotted off toward the far right of the Union line. The 9th Ohio cavalry used the unguarded road discovered by Northrop's scouts, passing through thick underbrush and scrub pines. The 10th Ohio cavalry followed in reserve.

As soon as the 9th Ohio cavalry gained the road, a heavy volley tore through its ranks, delivered by the 32nd Georgia and the 1st Georgia Regulars. Dense undergrowth had permitted the Georgians to approach undetected to within yards of the Federal cavalry. "I saw a line of infantry rise up and fire a volley," recounted Sergeant Andrews of the 1st Georgia, while "the cavalry moved toward our left." Andrews quickly ordered his men to fire, and they managed to get off three volleys before the Union cavalry took refuge in the safety of the swamp. Andrews's company commander rode over to find out why Andrews disobeyed orders by firing prior to reaching the left flank of the second line. "I told the Captain that I could not help it for the cavalry was too tempting a shot to let pass," explained Andrews, "He gave me Hail Columbia for disobeying orders."[51]

The 9th Ohio cavalry was both low on ammunition and unable to ascertain the strength of the enemy force in its front. The Buckeyes quickly retired to higher ground some 200 yards away. "We reformed and drove back the enemy who had followed us up," reported Colonel Hamilton.[52] Col. Thomas J. Jordan, whose brigade was the cavalry division's reserve, rushed several regiments to the front to reinforce the embattled 9th Ohio Cavalry. The Federal horsemen "opened so hot a fire upon the charging line that it fell back in confusion," reported Colonel Jordan.[53] The cavalrymen held this position until Selfridge's infantry brigade relieved them.

Taliaferro's undersized division was no match for a determined assault by three divisions of veteran infantry, one division of cavalry, and three batteries of artillery. Hardee and Taliaferro both recognized the hopelessness of trying to hold the second line, prompting Old Reliable to order Taliaferro to withdraw to the third, and main, defensive line.[54]

Concerned about the mounting number of casualties, Sherman ordered Williams not to press the retreating Confederates. The Northern soldiers therefore permitted the Southerners to retire largely unmolested. The fight for the second line was over. After nearly a full day of hard fighting, Sherman's blue-clad soldiers had driven the Confederates from two defensive lines. However, the victorious Federals still had to contend with Hardee's main line, which would prove far more challenging than the first two. Serious work remained.

SHERMAN'S ASSAULT ON THE THIRD LINE

Taliaferro's division retired to the third line with little difficulty. Taliaferro ordered Elliott's brigade to occupy the center of the third line, and he posted troops on either side of the road. Taliaferro also unlimbered a section of Brooks's battery in the road to support Elliott's brigade. Butler's battered brigade served as the third line reserve, holding a position 300 yards behind Elliott's brigade. Once Taliaferro's division had fallen back to the third line, McLaws's division shifted to the left, with Conner's brigade repositioning on Elliott's right. Harrison's brigade moved from its position in the center to Fiser's position, and, in turn, Fiser's brigade took Hardy's position. Hardy's brigade then extended the Confederate battle line to the Black River. In addition, McLaws also deployed a section of Brooks's battery in support of Fiser's brigade.[55]

Due to the broken terrain and a lack of troops, McLaws was unable to extend his line to the Cape Fear River, leaving his right flank vulnerable to being turned. McLaws faced a similar dilemma on the left, so he shifted pickets from Hardy's brigade to the banks of the Black River. McLaws also told Hardee that he lacked sufficient troops to cover the left flank. If the Federals launched an assault in that direction, McLaws warned, the third line would collapse, blocking his line of retreat. Hardee understood the risk but believed that the Federals would not attempt to assault his left flank. As a precaution, he repositioned Butler's brigade more to the east, where it could bolster the left flank if a threat developed. However, McLaws knew that Butler's 400 battle-weary survivors would not be able to stem a determined attack on the Confederate left flank.[56]

While McLaws looked after his left flank, the 1st Georgia Regulars and the 32nd Georgia withdrew to the third line under heavy Union pressure. When Sergeant Andrews returned to his former position, he was shocked to find that his regiment had moved. He found the line occupied by "a line of boys," with the Yankee line of battle no more than 40 yards away. Fortunately, a heavy volley unleashed by other Confederate troops further down the line brought the Yankee advance to a halt. In the meantime, Sergeant Andrews persuaded the lads to open fire on the Yankees. "The boys asked if the Yankees were coming which I told them yes," wrote Andrews. "I also told them if they did not fire that they would all be killed." The terrified boys were "stuck down in the trenches and poked their guns over the works and fired." The sergeant was not persuaded that they had taken aim when firing their ragged volley: "I doubt they ever saw the Yankees they were firing at."[57]

In the meantime, the advancing Union troops slowly pursued the Confederates toward the third line. Ward's division occupied the center, Jackson's division held the right, and elements of Morgan's XIV Corps division held the left. Because he had already taken heavy losses and with Goldsboro still a long way off, Sherman postponed launching an all-out assault on Hardee's strong third line. He ordered his subordinates not to push the Confederates until he could bring up the rest of the Left Wing. If the Confederates remained in position the next morning (March 17), he would attack with Slocum's entire force.

The Union advance on the third line slowed further when it struck the thick, marshy ground in front of the Confederate position. "The nature of the ground precluded a rapid advance," wrote General Ward, "it being very swampy and heavy." Although the nature of the terrain hindered their advance, Ward's troops slowly drove the Confederates back to their main line of defense, which extended along a commanding ridge on a flat plain.[58] Hardee had chosen his position well; the swampy ground provided protection from frontal assault, while the high ground provided a good platform for his artillery.

Sherman's strategy of "not pressing the enemy" did not please many of the Union soldiers. Pvt. Charles Castle of the 129th Illinois described his regiment's movements toward the Confederate line. "The bugle would sound the forward and we would advance a few steps and lie down," he recalled. The Union bugle calls also told the Confederate defenders where to direct their volleys of musketry and artillery. As the advancing Union line emerged from the swamp and crested the hill, Hardee's main line unloosed a violent volley of musketry and artillery that forced the Union troops to retire behind the cover of the ridge, where they halted to dress their lines.[59]

Williams decided to wait until Morgan's XIV Corps division was fully deployed before resuming his advance. While Morgan formed his division, Williams reorganized and repositioned his troops for the

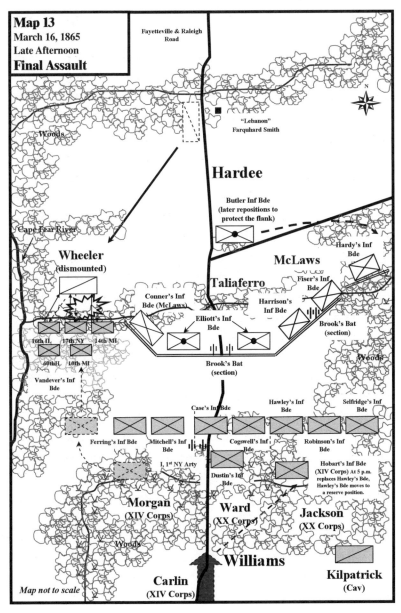

Map 13
March 16, 1865
Late Afternoon
Final Assault

Fayetteville & Raleigh
Road

N

Woods

"Lebanon"
Farquhard Smith

Hardee

Butler Inf Bde
(later repositions to
protect the flank)

Cape Fear River

Hardy's Inf
Bde

Wheeler
(dismounted)

McLaws

Fiser's Inf
Bde

Conner's Inf
Bde (McLaws)

Taliaferro

Harrison's
Inf Bde

Elliott's Inf
Bde

Brook's Bat
(section)

16th IL   17th NY   14th MI

Woods

60th IL   10th MI

Brook's Bat
(section)

Vandever's Inf
Bde

Case's Inf Bde

Hawley's Inf
Bde

Selfridge's Inf
Bde

Ferring's Inf Bde

Mitchell's Inf
Bde

Cogswell's Inf
Bde

Robinson's Inf
Bde

I, 1st NY Arty

Dustin's Inf
Bde

Hobart's Inf Bde
(XIV Corps) At 5 p.m.
replaces Hawley's Bde,
Hawley's Bde moves to
a reserve position.

Morgan
(XIV Corps)

Ward
(XX Corps)

Jackson
(XX Corps)

Woods

Williams

Kilpatrick
(Cav)

Map not to scale

Carlin
(XIV Corps)

Mark Smith

impending attack. Additionally, Battery I, 1st New York Artillery, with its four 3-inch ordnance rifles, deployed along the Fayetteville-Raleigh Road to provide artillery support for the attack. The poor road conditions made it difficult for Morgan to get his troops into position. Once Morgan's division deployed into lines of battle, his men connected with Ward's division, extending the Union line to the banks of the Cape Fear River. Morgan placed Bvt. Brig. Gen. John G. Mitchell's brigade to the left of Ward's division. Brig. Gen. Benjamin D. Fearing's brigade took up a position to the left of Mitchell, while Brig. Gen. William Vandever's brigade remained in reserve (See Map 13). Because it took time for these units to get into position, Williams did not give the order to renew the attack until late in the day. It is unclear why Williams elected to resume the attacks, since Sherman's orders were not to press the enemy. Perhaps they were merely probing attacks intended to find weaknesses in the Confederate position; Williams did not say. In any event, Williams ordered several assaults on Hardee's position.

When the order to attack finally came, the entire Union line lurched forward. Ward's and Jackson's divisions quickly encountered trouble. Cogswell's brigade had advanced only a few yards when a staff officer informed the brigade commander that he had broken connection with the brigade on his left. Cogswell ordered his brigade to halt and realign, the whole time "receiving the full fire of the enemy's line." Even under fire, halting his brigade was the lesser of two evils; advancing unsupported would have exposed Cogswell's left to enfilading fire, causing even more casualties. The intense Confederate fire eventually forced Cogswell to withdraw to a safer position.[60]

The Union attacks on the left fared no better. Morgan's skirmishers enjoyed initial success, driving "the enemy's outposts into the main works." Fearing's brigade made a "right half wheel," with Fearing believing that he had uncovered the Confederate right flank. Instead of uncovering the flank, Fearing "found works in our front…[which] extended far to our left to a very deep ravine."[61] Elsewhere, stiff resistance from the main Confederate line soon caused Morgan's advance to grind to a halt.[62] Sensing that his frontal assault was failing, Morgan ordered Vandever's brigade to advance from its reserve position, move to the left, and turn the Confederate right flank. Unfortunately for the Federals, Vandever's brigade soon encountered problems of its own.

MOTHER NATURE'S SURPRISE

As fighting raged all along the third line, Maj. Gen. Joseph Wheeler and part of his cavalry corps arrived on the battlefield. Wheeler had been covering the upper approaches of the Black River with a portion of his command, and now joined Hardee at Averasboro. Wheeler rode up to Hardee and asked whether his cavalry could be of any assistance. Aware that Sherman was massing his army to assault his undefended right flank, Hardee asked Wheeler to position his troopers on that flank and extend the Confederate line to the Cape Fear River. Wheeler readily agreed and rode off to comply.[63]

Vandever's Brigade at the Ravine
Drawing by Col. Darrell L. Combs, USMC (Ret.)

While Wheeler positioned his troopers, Vandever's Federal brigade was moving into position to assault the unprotected Confederate right flank. Initially, everything went according to plan. At first, Vandever's troops encountered little resistance as they advanced across an open field, but then they entered a deep ravine that lay directly across their line of attack. The forty-foot-deep ravine had nearly vertical walls and ran west toward the Cape Fear River. Vandever's men therefore could not bypass it. Two companies from the 16th Illinois and three companies from the 17th New York were sent forward as skirmishers. They scrambled down into the ravine and attempted to negotiate its far bank with little success.[64] Many became stuck in the bottom of the deep ravine, unable to climb the steep walls. The blue-clad soldiers grabbed onto roots and relied on the assistance of their comrades to climb to the top of the opposite side of the ravine. A private of the 10th Michigan recalled the extreme hardships his regiment in the ravine. "We could only descend by the help of bushes which grew from either bank," he wrote, "swing down from point to point, crossing a stream at the bottom, and again drawing ourselves up by the shrubbery on the opposite side." This arduous process caused the Federal flanking maneuver to grind to a complete halt.[65]

While Vandever's troops struggled in the ravine, Wheeler's horsemen hastily erected barricades in the field on the north side of the ravine. Wheeler's line rested only a few hundred yards away from the ravine and extended to the banks of the Cape Fear River. A twenty-yard buffer of woods provided the only cover available to those Union soldiers trapped between the ravine and Wheeler's line. As Vandever's skirmishers clawed their way out of the ravine and entered the field, Wheeler's dismounted horsemen unleashed a devastating volley into their ranks. The stunned Union skirmishers fell back to the cover of the woods. "Volley after volley was sent and returned," recalled a member of the 17th New York nicknamed "Old Rock." The firing was so heavy that the 17th New York was ordered to lie down and find shelter.[66]

In the meantime, the situation in the ravine grew tense. Vandever's skirmishers realized that they were pinned down and that they could not retreat across the ravine without being captured or killed. They had only one option: find cover and return fire. As casualities mounted, Morgan realized that further attempts to attack would only result in senseless waste of life, so he ordered Vandever to disengage. Daylight faded, and "it grew chilly and rained heavily," noted a soldier of the 17th New York. "We abandoned our line leaving only a skirmishing party under command of Capt. James B. Horner." Union losses at the ravine had been heavy. Vandever lost 66 men killed or wounded, while the 17th New York infantry suffered 32 casualties, including its regimental commander, Lt. Col. James Lake, who was severely wounded.[67]

Fortune had smiled on Hardee's outnumbered troops that afternoon, permitting them to hang on in the face of repeated Union assaults. All of Sherman's attempts to turn the third line had failed, and the Union commander was in no hurry to try his luck again. Slocum called a halt to further probing attacks that day, although heavy skirmishing continued until well after dark.

Unfortunately for the Confederates, the day's activities did not end with the termination of Federal efforts to drive Hardee from the third line. Union artillery and infantry directed a continuous fire on the third line. W. F. Johnson of the 2nd South Carolina Infantry recalled that "we stuck our flag staff into the breastworks," drawing the immediate attention of a Union battery. "The enemy battery had enfilading fire on my regiment," recounted Johnson. One shell from the battery "missed my back, passed between the arm of Lt. Col. Wallace and his body, grazed the back of the adjutant, [and] ricocheted along down the line hitting two men."[68]

Nevertheless, Hardee's third line had held. The Southerners' well-prepared breastworks, good selection and use of terrain, combined with favorable weather conditions contributed greatly to the success of Hardee's well-planned and well-executed defense in depth. Hardee's demoralized and largely untested command had performed beyond his wildest expectations. Taliaferro was justifiably pleased with the performance of his troops. "The enemy advanced several times on my position during the day but was always repulsed," he reported proudly. "His artillery shelled our lines at intervals, and was replied to by a section of Brooks' battery."[69]

"Old Reliable" was magnificent that day. Hardee had designed and implemented a masterful defense, and he had handled his troops skillfully. Hardee had accomplished all his objectives: he had stopped Sherman's advance in its tracks for an entire day and had bloodied the Northern veterans in the process. More importantly, Hardee's troops bought precious time for Johnston, allowing him to consolidate his forces around Smithfield. Hardee decided to withdraw before Sherman could find a weakness in the Confederate line and then exploit it.

Hardee had good reason to be concerned. Sherman was preparing to launch an all-out assault on the Confederate works the next morning. During the night, Sherman ordered up the rest of the Left Wing in anticipation of renewing the attack. General Hampton also advised Hardee that the Right Wing had crossed the South River, and that his position at Averasboro was in danger of being flanked.[70] If Sherman launched an assault with both wings, Hardee's little command would be destroyed. This was no time for Hardee to press his luck, and Old Reliable knew it.

HARDEE SLIPS AWAY

Johnston and Hardee corresponded throughout the Battle of Averasboro. With troops from the Army of Tennessee arriving at Smithfield, Johnston was now ready to concentrate his forces against one wing of Sherman's army in the hope of defeating it in detail. Accordingly, Hardee advised Johnston that he was abandoning his position and would move north toward a link-up with Johnston's forces at Smithfield. That night, Hardee ordered his infantry and artillery to abandon their entrenchments, while Wheeler's cavalry remained behind as a rear guard to cover Hardee's withdrawal. The Battle of Averasboro was over.[71]

As day broke on March 17, Union skirmishers cautiously approached the Confederate entrenchments and peered over the embankment. To their surprise, they found the breastworks empty. Nothing remained but the smoldering embers of the enemy's camp-fires. The Confederates were gone. Sherman's main body moved forward to occupy Hardee's line.

Upon learning that Hardee had retired north, Sherman turned again to his plan to mislead the Confederates into believing that his objective was the state capital at Raleigh and not the railhead at Goldsboro. XX Corps commander Bvt. Maj. Gen. Alpheus S. Williams ordered Kilpatrick's cavalry to pursue the retreating Confederates. To further the deception, Williams also instructed Ward's division to pursue Hardee as far as Averasboro before turning toward the northeast and then heading for Goldsboro.[72]

The last act of Confederate defiance at Averasboro came from an unlikely source. One of the artillery pieces on the Confederate first line was badly damaged in the previous day's artillery duel and was not worth removing from the battlefield. Union artillerymen were instructed to destroy the 12-pounder gun in order to ensure that the piece did not fall back into Rebel hands. Lt. Edward P. Newkirk of Battery M, 1st New York Artillery, drew the task of destroying the gun. "An attempt was made the next day to burst the captured 12-pound gun," recalled Newkirk. "Two cartridges were inserted, the bore filled with sand and pounded bricks, and the charge fired by a slow match, the piece being in a nearly vertical position." A giant explosion echoed across the surrounding countryside. Newkirk and his men patiently waited while the smoke cleared. To their amazement, the gun still stood defiantly intact in the field. "The only effect seemed to be the driving of the gun into the ground for more than half its length," remembered a frustrated Newkirk. When his battery moved out, Newkirk ordered the gun spiked. "A shell was rammed into the bore, the piece spiked and abandoned, and the carriage burned." As Lieutenant Newkirk departed the battlefield, the lone Confederate gun still stood on the battlefield, a silent monument to the stubborn Confederate resistance at Averasboro.[73]

The Battle of Averasboro cost the Union 682 casualties: 95 killed, 533 wounded, and 54 missing. The Confederates lost an estimated 865 killed, wounded, and missing. After two days of fierce resistance, Sherman lost his enthusiasm for bringing Hardee's Corps to battle. Consequently, Sherman ordered his commanders not to press the withdrawal of Hardee's command as it moved toward a link-up with Johnston's forces at Smithfield. Sherman had no interest in bringing on another general engagement. Content with his victory at Averasboro, he ordered his army to continue toward Goldsboro.[74]

RALEIGH OR GOLDSBORO?

On March 15, Johnston arrived at Smithfield and established his headquarters. He began at once to assemble his forces. If the opportunity presented itself, he intended to attack one of Sherman's wings in the hope of defeating the Federals in detail. He had already summoned Gen. Braxton Bragg's Department of North Carolina forces to Smithfield, while remnants of the Army of Tennessee were trickling in from Charlotte and Salisbury. As these forces assembled, Hardee's and Hampton's commands stubbornly contested the advance of Sherman's Left Wing at Averasboro, while Butler's cavalry division harassed the Union Right Wing.

On March 16, Johnston ordered Hardee to march his command to join him at Smithfield. That night, Hardee's Corps abandoned its defensive position along the ridge near Averasboro and headed north to link up with Johnston's army. Once Hardee arrived at Smithfield and the Army of Tennessee contingent joined them, all of Johnston's available forces would be concentrated, and Johnston could search for an opportunity to pounce upon one of Sherman's wings. Because

Johnston could not be sure of the Union commander's true objective, Hampton's cavalry remained in constant contact with both of Sherman's wings. Until Sherman made his intentions clear, Johnston intended to remain at Smithfield, where he could cover both Raleigh and Goldsboro. Once Sherman revealed his destination, Johnston could then strike Sherman on a field of the Virginian's choosing.

On March 17, Kilpatrick's cavalry and Ward's infantry division continued feinting northward toward Raleigh before turning east and resuming the march toward Goldsboro. Later that day, the entire Union Left Wing veered to the northeast. Johnston, uneasy about the speed at which events were unfolding, continuously queried Hardee and Hampton for information as to the enemy's intentions. By the evening of March 17, Morgan's division of the Union Left Wing was only 20 miles from Bentonville. Cox's XXIII Corps remained at Kinston, while Terry's Provisional Corps had begun its advance up the Wilmington and Weldon Railroad toward Goldsboro. Howard's Right Wing only covered six miles that day, awaiting news of the Battle of Averasboro. As Sherman moved toward Goldsboro, Johnston's golden opportunity to strike one of the Union wings was rapidly slipping away. Within a few days, the Union forces would be in united Goldsboro and any hope of defeating Sherman's army would be lost forever.[75]

On the evening of March 17, Hampton informed Johnston that he now believed that Sherman's forces were converging on Goldsboro. Hampton reported that he was at the Willis Cole house, a few miles south of Bentonville, and that the Union Left Wing was marching on the Old Goldsboro Road. Hampton therefore suggested that the Cole plantation was an ideal location to strike the flank of the Union Left Wing. Hampton assured Johnston that Brig. Gen. George G. Dibrell's division of Wheeler's Corps could delay the Left Wing's advance long enough for Johnston to deploy near the Cole house and pounce on the Left Wing. Johnston concurred, and immediately ordered his units to move toward the Cole plantation at first light. Lt.

Gen. A. P. Stewart's remnant of the Army of Tennessee, joined by Bragg's command, marched toward the Cole house early on March 18. Hardee's Corps, along with two divisions of Wheeler's cavalry, was camped near Elevation and did not receive their marching orders until late morning on March 18. Poor maps also plagued Johnston, who mistakenly believed that Hardee was closer to Bentonville than he was, and that a gap of 12 miles, or roughly one day's march, separated the two Union wings.[76]

Sherman correctly feared that Johnston would try to disrupt the Left Wing's movement toward Goldsboro. On March 18, Kilpatrick's scouts reported that Johnston's forces were assembling near Smithfield, and that Confederate cavalry had destroyed the bridge over Mill Creek on the Clinton and Smithfield Road.[77] Sherman's own faulty map indicated that this bridge was the only crossing available to Johnston should he decide to attack the Left Wing. Sherman's inaccurate map omitted the other routes to Bentonville, including Johnston's route from Smithfield. The combination of inaccurate maps and faulty intelligence persuaded Sherman that Johnston intended to defend Raleigh instead of contesting his advance on Goldsboro. Sherman was now convinced that his march into Goldsboro would be unopposed.

Luck was favoring Johnston. Some historians have speculated that Sherman received advance warning of an impending attack on his Left Wing from intelligence gathered by Brig. Gen. William P. Carlin, the commander of the First Division of the XIV Corps. Carlin's claims are questionable, however. On the morning of March 19, Carlin's division assumed the lead from Morgan's division. Although Carlin later claimed that he believed that the enemy was in his front in force, his words and actions that day indicate otherwise. When foragers reported increased Confederate resistance in his front and suggested that an engagement was imminent, Carlin scoffed at the idea and blindly marched his division right into Johnston's well-laid trap. Clearly, Carlin's actions did not reflect a commander who was concerned about reports of Johnston's army waiting to attack the Left Wing.[78]

Early on the morning of March 19, Sherman notified Slocum that he was transferring his headquarters to the Right Wing to facilitate communications with Terry and Schofield. Soon afterward, Union foragers engaged Dibrell's cavalry. Early reports from the lead elements of the Left Wing indicated only cavalry in their front. Consequently, Sherman ordered Slocum to shove the enemy horsemen aside quickly and move on to Goldsboro. Thus began the Battle of Bentonville, the last major infantry battle of the Carolinas Campaign.[79]

Chapter 6 | A Critical Analysis of the Actions from Fayetteville to Averasboro

B attles and campaigns often inspire many lingering ifs and whys, many of which are never fully answered. The Fayetteville to Averasboro phase of Sherman's Campaign of the Carolinas is no exception. This segment of the campaign offers an excellent study of the many facets and nuances of a brilliantly planned and well-executed military operation. We will highlight the importance of the actions at Fayetteville and Averasboro by analyzing the lessons learned there and by emphasizing their connection to the Battle of Bentonville.

Historians often ask why General Hardee did not attempt to slow Sherman's progress at the Cape Fear River. The truth is that Sherman was also puzzled by this mystery. Writing many years after the end of the war, Sherman commented in his memoirs that the Confederate forces did not take advantage of the major river systems that criss-cross the Carolinas in order to contest his advance. Sherman identified five major river systems: the Edisto, Broad, Catawba, Pee Dee, and Cape Fear. The Cape Fear River, which provided the direct logistical link with the important seaport town of Wilmington, provides a good illustration of Sherman's point.

In Sherman's assessment, "a comparatively smaller force, well handled, should have made the passage most difficult, if not impossible."[1] By picketing the fords and placing small infantry detachments and artillery in a defensive cordon, Hardee could have wreaked havoc on Sherman's attempt to cross the Cape Fear River. Once on the east bank of the river, Hardee had sufficient infantry and artillery on hand to resist any of Sherman's attempts to cross. Additionally, Hampton's cavalry could have served as a reserve in the event one of those detachments needed reinforcements. Unfortunately, Johnston and Hardee chose not to defend the river crossings, and instead lightly picketed the important river fords and crossings.

While they held Fayetteville, Hardee and Johnston were unsure of Sherman's intentions or ultimate objective. They assumed that Sherman was headed in a northeasterly direction, toward either Raleigh or Goldsboro. Had Hardee been able to delay Sherman's crossing of the Cape Fear, Sherman would have had three options: force a crossing, move north along the west side of the river until it was shallow enough to cross at any point, or move south to Wilmington and follow Terry's route of march along the Wilmington rail line. The second and third options would have eaten up inordinate amounts of time and resources, and would have moved his army farther away from its ultimate objective of Goldsboro. The first option, to force a crossing, was the most likely, but Sherman would have had to establish a beachhead first, provided that the Confederates permitted him to do so. In any event, Johnston and Hardee obviously felt that it was more critical for Johnston to concentrate his scattered force to fight the enemy than for Hardee to contest Sherman's crossing of the Cape Fear River.

The question of why Hardee chose to establish a defense in depth at Averasboro is often debated. As discussed in an earlier chapter, Hardee's stated goal was to "ascertain the strength and destination of the forces in his front." Battle reports and correspondence fail to disclose the reason why Hardee chose a defense in depth, considering that Hardee's command was suffering from desertions, low morale and the rapidly decreasing size of his Corps. Mark L. Bradley, a notable chronicler of the Carolinas Campaign, offers an explanation as to why Hardee fought a defensive battle at Averasboro. "Hardee's Corps was in danger of disintegrating," suggests Bradley, and if Old Reliable did not fight at Averasboro, "he would not have a command to fight with." Low morale was unquestionably an issue in Hardee's Corps, and Bradley's point is well taken—bleeding Sherman's army would certainly give morale a much-needed boost. Bradley also contends that Hardee failed to mention his primary reason for fighting at Averasboro: to buy time for the concentration of Johnston's army.[2]

Another factor that influenced Hardee's decision to stand and fight at Averasboro was operational tempo, meaning that his command was having difficulty staying ahead of Sherman's rapidly advancing columns. Hardee's men were not seasoned field soldiers accustomed to long and difficult forced marches, and their rate of march did not match that of Sherman's army. Additionally, they lacked an experienced and efficient engineer/pioneer system, and with the terrible road conditions, Hardee's column moved at a crawl. His trains were also slowing him down. On March 29, 1865, the *Hillsboro Recorder* reported, "the bad conditions of the roads and the proximity of the enemy as well as other circumstances induced Hardee to make a stand."[3]

By March 14, Sherman's army had ended its respite at Fayetteville and the army prepared to continue its march by conducting a reconnaissance-in-force on the Fayetteville-Raleigh Road. At Silver Run Creek, just north of the Bluff Church, elements of Wheeler's cavalry and Rhett's infantry brigade successfully engaged the Federal reconnaissance force, which consisted of a single brigade of infantry under Col. Philo Buckingham.[4] The next day, Sherman's army marched out of Fayetteville.

If Hardee's intended to delay and buy time for Johnston to concentrate his forces, the logical solution would have been the use of the cavalry with an attached infantry brigade, similar to the Confederate formation utilized at Silver Run Creek. This combined arms force was better suited to delay Sherman's advance by offering mobility, firepower, and economy of force. Additionally, this tactic exposed only a fraction of Hardee's command to the enemy, preserving the integrity of the remainder of his corps for future operations. The engagement at

Silver Run Creek demonstrates this point. The terrain in this portion of North Carolina was conducive to small unit delaying actions. Thus, Hardee did not need his entire corps to delay Sherman's Left Wing.

His trains were another possible reason why Hardee fought a defense in depth action at Averasboro with his entire corps. Understanding that Hardee's primary mission—which was to buy time for the concentration of Johnston's army—did not change, the pressure of Sherman's pursuit of his rear guard left Hardee with no choice but to delay Sherman long enough to allow his trains to move out of harm's way. Pvt. Daniel Miles Tedder of the 1st South Carolina Regulars, who served in Hardee's rear guard as a member of Rhett's brigade, reinforced the idea that the movement of the wagon trains triggered the decision to stand and fight at Averasboro. "On the 15th General Hardee halted the whole command, and built breast works, as his trains had not all got over the river in front of him in two days," wrote Tedder.[5] Taliaferro also suggested that, more than anything else, the balky wagon train induced Hardee to make his stand at Averasboro. Hardee himself explained, "my object in this was only to check the enemy until our trains should be beyond the reach of danger."[6] A defense in depth would buy the time needed to clear the trains and allow for an organized withdrawal. Finally, Maj. Gen. Lafayette McLaws noted in his diary that he had "never thought about making a stand at Averasboro," providing insight into why there are no surviving orders explaining Hardee's decision to defend Averasboro.[7]

The Battle of Averasboro can be broken down into five distinct phases: the initial deployment a few miles south of the town of Averasboro, followed by the actions at the first line, the retreat from the second line, the assaults on the third line and the withdrawal. In order to analyze phase one, we will employ the United States Army's (OCOKA) analytic framework to assess Hardee's defense in depth. OCOKA is an acronym meaning Observation and fields of fire, Cover and concealment, Obstacles (natural and man-made), Key terrain, and Avenues of approach.[8]

The Smithville area was ideally suited for conducting a defense in depth. The close proximity of the Black and Cape Fear Rivers channeled Sherman's Left Wing directly into Hardee's proposed position. The narrow peninsula of land between the two rivers meant that Hardee's position could not be outflanked. Additionally, Hampton's horsemen could constantly monitor the fords and crossings along the Black River and provide early warning should Sherman decide to turn east.

Observation and fields of fire: All three defensive lines offered the Confederates excellent observation and fields of fire to the front. The Confederate flanks were covered by thick swamps, and heavy vegetation aided in concealing the Confederate flanks. Conversely, while the undergrowth helped to protect them from large troop movements, it also restricted Confederate observation and fields of fire. As a result, all three Confederate lines were vulnerable to small unit flank attacks.

Cover and concealment: All three of Hardee's defensive lines provided excellent cover and concealment. At no time could Sherman's men detect the presence of successive lines of defense, meaning that the Union troops could not reconnoiter the subsequent Confederate defensive positions.

The terrain on the flanks and front of Hardee's third line was ideal for the Confederates defense. The flanks of Hardee's third line were hidden from prying Union eyes. As the blue-clad soldiers emerged from the swamps in front of McLaws's position, 150 yards of open terrain lay in front of them. The Federals drew constant rifle and artillery fire as they emerged from the swamp.

Obstacles: The Smithville area south of Averasboro offered numerous physical obstacles that hindered the progress of the Federals. The area's swamps and streams were ideal for conducting a defense. Hardee took full advantage of these natural obstacles in orchestrating his defensive plan. Nevertheless, the second line was not as good a position as the first or third. The only obstacle in front of the second line was a creek bed that rendered the second line extremely vulnerable to flank attacks. Mitigating this was the fact that Hardee did not intend to hold the first two lines for an extended period of time, so the lack of physical obstacles on the second line was not fatal to the success of his defensive scheme. As one position became untenable, its defenders simply fell back to the next prepared line.

Key terrain: The terrain surrounding Averasboro is mostly flat, interrupted by creek beds and swamps dispersed throughout the area. These terrain features channeled the enemy's movements and offered some protection for the flanks. Although the first two lines were not ideal for a strong defense, they were suitable for the task assigned by Hardee—his troops could hold there for a while, and thus buy time. Once they were driven from the first two lines, the Confederates could then fall back to the main defensive position atop the ridge. The key terrain was along the third line, because Hardee had decided to make his final stand there, and he had chosen his position well. A heavily wooded swampy area lay in front of the third line, which would hinder any potential Union movements against that line. Upon emerging from the swamp, Union troops faced a heavily fortified Confederate position only 150 yards from the wood line. The Union battle lines had to deploy under constant Confederate small arms and artillery fire. Additionally, the forty-foot deep ravine that ran to the Cape Fear River protected the right flank of Hardee's third line. Although the ravine was a formidable obstacle, it was still negotiable, albeit with great difficulty. This meant that the right flank of the third line was vulnerable to a turning movement because Hardee's line did not extend to the Cape Fear River. Had it not been for Wheeler's timely reinforcement of the third line, Sherman might easily have turned Hardee's right flank.

Avenues of approach: The river systems and swamps in the Averasboro area channeled all troop movements onto a single artery, the Fayetteville-Raleigh Road. One of the primary routes northward toward either Raleigh or Goldsboro was the Fayetteville-Raleigh Road, meaning that any movement north out of Fayetteville would logically be made on the Fayetteville-Raleigh Road. Thus, the Left Wing would have to pass through the Averasboro area, no matter what Sherman's ultimate destination might be. Additionally, the Goldsboro Road intersected the Fayetteville-Raleigh Road at Averasboro. This was a critical junction, because it was the Left Wing's main route of march toward Goldsboro. The flooded state of the rivers and creeks meant that Sherman's army could not go cross-country and would be forced to use the road network, meaning that the only logical route for the Left Wing was along the Fayetteville-Raleigh Road and through the Averasboro area. Thus, Hardee made the correct choice in selecting Averasboro, because it offered the only avenue of approach for the Left Wing.

Applying the OCOKA methodology for analyzing Hardee's defensive position, we conclude that the choice of battlefield was acceptable, but still had some risk. Hardee obviously mulled over his position at Averasboro and made dispositions to maximize his advantages in terrain. In order to capitalize on these advantages, he needed sufficient forces. Each line was undermanned, leaving his Averasboro defenses vulnerable. However, Hardee was fortunate: but for the combination of the the deep ravine on the right flank of the Confederate third line, Wheeler's timely arrival, and poor scouting of the Confederate left flank by Kilpatrick's cavalry, the third line would probably have suffered the same fate as the first two lines.

General McLaws performed his own assessment of the Averasboro battlefield. McLaws kept detailed field notes of his service in the Carolinas Campaign. He believed that the Averasboro defenses were lacking, noting that "Rhett's position [was] tolerable, Elliott's a bad position," and that his own position was not of his choosing. McLaws also correctly believed that Hardee's Corps lacked sufficient troops to defend the third line. Thus, while the third line was laid out on the battlefield's most defensible terrain, its weaknesses were obvious.[9]

Hardee's initial planning was skillfully executed, but the plan had flaws. Neither Hardee nor Taliaferro indicated what they expected to be the trigger for initiating each brigade's withdrawal to the next defensive position on the first and second lines, meaning that the decision to withdraw was apparently left to the discretion of the brigade commanders. However, the Confederate commanders were apparently unclear as to the objective of their defense in depth, and they did not indicate when Butler's troops should fall back to the second line. Knowing when to fall back was critical to success. Taliaferro intended to have his brigades fall back once the trains were secure, or, as he commented, "take such other positions as should be directed by the lieutenant general commanding."[10] According to Taliaferro, Hardee was to decide when to fall back upon each successive line of defense.

Hardee's initial success during the opening stage of the battle may have caused overconfidence on his part. When Butler's troops successfully delayed the Union advance, Hardee made the understandable but fatal mistake of becoming decisively engaged, leaving him unable to withdraw Butler's troops safely from the first line. Increasing Union strength in Butler's front should have made it obvious that he had achieved his objective on the first line, and that he should then have ordered Butler's men to fall back to the second line. Hardee's apparent overconfidence proved costly, because it enabled the Union forces to turn Butler's flank. The Federal assault on that flank routed Butler from the first line.

Hardee also grossly underestimated Sherman's ability to maneuver through difficult terrain, such as the swamp on the Confederate right flank. Throughout the Carolinas Campaign, Sherman's troops had demonstrated their ability to maneuver through seemingly impassable terrain. At the outset of the Carolinas Campaign, the Federals had made it clear that swampy areas would not stop them. If twenty-two miles of thick swamp in the Salkehatchie River basin could not halt Sherman's advance, then the small swamps on the Confederate right at Averasboro could hardly be expected to do so. Johnston himself marveled at the efficiency of Sherman's army. Upon learning that Sherman's army was building corduroy roads through the Salkehatchie Swamps at the rate of a dozen miles a day, Johnston "decided that there had been no such army since the days of Julius Caesar."[11] Thus, Sherman's successful flank attack on Butler's right should have come as no surprise to the Confederate defenders, who were accustomed to seeing the Federals accomplish seemingly superhuman feats. While Hardee, Taliaferro, and Butler should have recognized the weakness of the first line's right flank, they did not. Fortunately for the Confederates, Hardee did not make the same mistake on the second line.

The conduct of some of the units of Elliott's brigade on the second line offers an interesting study. Elliott's command had obvious problems with morale and leadership. As discussed in Chapter Four, Elliott's brigade was a hodgepodge of commands lacking unit cohesion. As a result, it appears that some of Elliott's regiments did not even fight. Issues of low morale, inexperience, and lack of unit cohesion came into play during the Federal assault on the second line, creating the potential for disaster. General Hardee had two options: either to fall back to the third line immediately and risk a rout, or to deploy veteran troops on the second line to facilitate the orderly retreat of Taliaferro's division. Old Reliable chose the latter course of action, raising the question of why he weakened his main line of defense, the third line, to reinforce the second. Considering that Hardee intended to fall back anyway, his risking additional losses or even disaster does not make sense. He should simply have abandoned the second line prior to the Federal assault.

Some commentators suggest that Hardee dispatched veteran units from McLaws's division in order to prevent the Federals from enveloping Taliaferro's flanks while they fell back to the third line. Others believe that Elliott's troops were extremely unsteady, and that, if pressed, they would break, resulting in a disastrous rout. Whatever the case may be, in order to prevent the potential loss of a significant portion of Taliaferro's division, Hardee realized that he would have to use veteran troops to fill the trenches. It is therefore obvious that

Hardee lacked confidence in the ability of Taliaferro's troops to execute the planned retrograde movement.

Hardee's fears proved well-founded at the Battle of Bentonville on March 19, where Elliott's brigade again broke. Late in the evening on March 19, General Elliott stopped to chat with Huguenin, who had known the general since boyhood. "We conversed freely," recalled Huguenin, and "he expressed great regret and chagrin at the conduct of his brigade." Huguenin defended his old friend: "The brigade (Elliott's) was organized after the evacuation of Charleston, he had not time to get it in shape and was not responsible for its conduct."[12] His untried units had broken at both Averasboro and Bentonville. Because Elliott's brigade lacked cohesion and combat experience, disaster was all but inevitable.

Nevertheless, Hardee was rightfully proud of his corps' performance at Averasboro. They had fought long and hard against superior numbers, and had given as well as they had gotten. The next day, Hardee issued a congratulatory order to his command:

> The lieutenant-general commanding thanks the officers and men of this command for their courage and conduct of yesterday, and congratulates them upon giving the enemy the first serious check he has received since leaving Atlanta. This command contended with the Fourteenth Army Corps, most of the Twentieth, Kilpatrick's cavalry command—three times their number—and while they sustained a loss of less than 500 men, they inflicted upon the enemy, by accounts of prisoners, a loss of 3,300. The lieutenant-general augurs happily of the future service and reputation of troops who have signalized the opening of the campaign by admirable steadiness, endurance, and courage.[13]

Sherman, on the other hand, had just as much reason to be proud of his troops. They had contended with terrible weather and wretched roads, and had driven the enemy from two defensive lines, holding the battlefield when the fighting was over. Sherman could justifiably claim victory.

Until Sherman visited his wounded at the "Oak Grove" hospital on the afternoon of March 16, his plan was flawlessly executed. But after achieving success on the Confederate first and second lines, Sherman lost his desire to press the attack. Union causalities were significantly higher than he had expected, and he was forced to empty vital supply wagons to transport his wounded. Sherman's decision to slow and then halt his attacks on the third line proved to be the turning point of the battle. When he did so, Sherman violated a basic modern military premise: "Fight the enemy, not your plan." Standing on the steps of the "Oak Grove" hospital, Sherman became obsessed with completing the execution of his grand plan, which was to consolidate his force with Schofield and Terry's commands and to re-supply his army at Goldsboro. However, Sherman overlooked the fact that General Johnston would also have some say in the execution of his plan. Sherman failed to finish the fight at Averasboro; he also failed to maintain a close eye on the movements of Johnston's army, which nearly spelled disaster at Bentonville on March 19.

General Hardee took many risks in setting up his third line of defense. As mentioned earlier, Hardee lacked sufficient troop strength to defend his third line adequately. His selection of terrain helped to protect his right flank, and only the timely arrival of Wheeler's cavalry sufficiently strengthened that sector. However, Hardee's left flank was the Achilles heel of the third line, and his more experienced division commander, Major General Lafayette McLaws, knew it. Late on the afternoon of March 16, Sherman unleashed several probing attacks along the Confederate left, increasing the potential for Confederate disaster. McLaws accurately observed that the Federals "probably would have turned that flank, if the day had not been so far gone."[14] Fortunately, Hardee's gamble paid off, because Sherman failed to uncover his weak left flank. Hardee was extremely lucky that he had only Kilpatrick's cavalry and not one of the veteran Federal infantry brigades on his left flank. Having fought all day, Kilpatrick's troopers were tired and low on ammunition, and in no condition to mount a serious threat. Had Hardee's gambit failed, his army could have been pinned against the Cape Fear River without an escape route.

One may ask what the Union cavalry and scouts were doing during the actions on the third line. Although they had been engaged all day and were tired and low on ammunition, this does not excuse them from not performing their duties of reconnaissance and screening—yet one more instance in a series of misjudgments and errors that plagued Kilpatrick and his command during the campaign. Sherman's loss of faith in Kilpatrick's abilities is therefore no surprise.

Hardee's corps performed better than anticipated, enabling Hardee to achieve all of the objectives set by Johnston. Hardee's well-planned defense delayed the Left Wing's advance for more than an entire day when his inexperienced troops stood their ground and fought like seasoned veterans, gaining valuable combat experience that paid off a few days later at Bentonville. The performance of Wheeler's veteran cavalry corps was particularly noteworthy. They conducted numerous delaying actions from Fayetteville to Averasboro, buying precious time for Hardee to prepare his defense at Averasboro. His troopers also monitored the fords along the Black River, providing Johnston and Hardee with early warning of changes in Sherman's route of march. Hardee carefully prepared his defense in depth with this important intelligence, meaning that he was in place and waiting for Sherman's arrival. Once the Union Left Wing arrived at Averasboro, it found a well-entrenched enemy holding three strong defensive positions.

Thus, we are left with the ultimate question: who won the Battle of Averasboro? The answer is that both armies won. It should be pointed out that Hardee never intended to defeat Sherman's army in battle; instead, his objective was to delay Sherman's advance long enough to give Johnston sufficient time to concentrate his army at Smithfield. In a tactical sense, Averasboro was a Union victory only because Sherman's men held the battlefield after Hardee's withdrawal. From a strategic and operational perspective, Averasboro was a Confederate victory because Hardee achieved all of his objectives. This interesting juxtaposition makes Averasboro a fascinating battle to study. It is one of those rare examples in which both sides could legitimately claim victory.

By the end of March 17, Hardee and Hampton were able to provide Johnston with critical intelligence, including the direction in which Sherman's army was heading. (Because of the northward advance of Ward's division, Hardee had remained uncertain as to Sherman's ultimate destination for most of March 17th). He had disrupted and delayed Sherman's Left Wing from March 15 into March 17, thereby giving Johnston's army invaluable time to concentrate near Bentonville. Additionally, while the armies slugged it out at Averasboro, Sherman's Right Wing had slowed its rate of march to only six miles on March 16.

The pieces of a large and complex puzzle were falling into place, and an accurate picture of the larger strategic and tactical picture was emerging. Sherman's feints toward Raleigh were exposed as just that, and his ultimate objective—Goldsboro—soon became apparent to Johnston and Hampton. Johnston had to move fast in order to attempt to strike a decisive blow to the Left Wing, setting the stage for the next and most critical phase of the campaign: The Battle of Bentonville.

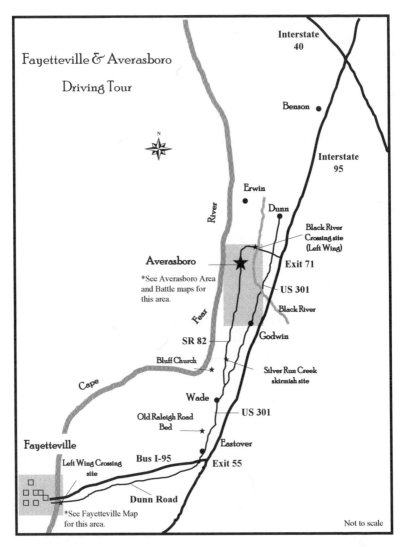

Mark Smith

Driving Tour

Fayetteville to Averasboro

This is a 16-mile driving tour covering key points of interest associated with this leg of Sherman's Carolinas Campaign, from Fayetteville to Averasboro. The tour begins at the former site of the U.S. Arsenal in Fayetteville, now home of the Museum of the Cape Fear.

Stop 1: *Museum of the Cape Fear/Old Arsenal Site: The Museum of the Cape Fear is located on Bradford St. just off Hay Street in Fayetteville, and is situated on the northeast corner of the Arsenal site. The old Arsenal was one of Sherman's main objectives on the march to Goldsboro.*

Behind the museum are the old Arsenal grounds; only the building foundations remain today. A highway bypass now bisects the arsenal grounds, though a footbridge connects the two halves. A reconstructed tower called the "Ghost Tower" on the northwest corner of the Arsenal, suggests the appearance of the four towers that once stood at each of the four corners of the arsenal. Early in the war, local militia seized the Arsenal, and from 1861 until Sherman's occupation in March 1865, the Arsenal produced small arms and ammunition for the Confederate army.

Sherman's army occupied the town of Fayetteville on March 11, 1865. During the army's four-day occupation, Sherman ordered his chief engineer, Orlando M. Poe, to destroy all the buildings and machinery at the arsenal:

> I shall therefore destroy this valuable arsenal, so the enemy shall not have its use; and the United States should never again confide such valuable property to a people who have betrayed a trust.

145

Ruins of the foundation of the Arsenal.

"Ghost Towers" replicating the original towers on the Arsenal grounds.

Unless otherwise indicated, all photos by Mark Smith

Pile of rocks from the Arsenal showing Sherman's engineers handiwork.

*After touring the Arsenal grounds and the Museum of the Cape Fear,
return to your vehicle. From this point on make sure to note your odometer
readings from stop to stop. Turn left onto Bradford Street and then right
onto Hay Street. You are now on the road Sherman's Left Wing used to
enter the city. From the corner of Bradford Street and Hay Street drive 1
mile to the Market House.*

Stop 1a: *As you start your descent, you can see downtown Fayetteville
before you. In March 1865, a Harper's Weekly artist drew a sketch of this
same view, showing the XIV Corps entering the town. (See drawing and
modern photo on page 148-149).*

Stop 2: ***Market House:*** Because of the Cape Fear River, its inland
port, as well as the early plank road system, Fayetteville was a thriving
center of commerce and county government. At the center of this
activity was the Market House; the present structure was built in 1832

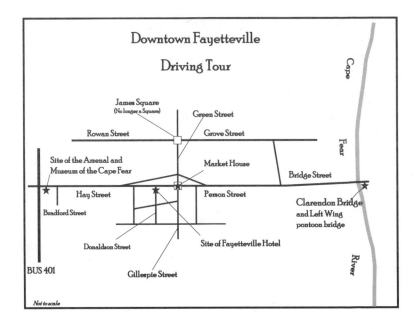

Fourteenth Corps Enters Fayetteville
Alfred R. Waud, Battles and Leaders

Market House looking east. Site of skirmish between
Wade Hampton and Union Scouts and Foragers.

Looking west from the Market House back towards the Arsenal.
The old Fayetteville Hotel was located 100 yards away on the left.

on the site of the previous courthouse. The upper floors were government offices and the lower portion was a market place. This site also
marks the location of a running street battle between Union scouts and
the Confederate rear guard commanded by Lt. Gen. Wade Hampton.
Hampton was eating his breakfast at the Fayetteville Hotel, 100-yards
west of the Market House, when he was surprised by Union soldiers.
A short but vicious fight occurred around the Market House.

*Continue east passed the Market House. Please note that the street
name changes to Person Street. Drive east on Person Street for 1.1 miles to
the Person Street bridge across the Cape Fear River.*

Stop 3: *Left Wing Crossing Site:* The Clarendon bridge across the
Cape Fear at this site was set afire by Hampton's troops when
Sherman's troops arrived. Sherman constructed a pontoon bridge to
the right of the bridge, and the Left Wing used this pontoon to cross
the Cape Fear River.

*Continue across the Person Street Bridge. Immediately after crossing
the bridge, make a left turn onto Dunn Road.*

View from the west bank of the Cape Fear River of Sherman's left wing pontoon
bridge. This was also the site of the Clarendon Bridge burnt by Hampton's Cavalry.

Stop 4: *Sherman's Route of March along the Raleigh Road:* Dunn Road *was one of the routes used by Sherman's Left Wing. Follow Dunn Road for 0.4 miles until you reach the intersection of Dunn and Middle Roads. At the Y intersection, you will continue to the right, staying on Dunn Road.*

Please note that the Left Wing used various roads for its northerly route of march, including the Middle and River Roads, which were used by smaller units. However, the two main routes were probably Dunn Road (Fayetteville-Raleigh Road) and Middle Road. Please note that Dunn Road runs to the town of Dunn, which is a post-Civil War town near the site of old Averasboro, which became a ghost town after the war.

Continue on Dunn Road for 4.5 miles until you come to an overpass where Business 95/US 301 crosses the Dunn Road. Continue through the town of Eastover.

Stop 5: *Old Raleigh Road bed:* *After traveling 2 miles from the overpass on the Dunn Road (now U.S. Route 301), turn left on to Flea Hill Road. After proceeding about 300 yards, you will spot a street sign marked the Old Raleigh Road on the right side of the road.*

The wartime road was narrow and, due to the heavy rainfall during the winter of 1865, in terrible condition. The passage of Hardee's Corps and the 30,000 troops and wagons of Sherman's Left Wing had transformed this road into a quagmire, requiring Sherman's troops to corduroy nearly its entire length as they moved north.

Turn around and head back to Dunn Road. Once you reach Dunn Road/ U. S. 301, turn left and continue north for 4.3 miles, passing through the town of Wade. When you reach the flashing light at Wade, pass through that intersection and continue on for 1.0 mile to a fork in the road. At the fork, you will bear left onto Sisk Culbreth Road (S. R. 1802). Be careful in crossing this intersection, as the road curves, limiting visibility. Once on Sisk Culbreth Road (S. R. 1802), you will see a State Historical Marker at the fork in the road on your right. Old Bluff Church Road is .8 miles north of the intersection of the Sisk Culbreth Road and U. S. 301. Turn left onto Old Bluff Church Road (S. R. 1709). This road dead-ends at Old Bluff Church.

Bluff Church graveyard where Hawley's Brigade camped.
The soldiers knocked over headstones to sleep on because of the sodden ground.

Stop 6: *Old Bluff Church:* Bluff Presbyterian Church was constructed in 1855 on bluffs over looking the Cape Fear River, behind the
church. On the night of March 15, 1865, Col. William Hawley's Union
infantry brigade briefly camped on this spot. As you look around the
church grounds, imagine the wet and miserable conditions faced by
Sherman's soldiers that spring. The combination of heavy rains and
lowland flooding left few dry spots on which to sleep. Some of the soldiers therefore pushed over headstones and bedded down on them. No
sooner had the troops made camp and started to cook their meals than
word arrived that they would be moving out. They learned that
Kilpatrick's cavalry had run into stiff resistance at Averasboro, and that
Kilpatrick had requested infantry reinforcements.

Janie Smith and other members of the Smith family are buried in
the church cemetery.

Turn around at Old Bluff Church and head back up Old Bluff Church
Road to Sisk Culbreth Road (S. R. 1802), and turn left. You are now heading

Bluff Church where Hawley's Brigade camped on the evening of March 15, 1865

Silver Run Creek skirmish site from Confederate position looking south.

north on S. R. 1802. After proceeding for 0.6 mile, you will see the bed of Silver Run Creek and the high ground to the north above a millpond on the right.

Stop 7: *Silver Run Creek:* Silver Run Creek is the location of a spirited skirmish between the Federals and elements of Maj. Gen. Joseph Wheeler's cavalry corps with the assistance of Col. Alfred M. Rhett's infantry brigade entrenched on the north side of the creek. Lt. Col. Philo B. Buckingham's 20th Connecticut, together with other Federal regiments, led the Union advance. The Union force failed to drive the Confederates from their works, and the Southerners withdrew toward Averasboro the next day.

Continue down S. R. 1802 for another 1.8 miles. Turn left onto Burnett Road (S. R. 1812). This road will become S. R. 82 in 0.9 mile. Proceed for 1 mile and then pull over for the first marker on the Averasboro Battlefield.

Stop 8: *First Marker at Averasboro/William Smith Plantation House:* This marker provides an excellent overview of the March 15 battle. As you look north, you will see the fork in the road mentioned by Capt. Theodore F. Northrop, Kilpatrick's Chief of Scouts. Rhett's skirmishers ventured to the banks of the Mill Creek about 50 yards south of the marker, (See map on p. 158) and were then driven north by the 9th Michigan cavalry. You can glimpse the William Smith house, located on the Ross West Road (to your right as you face the marker). The William Smith house was used as a field hospital during the battle. It is privately owned and not open to the public. (See Appendix C for details on the William Smith house).

Turn left and continue heading north. At 0.4 miles, you will come to the fork in the road mentioned by Captain Northrop in his post war accounts of the battle. Continue north on S. R. 82. At 0.1 miles you will see a cinder block church, Elizabeth Chapel A. M. E. Zion Church on the right, where Northrop left his scouts and foragers. Continue north on S. R. 82 to a slight rise at 0.2 miles. This rise marks the location of Kilpatrick's and Hawley's line on the night March 15–16, 1865.

Looking south at the front of the William Smith Plantation house.

Looking north. This is the location of Kilpatrick and Hawley's
defensive line on the evening of March 15th.

Stop 9: *Location of Kilpatrick's Defensive Line on the Night of March 15–16:* Early on the morning of March 16, Hawley and Kilpatrick initiated the attack by driving in Huguenin's skirmishers near this spot. The rise on the left side of the road marks the approximate location of Lieutenant Fowler's section of the 10th Wisconsin Battery.

Continue for another .2 miles to the Mill Creek area, defended by Captain Huguenin on March 15–16, 1865.

Stop 10: *Huguenin's Creek Bed Defense on March 15 and 16:* Captain Huguenin's skirmishers held the north side of the creek on the evening of March 15 and the morning of March 16. Lt. Edward Middleton and a few of his men picketed the south side of the creek that night and enjoyed the music of the 2nd Massachusetts' regimental band.

Continue on for another 0.1 mile until you reach the high ground near the position of the XX Corps artillery and the site of Rhett's capture on your left. Again, there is no wayside pullover area, so please be careful.

Stop 11: *XX Corps Artillery Position/Rhett's Capture Site:* On this spot, on the left side of the road, three Union batteries deployed hub to hub: from left to right, they were Battery C, 1st Ohio, Battery I, 1st New York and Battery M, 1st New York. The first Confederate defensive line, manned by Rhett's Brigade, lay 500 yards to the north of this position. On the morning of March 16, the twelve Union guns blasted away at the Confederate position.

Another point of interest is the site of Col. Alfred M. Rhett's capture. On the afternoon of March 15, Rhett was captured a few hundred yards southeast of the Oak Grove. Rhett and an aide unwittingly rode up to Captain Northrop and his scouts, who were trying to return to their lines after reconnoitering the Confederate position. The Federal scouts captured Rhett and escorted him back to Union lines.

Continue north on S. R. 82 for 0.1 mile to the entrance to the Oak Grove house. Please note that the Oak Grove is privately owned and not open to the public. Oak Grove sits behind the modern red brick ranch house. It is best to view "Oak Grove" from the next stop.

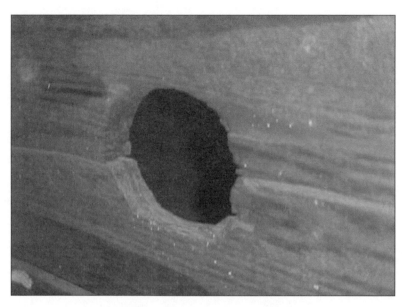

Attic of the Oak Grove Plantation House.
The cannonball holes made by Confederate artillery on the 1st line.

Front porch of the Oak Grove showing the bullet holes from the battle.
Photos by Wade Sokolosky

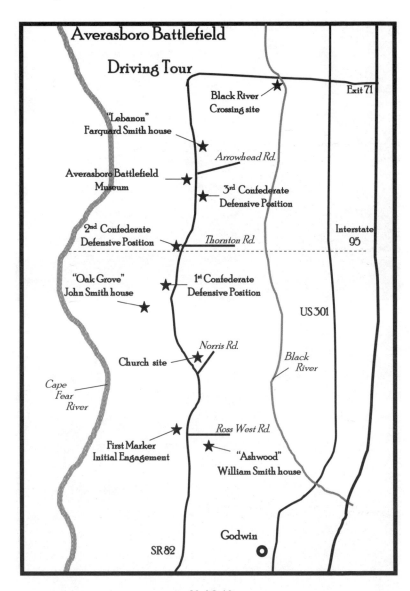

Averasboro Battlefield

Driving Tour

Black River
Crossing site

Exit 71

"Lebanon"
Farquard Smith house

Arrowhead Rd.

Averasboro Battlefield
Museum

3ʳᵈ Confederate
Defensive Position

2ⁿᵈ Confederate
Defensive Position

Thornton Rd.

Interstate
95

"Oak Grove"
John Smith house

1ˢᵗ Confederate
Defensive Position

US 301

Church site

Norris Rd.

Black
River

Cape
Fear
River

First Marker
Initial Engagement

Ross West Rd.

"Ashwood"
William Smith house

Godwin

SR 82

Mark Smith

Looking east along the Confederate defensive position of the first line.

Looking south from the 1st Confederate line at the "Oak Grove" plantation house.

Stop 12: *Oak Grove Plantation House:* The "Oak Grove" (also known as the John Smith house), was built around 1793, and is one of the three Smith homesteads in the area once known as Smithville. This wonderful old house is a classic example of Colonial architecture. "Oak Grove" served as a field hospital for both Union and Confederate wounded. There are cannon ball holes in the attic and numerous bullet holes in the front of the house (See photos). During the battle, Sherman visited the wounded at Oak Grove.

Continue for another 0.3 miles. On your left there is an historical marker and some reconstructed earthworks, marking the location of the first Confederate defensive position. Turn left and park your car in the roadside pull off.

Stop 13: *First Confederate Defensive Line:* Walk over to the Union marker on the field (west) side of the earthworks, where Case's brigade of the XX Corps struck Rhett's brigade. Monuments at each end of the trenches commemorate the Union and Confederate forces engaged at this location. To your right front, you will have an excellent view of the front of the Oak Grove. The two Confederate artillery shells that penetrated the attic of Oak Grove were fired from this spot. (See Appendix C for details).

From this location, face south and look over the open fields. You are at the approximate location of the 1st South Carolina Heavy Artillery, and are seeing the battlefield from the perspective of a Confederate soldier. On the morning of March 16, the fields in your front would have been a virtual sea of blue, as battle line after battle line of the XX Corps filed into position. Artillery shells burst overhead as the Union gunners worked their pieces with deadly efficiency. There would have been Confederate dead and wounded lying all around you. Now face to your right (west). Case's infantry brigade emerged from the woods in front of you and launched its surprise attack on the unsuspecting Confederate right flank. To your rear the east, across S. R. 82, is the 1st South Carolina Regulars position, where Lt. Col. Robert Detreville of the Regulars was killed early in the battle.

Face north and look up S. R. 82. In the tree line about 400 yards distant is the location of the Confederate second defensive position, held by Elliott's brigade.

Return to your car and turn left back onto S. R. 82 for 0.3 miles. You will find a historical marker on the right side of the road, indicating the location of the second Confederate defensive position. (There is no wayside pullover at this location).

Stop 14: *Second Confederate Defensive Line:* At this location, Taliaferro's division (Elliott and Butler's brigades) briefly defended this slight ridgeline. Union cavalry quickly flanked this position on the left while elements of the newly-arrived XIV Corps turned the right. Taliaferro's division had no choice but to withdraw to the third defensive line.

Continue driving north on S. R. 82 for another 0.6 miles until you come to the Chicora Cemetery on the right. Pull into the gravel parking lot, park your car, and feel free to walk around.

Stop 15: *Third Confederate Line/Confederate Cemetery/Union Flank Attack into the Ravine:* Walk to the front of the cemetery along S. R. 82. You will find several monuments and an informational marker describing the last phase of the Battle of Averasboro. As you face the cemetery, you will see a large boulder to your far left marking the forward site of the third Confederate line. General Hardee's small corps was deployed along the ridge on either side of S. R. 82. As you look south down S. R. 82, you are viewing the terrain from the perspective of one of Hardee's defenders. You will see a plateau about 200 yards in your front where Union troops deployed after emerging from the low ground. Hardee's forces unleashed volley after volley of small arms and artillery fire into the Union ranks, eventually compelling the Federals to withdraw to the safety of the low ground. As darkness fell on March 16, Hardee informed General Johnston that he would withdraw his forces and march to Smithfield to link up with Johnston's army.

Chicora Cemetery

The 40-foot-deep ravine that Vandever's brigade encountered while attempting to
turn the Confederate right flank. Note the steep banks of slippery clay.
Union soldiers had to climb on each other's shoulders and
use tree roots and vines to scale the banks. The young man
in the light-colored shirt in the center of the photo is 6 ft tall.

The third line also marks the site of the Confederate (or Chicora) Cemetery. ("Chicora" is the Indian word for "Carolina"). This is the site of the mass graves of 54 Confederate soldiers who were killed at Averasboro. In 1872, the cemetery, iron fence, and the small obelisk honoring the Confederate dead were dedicated by the ladies of the Smithville Memorial Association, which became the Chicora Chapter of the United Daughters of the Confederacy in 1904. Lt. Col. Robert Detreville of the 1st South Carolina Regulars is buried in the cemetery, as is Alfred Henry Angel, an eighteen-year-old who succumbed to wounds received during the battle. Angel's remains were relocated from the Averasboro town cemetery to Chicora cemetery during the centennial in 1965.

Your next stop on the third line will be the ravine where Brig. Gen. William Vandever's brigade attempted to attack the Confederate right flank. To see the ravine, face the road and cross S. R. 82. Proceed west on foot beside the cable and low wooden post. Continue along the fence line, which will bring you to the wood line to your front. Follow the wood line to the west. As you crest the hill, you will see large power lines. Continue following the wood line until you reach the right of way under the power lines, where to your right you will be able to observe the 40-foot deep ravine encountered by Vandever's brigade.

Return to your car at the cemetery. Exit the parking lot and make a right. Drive 0.2 miles, where you will find the Averasboro Battlefield Museum in the red brick house on the left

Stop 16: *Averasboro Battlefield Museum:* The museum is well worth a visit. You will find a wonderful artifact collection from the battle and miniatures depicting the battle. One of the key attractions at the museum is the uniform of Col. Thomas J. Purdie, whose North Carolina regiment tragically and accidentally fired on General Thomas J. "Stonewall" Jackson, mortally wounding him at Chancellorsville in May 1863. Colonel Purdy was also killed at Chancellorsville. The museum is open daily except on Monday.

Averasboro Museum.

After touring the museum, return to your car and turn left onto S. R. 82, and head north again. Continue for another 0.4 mile, where you will find the "Lebanon" on the right side of the road. The house is a private residence and is not open to the public. There is no roadside pull off.

Stop 17: *Lebanon Plantation House:* Lebanon house was the home of Farquhard Smith and was also used as a field hospital by the Confederates. This was the home of 18-year-old Janie Smith, whose colorful letter appears in Appendix D of this book. During the Union assault on the third line, stray bullets and artillery shells forced the family to take shelter in the ravine to the left (north) of the house. Descendants of the Smith family live in the house today.

Continue north on S. R. 82 for 1.7 miles, until you come to a stop sign. Cross the road. You are now on S. R. 1777. Continue for 1.6 miles until you come to the Black River. Note just before you reach the river crossing, the designation of the road will change to S. R. 1780.

"Lebanon" Plantation house. This is the site of the Confederate hospital

Stop 18: *Black River Crossing Site.* The Union Left Wing crossed the Black River on pontoons at this location after the retreating Confederates destroyed the original bridge. On March 17, 1865, this unimposing little river was at flood stage, and the flood plain was underwater. The Union engineers easily bridged the river here, and the Union Left Wing once again moved out toward Goldsboro.

Continue across the river on S. R. 1780 for 0.7 mile until you come to a traffic light at the intersection of S. R. 301 and S. R. 1780. Continue on S. R. 1780 for 0.8 miles until you reach Interstate 95. To return to Fayetteville, take I-95 South and follow the highway signs. To tour the Bentonville Battlefield, follow the signs on I-95. If you continue past the intersection of I-95 North and I-40, you will come to Smithfield, where General Johnston assembled his army to attack Sherman's Left Wing at Bentonville. You can also take SR 55 to Newton Grove and then north on US 701 to Harper House Road, which takes you to the Bentonville Battlefield Visitors Center.

This ends your driving tour of the Fayetteville-to-Averasboro portion of the Carolinas Campaign. You should now have a greater appreciation and understanding of the Battle of Averasboro and its significance in the Carolinas Campaign.

Black River crossing site.
Here Sherman's left wing crossed the river on a pontoon bridge.

Washington Artillery in Action
Charles and Richard B. Townsend Collection

Appendices

Appendix A
ORDER OF BATTLE AT AVERASBORO
March 15-16, 1865

UNION FORCES:
Maj. Gen. William T. Sherman

LEFT WING: ARMY OF GEORGIA
Maj. Gen. Henry W. Slocum

FOURTEENTH CORPS:
Bvt. Maj. Gen. Jefferson C. Davis

First Division:
Brig. Gen. William P. Carlin

First Brigade:
Bvt. Brig. Gen. Harrison C. Hobart
104th Illinois
42nd Indiana
88th Indiana
33rd Ohio
94th Ohio
21st Wisconsin

Second Brigade:
Bvt. Brig. Gen. George P. Buell
13th Michigan

21st Michigan
69th Ohio

Third Brigade:
Lt. Col. David Miles
38th Indiana
21st Ohio
74th Ohio
79th Pennsylvania

Second Division:
Brig. Gen. James D. Morgan

First Brigade:
Brig. Gen. William Vandever
16th Illinois
60th Illinois
10th Michigan
14th Michigan
17th New York

Second Brigade:
Brig. Gen. John G. Mitchell
34th Illinois
78th Illinois
98th Ohio
108th Ohio
113th Ohio
121st Ohio

Third Brigade:
Bvt. Brig. Gen. Benjamin D. Fearing
22nd Indiana
37th Indiana
85th Illinois

86th Illinois
110th Illinois
125th Illinois
52nd Ohio

TWENTIETH CORPS:
Bvt. Maj. Gen. Alpheus S. Williams

First Division:
Brig. Gen. Nathaniel J. Jackson

First Brigade:
Col. James L. Selfridge
5th Connecticut
123rd New York
141st New York
46th Pennsylvania

Second Brigade:
Col. William Hawley
2nd Massachusetts
13th New Jersey
107th New York
150th New York
3rd Wisconsin

Third Brigade:
Brig. Gen. James S. Robinson
82nd Illinois
101st Illinois
143rd New York
61st Ohio
82nd Ohio
31st Wisconsin

Third Division:
Bvt. Maj. Gen. William T. Ward

First Brigade:
Col. Henry Case
>   70th Indiana
>   79th Ohio
>   102nd Illinois
>   105th Illinois
>   129th Illinois

Second Brigade:
Col. Daniel Dustin
>   33rd Indiana
>   85th Indiana
>   19th Michigan
>   22nd Wisconsin

Third Brigade:
Bvt. Brig. Gen. William Cogswell
>   20th Connecticut
>   33rd Massachusetts
>   136th New York
>   55th Ohio
>   73rd Ohio
>   26th Wisconsin

Artillery:
Maj. John A. Reynolds
>   Battery I, 1st New York
>   Battery M, 1st New York
>   Battery C, 1st Ohio
>   Battery E, Independent Pennsylvania

Third Cavalry Division:
Bvt. Maj. Gen. Judson Kilpatrick

First Brigade:
Col. Thomas J. Jordan
   3rd Indiana
   8th Indiana
   2nd Kentucky
   3rd Kentucky
   9th Pennsylvania

Second Brigade:
Bvt. Brig. Gen. Smith D. Atkins
   92nd Illinois Mounted Infantry
   9th Michigan
   9th Ohio
   10th Ohio
   McLaughlin's (Ohio) Squadron

Third Brigade:
Col. George E. Spencer
   1st Alabama (US)
   5th Kentucky
   5th Ohio

Horse Artillery:
10th Wisconsin Battery

CONFEDERATE FORCES
Lt. Gen. William J. Hardee

Taliaferro's Division:
Brig. Gen. William B. Taliaferro

Elliott's Brigade:
Brig. Gen. Stephen Elliott, Jr.
    22nd Georgia Battalion Artillery
    27th Georgia Battalion Artillery
    2nd South Carolina Artillery
    Manigault's (S.C.) Battalion
    2nd Battalion North Carolina Local Defense Troops
        (Fayetteville Arsenal Battalion)

Rhett's Brigade:
Col Alfred M. Rhett (captured)
Col. William Butler
    1st South Carolina Regulars
    1st South Carolina Heavy Artillery
    Lucas's (S.C.) Battalion

McLaws's Division:
Maj. Gen. Lafayette McLaws

Harrison's Brigade:
Col. George P. Harrison, Jr.
    1st Georgia Regulars
    5th Georgia
    5th Georgia Reserves
    32nd Georgia
    47th Georgia

Conner's Brigade:

Brig. Gen. John D. Kennedy
  2nd South Carolina
  3rd South Carolina
  7th South Carolina
  8th South Carolina
  15th South Carolina
  20th South Carolina
  3rd South Carolina Battalion

Artillery:

Maj. A. Burnet Rhett
  Georgia Battery: Capt. Ruel Wooten Anderson
  Georgia Battery: Capt. John Brooks
  Louisiana Battery: Capt. Gustave LeGardeur Jr.
  South Carolina Battery: Capt. Edward L. Parker
  South Carolina Battery: Capt. H. M. Stuart
  Georgia Battery: Capt. John F. Wheaton

Cavalry:

Lt. Gen. Wade Hampton
Consisted of Maj. Gen. Joseph Wheeler's Corps and the division of Maj. Gen. Matthew C. Butler.
Confederate Cavalry units present at Averasboro consisted of the following organizations:

Wheeler's Corps:

Maj. Gen. Joseph Wheeler

Humes's Division:

Col. Henry M. Ashby

Harrison's Brigade:

Col. Baxter Smith
  3rd Arkansas

4th Tennessee
8th Texas
11th Texas

Ashby's Brigade:
Lt. Col. James H. Lewis
1st Tennessee
2nd Tennessee
5th Tennessee
9th Tennessee

Allen's Division:
Brig. Gen. William W. Allen

Hagan's Brigade
Col. D. G. White
1st Alabama
3rd Alabama
5th Alabama
9th Alabama
12th Alabama
51st Alabama
53rd Alabama
24th Alabama Battalion

Anderson's Brigade:
Brig. Gen. Robert H. Anderson
3rd Confederate
8th Confederate
10th Confederate
5th Georgia

Appendix B
Sherman's Concept of Logistics for the Carolinas Campaign

During the Carolinas Campaign, Maj. Gen. William T. Sherman's army conducted military operations ranging from intense combat, such as the Battle of Bentonville, to civil operations in the handling of thousands of displaced civilians and contraband slaves. The campaign is best remembered for Sherman's ability to conduct such operations independent of any established supply base or lines of communications. The forty-five-day campaign carried an army of more than 60,000 men through two states without the security of an established rear line of communication. The success of this operation is in part due to Sherman's understanding of logistics. Previous historical works on the Carolinas Campaign have focused on Sherman's use of the system of foraging and of the role played by his notorious "bummers" as the answer to logistics support. While foraging played a significant part in the campaign at the tactical level, other key aspects of logistics ensured Sherman's success. The War Department invested significant energy and resources into supporting Sherman at the operational and strategic levels as well.[1]

Sherman's Carolinas Campaign is one of the United States Army's most successful military operations of the Civil War. The ability to move a formation of over 60,000 men through the heart of the enemy's country, despite difficult terrain and weather, was nothing short of a logistical triumph. Sherman's movement through the Carolinas required his army to cross nine major rivers and numerous swollen streams, tributaries, and swamps during the rainiest winter in the Carolinas in decades.[2] "No one ever has and may not agree with me as to the very importance of the march north from Savannah," wrote Sherman after the war. "The march to the sea seems to have captured everybody, whereas it was child's play compared with the other."[3] The greatest compliment accorded Sherman's feat came from his old antagonist, Confederate General Joseph E. Johnston, who declared, "There had been no such army since the days of Julius Caesar."[4]

Martin Van Creveld, in his *Supplying War*, uses nineteenth-century military theorist Antoine-Henri Jomini's definition of logistics: "The practical art of moving armies and keeping them supplied."[5] In Georgia and the Carolinas, Sherman demonstrated the feasibility of conducting operations independent of a supply base or lines of communications. Sherman's Carolinas Campaign was a logistical success, but problems nevertheless arose. After-action reports and soldiers' journals illustrate that supply shortfalls occurred during the campaign.[6]

Sherman and his staff faced many of the same logistics challenges and issues faced by military commanders and logisticians in the twenty-first century. Sherman's anticipation of his army's future supply requirements and the coordination and support of strategic transportation assets, such as the navy and railroads, were necessary to the success of Sherman's campaigns.[7]

Sherman's capture of Savannah and his ability to begin the Carolinas Campaign soon afterward occurred because supplies needed to refit his army were awaiting him in vessels off the coast. The War Department's efforts to forecast future requirements and pre-position such assets along the coast enabled Sherman to begin re-supplying his army immediately upon his capture of Fort McAllister. The following order by the Quartermaster General of the U. S. Army, Bvt. Maj. Gen. Montgomery Meigs, illustrates the steps taken by the army to support Sherman upon his arrival at the coast:

DECEMBER 6, 1864.

Bvt. Brigadier General S. VAN VLIET,
Quartermaster, New York:

GENERAL: General Sherman appears to be approaching the Atlantic coast, and it is determined to send supplies to meet him at Port Royal, or rather to await there until he establishes his base of supplies. In the letter of this office date November 3 last an estimate of supplies was sent to you for a force of 30,000 men. It is believed that the force with General Sherman will reach 60,000 men, of which 10,000 will be cavalry, and that he will have with him from sixty to eighty pieces of artillery, and about 30,000 horses and mules...Colonel S. L. Brown, chief of the forage division, has been ordered to send daily to Port Royal forage for 30,000 animals. I notice that in the letter of 3rd of November last no blankets were ordered. I presume, however, that under the general order to send clothing to refit 30,000 men, General Vinton turned over to you a proper proportion of blankets. You will call upon General Vinton for the following clothing and equipage, which you will send to Port Royal as soon as possible, there to await news from General Sherman, which will determine the ultimate destination of the supplies...

Clothing.—30,000 sack coats; 30,000 trousers; 60,000 shirts; 60,000 pairs drawers; 60,000 pairs socks; 100,000 pairs shoes and boots; 20,000 forage caps; 10,000 greatcoats; 20,000 blankets, unless this number has already been shipped; 10,000 waterproof blankets...

I am, respectfully, your obedient servant,

M. C. MEIGS,
Quartermaster-General, Brevet Major-General.[8]

One must first understand Sherman's successful march from Atlanta to Savannah to gain insight into why Sherman considered such a risky undertaking as the Carolinas Campaign. In Georgia, Sherman had established priorities regarding logistics and support assets that remained essentially the same throughout both his Savannah and Carolinas Campaigns. In order to sustain such a large force in the field, Sherman issued Special Field Order Number 120, which established procedures for how the army would organize and operate to sustain itself while on the march.[9]

Sherman developed detailed plans for how transportation would be utilized within the army. He did not permit personal baggage or tentage to be carried in the trains in order to eliminate excess weight. Each corps wagon train consisted of only those wagons necessary for the transport of ammunition and provisions for the troops and animals. The army's wagon trains carried twenty days' rations, five days' forage for the animals, and enough ammunition to provide 200 rounds per man and per field piece. The result was an army that could move freely, without the burden of superfluous wagon trains.[10] When the army departed Atlanta, it numbered 62,000 men, 14,700 horses, 19,400 mules, and about 2,500 wagons.[11]

The absence of a supply line compelled Sherman to authorize a system of foraging in order to feed his troops and animals. Sherman adopted foraging as a means of supplementing or, even replacing, his army's standard supply system, depending on the situation. Wherever Sherman's army maneuvered, the local population and its resources were at the mercy of his foragers. In a sparsely settled region, foraging could quickly drain an area's resources. It was therefore important for Sherman's army to move swiftly in order to find new resources.[12]

Sherman's Special Field Orders No. 120 authorized his army to "forage liberally on the country." The order specified that each brigade commander should organize foraging parties, commanded by a commissioned officer, to gather food for the men and forage for the animals. Sherman hoped that the foragers would be able to maintain at least ten days' provisions and three days' forage. The order also authorized Sherman's infantry, cavalry and artillery units to confiscate any horses, mules, and wagons deemed necessary.[13]

In his memoirs, Sherman stated that he gave the greatest possible attention to the artillery and the wagon trains. The number of guns in the army was reduced to sixty-five and were generally organized into batteries of four guns each rather than the standard six guns.[14] By reducing the number of artillery pieces, Sherman also reduced the amount of ammunition and forage to transport. This reduction also reduced the number of draft animals necessary to move the army's batteries, thereby shortening his logistical tail. Sherman maintained this reduction for the rest of the war.

All told, the army had about 2,500 wagons and 600 ambulances. The wagon trains were dispersed among the four corps, so that each corps commander was responsible for about 800 wagons. A corps wagon train typically stretched for five or more miles.[15] To grasp the significance of the reduction in wheeled transportation, a comparison of Sherman's Savannah Campaign and Maj. Gen. William S. Rosecran's Chickamauga Campaign of 1863 is useful. Both generals had roughly 65,000 men to support, yet Rosecrans's army had about 4,800 wagons and ambulances compared to Sherman's 3,100.[16]

To ensure that only fit men began the march, Sherman's medical officers undertook a thorough screening to purge the army of any men deemed too weak to reach the coast. Sherman knew that he could ill-afford to have sick men filling the army's ambulances. He wanted to fill his ranks only with men who were "able-bodied experienced soldiers, well armed, well equipped and provided, as far as human foresight could, with all the essentials of life, strength, and vigorous action."[17]

Sherman had already demonstrated that armies do not have to be tied to supply bases in order to prosecute successful campaigns. In truth, Sherman's March to the Sea was merely a change of base, a significant departure from his Atlanta Campaign, in which he had relied upon Nashville and Chattanooga for his supplies. While Sherman had reduced his army's logistical requirements, he had never severed his supply line. Throughout the campaign, he depended on maintaining a secure line of communication with Chattanooga and thus had to commit substantial combat resources to maintain that line. Such was not the case in his March to the Sea. Sherman had organized and prepared his army so that it required no supply base. "The railroad and telegraph communications with the rear were broken, and the army stood detached from all friends, dependant on its own resources and supplies," Sherman later wrote.[18]

Sherman's ability to accomplish such a campaign was possible only because he faced a weak enemy. When Sherman departed Atlanta, he left his only significant military threat—Gen. John B. Hood's Army of Tennessee—far behind. Between Atlanta and Savannah, the Confederacy could muster a force of only 20,000, consisting of Hardee's force at Savannah, Wheeler's veteran cavalry, and elements of the Georgia State Militia.

After capturing Savannah, Sherman immediately began moving his force into South Carolina as a precursor to his Carolinas Campaign. By early February, Sherman had amassed enough supplies to initiate northward movement. The army's trains had been loaded with ten to twelve days' rations, and each soldier carried an additional three or four days' in his haversack. The army also carried seven days' supply of forage in its wagons. Table 1 shows the initial supply level of Maj. Gen. John W. Geary's Second Division, XX Corps at the start of the campaign, which is typical for Sherman's divisions at the start of the campaign.

Table 1. Government Supplies

Ration Type	Days of Supply
Salt Meat	3
Hard Bread	15
Coffee	30
Sugar	15
Salt	30
Pepper	15
Soap	10

Source: United States War Department, *The War of the Rebellion: A Compilation of the Official Records of the Union and Confederate Armies,* ser. 1, vol. 47, pt. 1 (Washington, D.C.: Government Printing Office, 1884–1891), 36.

As Table 1 illustrates, government-issued supplies alone could not sustain Sherman's army. Upon departing the coast of South Carolina, the army would have to "forage liberally" until Sherman reached Goldsboro, where he could exploit the town's rail connections to Morehead City and Wilmington. Contingency planning also called for re-supply via the Cape Fear River at Fayetteville. A worst case scenario envisioned re-supply at other points along the Carolinas coast. While Sherman was concerned about cutting his line of communication at Savannah, he "reasoned that we might safely rely on the country for a considerable quantity of forage and provisions, and that, if the worst came to worst, we could live several months on the mules and horses of our trains."[19] He wrote to Grant, "I will start with my Atlanta army (sixty thousand), supplied as before, depending on the country for all food."[20] The plan called for consuming government-issued supplies only when foraging failed to meet the army's demand.

Bummer
G. W. Nichols, The Story of the Great March (New York: Harper and Brothers, 1866)

While Special Field Order No. 120 called for each brigade to organize a foraging detail, this scheme soon proved unsatisfactory because too many division commanders sent out only fifty men per brigade, an insufficient force for the task at hand. As the brigade foraging organization began to break down, many commanders further decentralized the system by having regimental commanders assign the task to one or two companies. The supplies they gathered no longer went to the brigade commissary; instead, they went directly to the men of each regiment.[21] Their efforts proved most successful once the army reached the interior of South Carolina, leaving a fifty-mile-wide swath so bare of edibles that a Rebel prisoner claimed "a crow could not fly across it without carrying a haversack."[22]

The practice of foraging for the army was not without its dangers: the possibility of Confederate cavalry on the lookout loomed around every bend. Throughout the campaign, "a minimum of one hundred and nine [of Sherman's foragers] were either hanged, shot in head from very close range, or killed with their throats slit, and in a few cases someone had actually been butchered."[23] The Confederates usually left the bodies of these unfortunates along the road for Sherman's men to see. As a result, foragers fought with a ferocity that enabled many of them to avoid the fate of their less fortunate comrades.

While Sherman advanced into central South Carolina, logistical activity along the North Carolina coast increased. By mid-February, the tempo of support operations had increased significantly (see map below). From his headquarters in New Bern, Schofield integrated the arrival of his XXIII Corps from Tennessee with the buildup of supplies for Sherman's army. The ports of Wilmington, Morehead City, and New Bern saw the endless arrival of men and materiel. This activity began to strain the limited transportation network of eastern North Carolina. Nevertheless, the stockpiling of supplies along the coast prior to Sherman's arrival held the key to the success of future operations.

North Carolina Logistics Sites in Support of Campaign

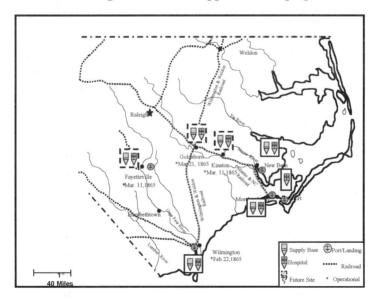

The task proved difficult. Confederate forces commanded by Gen. Braxton Bragg had recently evacuated the town of Wilmington, moved north along the Wilmington and Weldon Railroad line to Kinston, where they blocked Schofield's direct route to Goldsboro.

While preparing for combat against Bragg, Schofield and his staff also faced logistical problems, including the repair of the railroad west toward Goldsboro, and the buildup of supplies for Sherman's army. Chief quartermaster Brig. Gen. Langdon C. Easton and Col. W. W. Wright of the Railroad Department assisted Schofield in these critical tasks. As a result of a recent conference between Grant and Schofield, the seaport at Morehead City was chosen as the site for the grand depot, because it provided easy access for ocean going transports as well as a railroad linking the coast to the interior of the state.[24]

Because of Morehead City's logistical importance, Easton established his headquarters there and oversaw the construction of the advanced supply depot. By this phase of the campaign, rail transportation requirements began to overwhelm Easton's resources. On March 10, in order to alleviate the pressure on the railroad, Schofield instructed Easton to cease all movement of men and materièl not necessary for the support of future operations at Goldsboro.[25]

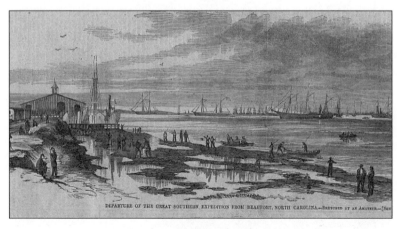

The Port at Morehead City
Harpers Illustrated Weekly, February 21, 1863

Nevertheless, some transportation issues were beyond Easton's control. In a letter to Maj. Gen. Quincy Gilmore at Hilton Head, Quartermaster General Meigs observed that the "demands upon the ocean transports of the country are now enormous," and he further complained that the "Southern ports have been nearly bare of vessels suited to our uses."[26] Table 2 illustrates the number of vessels allotted by the quartermaster general for the support of Sherman's Carolinas Campaign.

Table 2. Quartermaster Department Vessels in Support of General Sherman

Vessel Type	Number of Vessels
Steamers	73
Tugs	8
Ships	2
Brigs	1
Schooners	12
Pilot Boats	2
Total	98

Source: O.R., ser. 3, vol. 5, pt. 1, 293.

Gilmore's problem surfaced when he tried to procure transportation for the transfer from Savannah of nearly 5,000 men of Sherman's army who were either returning to duty after convalescing in local hospitals or who were replacements sent to Sherman's army from the north.

When Sherman's command was expanded to include the Department of the South and the District of North Carolina, he also gained responsibility for the control of all vessels operating under contract with the War Department in the littoral regions of the two departments. Sherman assigned the responsibility for managing these transportation resources to Easton.

The War Department's transfer of additional railroad assets to Morehead City enabled Easton and Wright to increase the distribution capability of the Atlantic and North Carolina Railroad. Sherman's staff had noted that the railroad lacked the capacity to sustain the large movement of men and materièl inland required for the next phase of the Carolinas Campaign. In response, the War Department provided additional assets that allowed the Construction Corps, augmented by detailed men from available forces, to put the railroad in suitable working order. The expansion of the wharf at Morehead City also allowed for the simultaneous discharge of up to eight vessels.[27] Table 3 indicates the volume of personnel and materiel shipped from the coast to Goldsboro.

Table 3. Rail Movement from 15 February to 1 May 1865

From	To	Contents	Number of Cars
Morehead City	Front	Supplies	1841
New Berne	Front	Supplies	850
Morehead City	Front	Troops	400
Total			3091

Source: O.R., ser. 3, vol. 5, pt. 1, 36.

Schofield's medical staff also prepared to treat Sherman's sick and wounded. To meet the anticipated demand, their plan called for the establishment of temporary hospitals at or near Goldsboro for those men not requiring evacuation. The soldiers with more serious illnesses or wounds would be transported to Foster General Hospital at New Bern. The capacity of Foster General Hospital was immediately increased to 1,500 beds and was later increased to 3,000 beds because of the hospital's proximity to the rail line connecting New Bern and Goldsboro.[28]

In addition to Foster Hospital, Mansfield Hospital was established at Beaufort, North Carolina, to accommodate patient overflow and facilitate evacuation from the seaport. Mansfield Hospital had 600 beds. Ironically, Easton had transformed the old Mansfield Hospital complex at Morehead City into supply warehouses.[29]

Writing to Schofield from Fayetteville on March 12, Sherman outlined his intentions for carrying out the remainder of the campaign. Sherman intended to refit the army as much as possible while still at Fayetteville. He intended to resume movement no later than March 15, and anticipated a link-up with Schofield about ten days later at Goldsboro. He ordered that repairs continue on the railroads from New Bern and Wilmington to Goldsboro. Thus far, Sherman's army had collected enough wagons and mules to support an army of 100,000, relieving Schofield of this burdensome task. Sherman still envisioned New Bern as the army's main depot, unaware that Grant and Schofield had already established Morehead City as the site for his primary depot. In a letter to Schofield, Sherman demonstrated his confidence: "With my present force, and with yours and Terry's added we can go wherever we can live. We can live where the people do, and if anybody has to suffer let them suffer."[30]

Also on March 12, Sherman sent a separate message to Wilmington for Easton and Beckwith, although he was unsure of their location. Sherman described the condition of his army, detailed what he needed for the next phase his campaign, and then outlined the conduct of future logistics operations. Sherman's immediate re-supply priority was shoes, socks, drawers, and trousers. Sherman expected his men to receive an "entire equipment of clothing" upon the army's arrival at Goldsboro.[31] The march through the Carolinas had required the men to spend much of their time wading through cold, muddy water or marching in the rain, thus quickly wearing out their clothing and footwear.

Sherman ordered Easton and Beckwith, "The moment you hear I am approaching Goldsborough forward to me clothing and bread, sugar and coffee [,] and empty wagons will meet them."[32] As with Schofield, Sherman relieved the two men of any responsibility for providing wagon transportation.

During the Battle of Averasboro less than a week later, several logistical problems occurred because of the terrible condition of the roads. Unfortunately for the Federals, the Fayetteville-Raleigh Road was narrow and offered the only route for both Kilpatrick's cavalry division and Slocum's Left Wing. The heavy traffic quickly turned the road into a quagmire, hindering the movement of troops and supplies to the front. Competition for road space ensued between combat units and supply wagons, and aggravating delays inevitably resulted.[33]

Ammunition re-supply problems occurred because the ordnance trains of several units were unable to move forward swiftly due to the muddy road. For example, the lack of ammunition hindered the performance of the 9th Ohio Cavalry Regiment. The rain had rendered the unit's ammunition "utterly worthless" and had also made re-supply impossible.[34] The 9th Ohio was one of the few regiments in Sherman's army armed with the Smith carbine, and because the Smith fired a special round, immediate re-supply was out of the question. On the Federal side, the fighting at Averasboro consumed enough ammunition to require a re-supply of twenty wagonloads of small arms rounds and six wagonloads of artillery rounds.[35]

Yet another logistical problem arose at Averasboro, where Hardee's determined resistance resulted in a large number of wounded for Sherman. The total losses in Slocum's Left Wing and Kilpatrick's cavalry were 95 killed and 533 wounded.[36] These casualties created significant problems in treating and evacuating the wounded for the medical staffs of both armies. The 533 wounded Federals far exceeded the capacity of the ambulances traveling with the light divisions of both the XIV and XX Corps.

Fourteen miles to the southeast, Geary's division of the XX Corps escorted the remainder of the corps' wagon train. As a result of the intense combat on March 16, Geary received instructions from XX Corps headquarters that evening to immediately "send all empty wagons and ambulances possible to the corps to transport wounded."[37] The train was placed under the charge of Capt. Moses Summers, the assistant quartermaster for Geary's Third Brigade. Because of the congested traffic conditions on the Fayetteville-Raleigh Road, Summers's wagons did not depart until about 6:00 A.M. the following morning. By noon on March 17 Geary received another message from XX Corps headquarters ordering him to send additional wagons "loaded with hard bread and coffee for the wounded."[38]

The morning of March 17 revealed the ugly reality of war. Sherman's men discovered the abandoned Confederate positions, and with them, the disturbing aftermath of battle: hundreds of Confederate wounded had been left to the tender mercies of the local residents and the Federal surgeons. John McBride of the 33rd Indiana described the Confederate retreat on the road from Smithville to the town of Averasboro as "disorderly and demoralizing…rejected wagons and ambulances were filled with the enemy's dead and dying and wounded."[39] Only minimal health care had been provided, and those wounded Confederates lucky enough to survive became dependent upon the locals. Worse yet, no rations or medical supplies had been left behind for the wounded. The Federal surgeons remained behind only long enough to stabilize Sherman's wounded and to ensure their evacuation. To make up for the shortfall in ambulances, the wounded men were transported in supply wagons (see p. 190).

Because of the wagon shortage, the ninety-five men killed in action were temporarily buried near the makeshift field hospitals. Slocum directed Bvt. Maj. Gen. Alpheus S. Williams, the XX Corps commander, to "make details for interring all the dead, keeping an

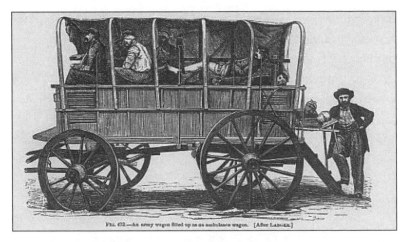

Army Supply Wagon
The Medical and Surgical History of the Civil War, vol. 12,
Wilmington, N. Car.: Broadfoot Publishing, 1991

exact account of the number, our own and rebel."[40] The burial details performed their unpleasant task under the direction of the provost marshal. Abel C. Stelle of the 31st Wisconsin served on the burial detail and remembered how he helped bury "thirty-nine Johnnies in one line of works."[41] Those Union soldiers buried at Smithville were later transferred to the National Cemetery at Raleigh, North Carolina.[42]

The logistical analysis conducted by both Sherman's staff and War Department bureaucrats prior to the campaign illustrates the benefit of accurate calculations and careful planning. Sherman and his staff had an excellent understanding of the expected logistical support. Their ability to conceptualize the campaign through the Carolinas allowed them to anticipate the necessary support to refit Sherman's army upon its arrival at Goldsboro.[43]

Nevertheless, supply problems sometimes arose during the campaign. Supplying the men often proved difficult, and demonstrated the pitfalls of maneuvering an army without a line of communications. Sherman's plan failed to allow for all the hardships that accompany a campaign of this magnitude, particularly regarding the wear and tear to uniforms and shoes. Foraging proved effective most of the time, but shortages of food and forage sometimes occurred.[44]

The Carolinas Campaign posed considerable challenges to Union logisticians. The campaign succeeded because Sherman anticipated his army's needs and coordinated the necessary logistical support. Quartermaster General Meigs's report to Secretary of War Edwin M. Stanton neatly summarizes the logistical success of the campaign:

> This army of nearly 100,000 men needed to be entirely reclad and reshod; the troops were to be fed while resting, for as soon as the army ceased its march it ceased to supply itself by foraging, and depended upon the supplies from the coast. Nevertheless, on the 7th of April I was able to inform General Sherman that the necessary supplies were in his camps. Every soldier had received a complete outfit of clothing and had been newly shod. The wagons were loaded with rations, and forage.[45]

Union Hospital at Savage Station
The scenes around the "Oak Grove" would have looked very similar.
The man in the straw hat in the middle foreground is a surgeon.
Library of Congress

Appendix C
AVERASBORO FIELD HOSPITALS

The Averasboro battlefield is located at "Smithville," so named because of the three interrelated Smith families who lived there. The site of the Oak Grove plantation was selected for its access to "Smith's Ferry" across the Cape Fear River, and for its proximity to the Raleigh-Fayetteville Road. The elder John Smith (1772–1851) built Oak Grove in 1793. He later willed the property of over 8,300 acres to his three sons, Farquhard, John, and William. Farquhard and William built their own homes, while John resided in Oak Grove. Farquhard built and established the Lebanon plantation, and William built his house south of Oak Grove plantation house.

On March 15–16, 1865, the Civil War came to Smithville, and the Smiths found themselves trapped in a major battle. Union surgeons established hospitals at the William Smith house and the John Smith house, where the wounded of both armies were treated. Confederate surgeons established a third hospital at Lebanon, the Farquhard Smith house, where they treated mostly Confederate soldiers.

The John Smith House: OAK GROVE
The largest hospital on the Averasboro battlefield was at Oak Grove house. One Union soldier left an account of his wounding and his treatment at Oak Grove. Late on March 16, Cpl. Thomas Simpson of Company E, 102nd Illinois, was wounded during the Federal assaults on the Confederate third line. "I was wounded in the left arm breaking the bone," wrote Simpson. Along with his friend Pvt. Ed Chilson, Corporal Simpson made the mile-long trek back to Oak Grove. "I walked most of the way, arriving at the hospital feeling pretty bad," he remembered. Because his arm was too badly shattered to be saved, Simpson was immediately placed on the amputating table. Dr. William Hamilton, the regimental surgeon of the 102nd Illinois, gave Simpson chloroform and then amputated his arm.

Sherman Visiting Wounded at Oak Grove
Drawing by Col. Darrell L. Combs, USMC, (Ret.)

Simpson survived the surgery. "I feel quite well this morning considering what I have come through," he wrote. "I didn't sleep much last night on the account of my arm, although I laid on my first bedstead that I have laid on since I left home two and half years ago."[1]

Simpson's brief statement is particularly noteworthy: it speaks volumes about the character and hardiness of the men who fought in the Civil War. That Simpson walked nearly a mile to a hospital with a shattered arm is impressive but not unique. However, his passing comment about not having slept on a bed in over two-and-a-half years reveals a great deal about the hard life of Civil War soldiers.

Sherman took time during the battle to visit the wounded at "Oak Grove." "Amputated arms and legs lying around loose, in the yard and on the porch," he later wrote. "Sherman went through every ward and tent, and talked to his brave Boys, and the poor cripples seem to lifen [sic] up when they heard and seen the Commander in Chief. They all smiled at him," noted hospital steward Charles Gottlieb Michael. Sherman's personal concern lifted the spirits of the mangled men who had followed him into battle.[2]

Sherman spotted a handsome young man lying on a bed in one of the rooms of Oak Grove. The young man was pale and weak after having his left arm amputated at the shoulder. In a frail voice, the young man asked if he was speaking to General Sherman. The general replied that he was. The young man announced that he was

Captain Macbeth of the 1st South Carolina Artillery, and that he remembered the General from the days when he was stationed at Charleston and would visit his father's house. Sherman replied that he remembered too, and inquired about his family. Macbeth asked whether Sherman would see to it that a letter he had written would get to his mother. Sherman agreed, and mailed it once he reached Goldsboro.[3]

After visiting the large number of casualties at the hospital, Sherman's focus apparently shifted from fighting the enemy to reaching Goldsboro as quickly as possible. The Sandhills region of North Carolina could not feed his army for long, and the large number of wounded would slow his progress. He was therefore anxious to avoid another battle before reaching Goldsboro.

On March 16, Maj. Henry Clay Robbins, surgeon of the 101st Illinois, was one of many regimental surgeons caring for the wounded at Oak Grove. Regimental surgeons often came from the same areas as the men in their units and knew them well. This familiarity sometimes made it difficult for surgeons to treat their wounded charges. Robbins recalled an incident at Oak Grove that was forever burned into his memory. "After working many hours at the operating tables and getting a little over the rush, I took a turn through the hospital," recalled Robbins. He wanted to make sure that there were no more soldiers needing his attention. Robbins recalled hearing a faint voice call, "Major."

When he turned in the direction of the voice, Robbins realized that a man from his own regiment was calling him. "What is it, Mike?" asked the major as he approached the wounded man's side.

"I am wounded in the leg," replied Mike, whose last name escaped Robbins. (The wounded man was probably Pvt. Michael Hurley. Only three members of the 101st Illinois were wounded at Averasboro, including Hurley, who was still listed as wounded when the regiment was mustered out in June 1865.) Robbins inquired whether the man had been attended to, and was surprised to hear that the answer was,

"No." Major Robbins immediately moved the man to the operating table for a closer examination.

The wound was serious, and Mike was weak from loss of blood. "A ball had shattered his ankle breaking all the bones into fine fragments," noted Robbins. Robbins ordered that the man be given ether and then prepared the foot for amputation.

"Doctor, don't you cut my foot off; if you do I'll never forgive you," exclaimed Mike.

Robbins briefly tried to convince the man that the operation was necessary. In any event, Robbins ignored the man's threat, hoping that the man would later realize the necessity of amputating his foot. Several hours after the operation, the man awoke and realized that his foot was gone.

"Looking me in the face he said 'Doctor I will never forgive you,'" recalled Robbins.

"I tried to reason with him," recalled Robbins, who explained that the foot had to come off. Robbins ordered the assistant surgeon to show the amputated foot and to Mike: Only then did the man understand. "I guess it is all right," remarked Mike, much to Robbins's relief.[4]

Another surgeon on duty at Oak Grove that day was Dr. George Martin Trowbridge of the 19th Michigan. "I have been very busy all day with the wounded and have only an hour or so before I go back on duty," Trowbridge wrote his wife. He was on duty from 12 A.M. to 4 A.M. During some slack time, Trowbridge scrawled a few lines describing the Oak Grove hospital to his wife. "I sheltered up great in a fine plantation residence, the people are all from home and left bedding, etc. very convenient for us and assure you we used what we wanted," he remarked. "It would be pleasant were it not for the cries and groans of the wounded and dying, so great as to disturb sleep." The next morning, March 17, Trowbridge returned to his regiment, which was under marching orders. The Confederates had retired during the night, and the 19th Michigan was moving north to Averasboro. "We found a Reb left in an ambulance at the road to die and some 20–30 others left in town for want of transportation," Trowbridge reported.[5]

Corporal Simpson of the 102nd Illinois also departed "Oak Grove" on March 17. "I still feel some of the effects of the chloroform," recalled Simpson when he awoke on the morning of March 17. "About noon we loaded up the ambulances. I was put in an ambulance on a good tick with William H. Sanford, of Co H 19th Michigan Regiment. He lost his left leg."[6] The wounded suffered mightily as they moved north toward Goldsboro. Each bounce on the corduroyed roads caused excruciating pain to the wounded.

Oak Grove remains one of the most interesting houses in the area today, not only for its colonial architecture, but also because it still bears the scars of battle. The front of the house has numerous bullet holes in the walls and rails. However, the attic holds the most interesting battle scars: cannon ball holes made by two 12-pound shells fired from the Confederate first line.

Oak Grove Bloodstained Floor
Wade Sokolosky

CANNONBALL CONTROVERSY

There is some dispute as to who fired the artillery shells that entered the roof of Oak Grove. One theory states that Union artillery fired upon the house, but this is unlikely for two reasons. First, no Union artillery was in position to fire rounds into the roof at such an angle. Second, until the XX Corps artillery unlimbered in the orchard southeast of the Oak Grove house, a section of the 10th Wisconsin Battery was the only Union artillery on the field. The round that passed through the flat wallboards of the attic was 4.5-inches in diameter—that is, a 12-pound shell. The 10th Wisconsin had 3-inch ordnance rifles, which fired a 2.92-inch shell, so the hole could not have been caused by a round fired by the 10th Wisconsin Battery.

Visitors often ask why Confederate artillery fired into the attic of Oak Grove. The most likely explanation is that Union sharpshooters were using the second floor as a haven. The Confederate gunners, knowing that some of their wounded were also in the house, fired two non-explosive solid shots into the attic as a clear message to the Union snipers: stay out of the house.

Another controversy involves the location of the Confederate artillery. Some historians believe that all three Confederate guns were located on the Confederate right flank. The Union engineers who mapped the battlefield noted the placement of three guns in two locations: one section on the Fayetteville-Raleigh Road, and one gun in the field. Captain Huguenin's sketch shows the deployment of two guns on the Fayetteville-Raleigh Road.

A more scientific approach puts to rest any doubts about where the shots came from and also pinpoints the location of the Confederate artillery on the first line. The author took string and ran it from the entrance hole to the exit hole for each of the two shells, taping it at each end. A magnetic compass reading was taken at each shell location. The author then moved to the front of the house and shot an azimuth from the approximate entrance location of each shell hole. These measurements revealed that the shell that entered the

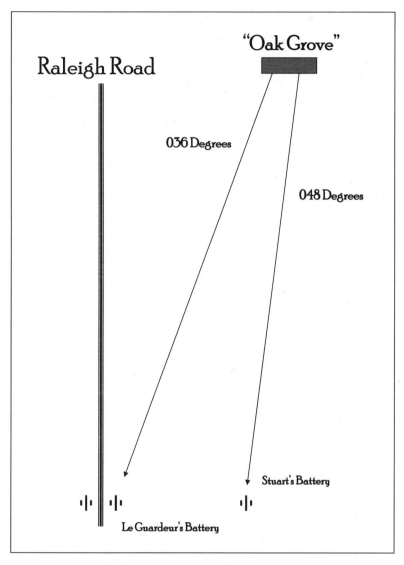

Oak Grove Shell Hole Table
Mark Smith

right front portion of the house came from the Fayetteville-Raleigh Road, while the shell that entered the left front portion of the house came from the field (See Table). The Union engineers' maps were in fact accurate, placing two Confederate guns on the Fayetteville-Raleigh Road and one in the field. Judging from the trajectory of the entrance and exit holes in the attic, it is likely that one of the shells came from the gun of Stuart's Battery, in the field, and that the other came from one of the two guns of LeGardeur's Battery in the Fayetteville-Raleigh Road.

Years later, Smithville resident Jessie Slocumb Smith recalled the incidents that swirled around Oak Grove during the battle. "In the attic are still to be seen the holes made by the cannon balls," she wrote, "and on the upstairs bedroom floor are still discernible the blood stains left by the wounded Confederate and Union soldiers." Those artillery shell holes in the attic, noted in Jessie Smith's letter, are still visible today in Oak Grove.[7]

The William Smith House:

The scene at the William Smith house was as horrendous as at Oak Grove. The William Smith house was the first of the three Smith houses to be used as a hospital. Most of the causalities treated at the William Smith house were wounded on March 15 or early on March 16. Jessie Slocumb Smith recalled, "The parlor on which the bloodstains are yet to be seen was used as an operating room. The piano was used for an operating table." The Union soldiers who died at the hospital were buried on the grounds of the house. Much to Smith's dismay, "the Federal soldiers dying here were first buried in the garden." They were later disinterred and moved to the National Cemetery in Raleigh.[8]

The Farquhard Smith House: LEBANON

During the fighting on the March 16, the Confederates established their field hospital at Lebanon, the Farquhard Smith house. As at the other two hospitals, the conditions at Lebanon were terrible. The casualties who flooded into the hospital quickly overwhelmed the surgeons. The Smiths helped wherever they could, but they were ordered to leave the house and seek shelter in a nearby creek bed. Janie Smith, the eighteen-year-old daughter of Farquhard Smith, tended to the wounded. Janie described the gruesome scenes around Lebanon. "Ambulance after ambulance drove up with our wounded," she wrote. "One half of the house was prepared for the soldiers, but owing to the close proximity of the enemy, they only sent in the sick, but every barn and out house was filled and under every shade tree." Janie was deeply moved by the carnage. "The scene beggars description, the blood lay in puddles in the grove," she recalled, "the groans of the dying and the complaints of those under amputation was horrible." The house's tables were "carried for amputating the limbs." She declared, "Oh! It makes me shudder when I think of the awful sights I witnessed that morning."9

Late in the day on March 16, during the battle for the third line, Lt. Oscar Laborde of the 1st South Carolina Artillery, who survived the violent assaults on the first and second lines, was killed instantly "while sitting on a fence" in the lane leading to the "Lebanon" house when "a stray ball pierced his head." Janie Smith cared for Laborde's grave until his family could remove his remains. He now rests in the Trinity Episcopal Church Cemetery in Columbia, South Carolina.10

Early on the morning on March 17, Union troops advanced and occupied the abandoned Confederate third line. As Ward's division moved north toward Averasboro, his men found the wounded Confederates left behind at Lebanon by the retreating Southerners. During the push toward Averasboro, Pvt. William Grunert of the 129th Illinois recalled finding the road "strewn with the rebel dead. We found the greater part of the wounded in the frame houses on both sides of the road, all alone and without attendants, medicine, or provisions." To Grunert's horror, he found, in one of the abandoned ambulances, "a wounded rebel almost dead, who a shot had struck in the forehead, the brain oozed out of the wound over his eyes, and a few faint groans were all the poor fellow could utter." Grunert concluded that the Confederates had abandoned the man because he was too far gone to save.[11]

All three field hospitals survive today and are currently in private hands. Oak Grove is the only house not currently occupied. It is in an advanced state of disrepair, due to lack of maintenance and to extensive hurricane damage. Please obtain prior permission before visiting these sites and respect the rights and privacy of the landowners.

Although Hardee left a portion of his wounded at Averasboro, the Confederate evacuation system was not a total failure. As Hardee prepared to engage Sherman's Left Wing, others anticipated the need for general hospitals to support the wounded. Under the direction of the Medical Director of North Carolina, Dr. Peter E. Hines, other surgeons were preparing hospitals to care for the wounded of the campaign.

Dr. Simon Baruch was ordered to set up a general hospital in Thomasville, North Carolina, a small town that had sprung up around a railroad depot. Dr. Baruch immediately went to work, using two churches and a tobacco warehouse as hospitals. Within a few days of his arrival, and with the help of local citizens, Baruch built a bake oven and cleared more buildings, including a hotel, for the wounded. No sooner had he finished when word arrived from Medical Director Hines, announcing that "two hundred wounded from the fighting at Averasboro were on a train to Thomasville." With no time to lose, Baruch mobilized nearly the entire town to support the hospital; wagons were commandeered, women stuffed straw into sacks for makeshift beds, while others stayed at home "baking bread, preparing rye coffee and bacon" for the wounded. All was ready when the train bearing the wounded arrived in Thomasville. Only two surgeons accompanied the wounded men.

Joined by Baruch, the three surgeons immediately attended to the wounded, working through the night with the assistance of numerous older women of Thomasville. This process continued for two days, until they had tended to all of the wounded.[12]

Janie Smith
Courtesy of Walt Smith

Appendix D
Janie Smith's Letter

Almost a month after the Battle of Averasboro, eighteen-year-old Janie Smith wrote a letter to her friend, Janie Robeson of Bladen County. Janie Smith was the daughter of Farquhard and Sarah Slocum Grady Smith, and she lived at Lebanon, with her eight brothers and two unmarried sisters. In 1865, as Sherman's forces threatened North Carolina, Janie was attending Burwill Female Seminary in Charlotte, North Carolina. She returned home to Lebanon in order to be with her father and two sisters (her mother had died in 1861) until the danger had passed. Janie's brothers were all in Confederate service at the time of the battle, and none were at home. In her April 12, 1865 letter, Janie detailed the events she witnessed during and after the battle. Janie Smith's letter is currently in the Mrs. Thomas H. Webb Collection, North Carolina Division of Archives and History, Raleigh, North Carolina.

Where home used to be.
April 12th, 1865.

Your precious letter, My dear Janie, was received night before last, and the pleasure it afforded me, and indeed the whole family, I leave for you to imagine, for it baffles words to express my thankfulness when I hear that my friends are left with the necessities of life, and unpolluted [sic] by the touch of Sherman's Hell-hounds. My experience since we parted has been indeed sad, but I am so blessed when I think of the other friends in Smithville that I forget my own troubles. Our own army came first and enjoyed the cream of the country and left but little for the enemy. We had a most delightful time while our troops were camped around. They arrived here on the first of March and were camping around and passing for nearly a week. Feeding the hungry and nursing the sick and looking occupied the day, and at night company would come in and wait until bed-time.

I found our officers gallant and gentlemanly and the privates no less so. The former of course, we saw more of, but such an army of patriots fighting for their hearthstones is not to be conquered by such fiends incarnate as fill the ranks of Sherman's army. Our political sky does seem darkened with a fearful cloud, but when compared with the situation of our fore-fathers, I can but take courage. We had then a dissolute and disaffected soldiery to contend with, to say nothing of the poverty of the Colonies during the glorious revolution of '76. Now our resources increase every year and while I confess that the desertion in our army is awful, I am sanguine as to the final issue to the war.

Gen. Wheeler took tea here about two o'clock during the night after the battle closed, and about four o'clock the Yankees came charging, yelling and howling. I stood on the piazza and saw the charge made, but as calm as I am now, though I was all prepared for the rascals, our soldiers having given us a detailed account of their habits. The paling did not hinder them at all. They just knocked down all such like mad cattle. Right into the house, breaking open bureau drawers of all kinds faster than I could unlock. They cursed us for having hid everything and made bold threats if certain things were not brought to light, but all to no effect. They took Pa's hat and stuck him pretty badly with a bayonet to make him disclose something, but you know they were fooling with the wrong man. One impudent dog came into the dining room where Kate and I were and said "Good morning girls, why aren't you up getting breakfast, it's late?" I told him that servants prepared Southern Ladies breakfast. He went off muttering something about their not waiting on us any more, but not one of the servants went from here, they remained faithful through it all, with one exception, and Pa has driven him off to the Yankees.

Mr. Sherman, I think is pursuing the wrong policy to accomplish his designs. The Negroes are bitterly prejudiced to his minions. They were treated, if possible, worse than the white folks, all their provisions taken and their clothes destroyed and some carried off.

They left no living thing in Smithville but the people. One old hen played sick and thus saved her neck, but lost all of her children. The Yankees would run all over the yard to catch the little things to squeeze to death.

Every nook and corner of the premises was searched and the things that they didn't use were burned or torn into strings. No house except the blacksmith shop was burned, but into the flames they threw every tool, plow etc., that was on the place. The house was so crowded all day that we could scarcely move and of all the horrible smelling things in the world the Yankees beat. The battlefield does not compare with them in point of stench. I don't believe they have been washed since they were born. I was so sick all the time that I could not have eaten had I had anything. All of Uncle John's family were here and we lived for three days on four quarts of meal which Aunt Eliza begged from a Yank. Didn't pretend to sift it, baked up in our room where fifteen of us had to stay. When and how we slept, I don't know. I was too angry to eat or sleep either and I let the scoundrels know it whenever one had the impudence to speak to me. Gen. Slocum with two other hyenas of his rank, rode up with his body-guard and introduced themselves with great pomp, but I never noticed them at all. Whenever they would poke out their dirty paws to shake my hand, I'd give the haughtiest nod I could put on and ask what they came for. I had heard that the officers would protect ladies, but it is not so. Sis Susan was sick in bed and they searched the very pillows that she was lying on, and keeping such a noise, tearing up and breaking to pieces, that the Generals couldn't hear themselves talk, but not a time did they try to prevent it. They got all of my stockings and some of our collars and handkerchiefs. If I ever see a Yankee woman, I intend to whip her and take the clothes off of her very back. We would have been better prepared for the thieves but had to spend the day before our troops left in a ravine as the battle was fought so near the house, so we lost a whole days hiding. I can't help laughing, though the recollection is so painful when I think of that day. Imagine us all and Uncle John's family trudging through the rain and mud down to a ravine near the river, each one with a shawl, blanket and basket of provisions. The battle commenced on the 15th of March at Uncle John's. The family were ordered from home, stayed in the trenches all day when late in the evening they came to us, wet, muddy and hungry. Their house was penetrated by a great many shells and balls, but was not burned and the Yankees used it for a hospital, they spared it, but everything was taken and the furniture destroyed. The girls did not have a change of clothing. The Yankees drove us from two lines of fortifications that day, but with heavy loss, while ours was light. That night we fell back to the cross roads, if you remember where that is, about one sixth of a mile from here, there our men became desperate and at day-light on the sixteenth the firing was terrific. The infirmary was here and oh it makes me shudder when I think of the awful sights I witnessed that morning. Ambulance after ambulance drove up with our wounded.

One half of the house was prepared for the soldiers, but owing to the close proximity of the enemy they only sent in the sick, but every barn and out house was fill and under every shed and tree the tables were carried for amputating the limbs. I just felt like my heart would break when I would see our brave men rushing into the battle and then coming back so mangled.

The scene beggars description, the blood lay in puddles in the grove, the groans of the dying and the complaints of those undergoing amputation was horrible, the painful impression has seared my very heart. I can never forget it. We were kept busy making and rolling bandages and sending nourishment to the sick and wounded until orders came to leave home. Then was my trial, leaving our poor suffering soldiers when I could have been relieving them some. As we passed the wounded going to the woods they would beseech us not to go. "Ladies, don't leave your home, we won't let the enemy fire upon you." But orders from headquarters must be obeyed and to the woods we went. I never expected to see the dear old homestead again, but thank heaven, I am living comfortably in it again.

It was about nine o'clock when the courier came with orders. The firing continued incessantly up and down the lines all day, when about five in the evening the enemy flanked our right, where we were sent for protection, and the firing was right over us. We could hear the commands and groans and shrieks of the wounded.

A line of battle was formed in front of us, and we knew that was certain death to us should we be unsuccessful in repelling the charge. Lou and I started out to do the same thing, when one of the vedetts [*sic*] saw my white flag (my handkerchief (sic) on a pole) and came to us. I accosted him, "Are you one of our men or a Yankee?" "I am a Reb, Mam." "Can't you go and report to the commanding officer and tell him that the hillside is lined with women and children he sent here for protection, and the line of battle over there will destroy us?" "I'll do all I can for you," was the gallant reply and in a short time we were ordered home.

Well, Janie dear, I am really afraid of wearying you with my long epistle, but if you feel as much interested in Smithville as I do in the welfare of Ashwood, I know you won't complain. You inquired after Cam. I believe the excitement cured her. She is better now than she has been for years.

Their house is ruined with the blood of the Yankee wounded. Only two rooms left, Aunt Mary's and the little one joining, which the family occupied. The others she can't pretend to use. Every piece of bed furniture, etc. is gone. The scamps left our piano, used Aunt Mary's for an amputation table.

The Yanks left fifty of our wounded at Uncle John's whom we have been busy nursing. All that were able have gone to their homes, and the others except four, are dead. The poor things were left there suffering and hungry with only one doctor. I felt my poverty keenly when I went down there and couldn't even give them a piece of bread. But, however, Pa had the scattering corn picked up and ground, which we divided with them, and as soon as the Country around learned their condition, delicacies [sic] of all kinds were sent in. I can dress amputated limbs now and do most anything in the way of nursing the wounded soldiers. We have had nurses and surgeons from Raleigh for a week or two. I am really attached to the patients of the hospital and feel so sad and lonely now that so many have left and died. My favorite, a little black-eyed boy with the whitest brow and thick curls falling on it, died last Sunday, but the Lord has taken him to a better land. He was the only son of his widowed mother. I have his ring and a lock of his hair to send her as soon as I can get an opportunity. It is so sad to receive the dying messages and tokens for the loved ones at home. It grieves me to see them buried without coffins, but it is impossible to get them now. I have two graves in my charge to keep fresh flowers on, the little boy just mentioned and Lieutenant Laborde, the son of Dr. Laborde of Columbia College. The latter had passed through the fight untouched, and while sitting on the fence of our avenue resting and making friends with his captain, whom he had challenged, a stray ball pierced his head. His with three other Confederate graves are the only ones near the house. But the yard and garden at Uncle John's, the cottage and Aunt Mary's are used for Yankee grave yards, and they are buried so shallow that the places are extremely offensive. The Yankees stayed here for only one day, a few for a day or two would come. "We had a romantic time feeding the Confederate captain they brought here, hiding the bread from the rogues."

We had to walk about three miles going to the hospital at first to avoid the Yankee pickets. Our soldiers were there suffering and we were determined to help them.

Cousin Rice came home yesterday wounded by a pistol shot in the fleshy part of his shoulder. He looks well considering his long walk. We have no way of sending for our wounded brothers now. Bros. Henry and Fark came about a week after the Yanks left. I never was so glad to see folks in my life, but they are so saddened by the dissolution in Smithville that they don't seem like the same boys. Cousin Walter is also at home. Each one of the boys brought their rations and it looked so strange. Cousin Rice was wounded on the 6th inst. at Petersburg. Tom's horse was lost. The others were all safe at that time. It sickens me when I think of the bloody battles they have been in since, and we can't hear from them. I think you ought to be thankful that your brother is captured, though I know how you feel about him. All things are for the best and I feel it is so. Your Uncle David spent the night with us as he passed on a sad mission. I was so glad to see him and hope that he will bring his wounded son here on his way back. I reckon he thought there was no end to my questions. Sloke was in the battle of Bentonville, but escaped unhurt. He had to leave home in spite of our entreaties, volunteered for the emergency, says he and his horse had a funny time dodging behind each other. This is the only "critter" he saved, but our army got them. We plow old bags of bones the Yanks would not trouble to kill, pick them up from the battle field. We are getting on very well in the eating line. As you suppose, we had little corn left at the plantation and a cow or two. I am not afraid of perishing though the prospects for it are very bright. When our army invade the North, I want them to carry the torch in one hand, the sword in the other. I want desolation carried to the heart of their country, the widows and orphans left naked and starving just as ours were left. I know you think this a very unbecoming sentiment, but I believe it is our only policy now.

I will wait until tomorrow to finish my volume as Jess can't bear the light in his eyes and it is too dark for me. Sloke is quite sick with measles, took cold and I am staying with him while sister and Louise are out enjoying the lovely spring evening. All nature is gay and beautiful, but every Southern breeze is loaded with a terrible scent from the battle field, which renders my home very disagreeable at times.

Appendix E
The Lost Gunners Quadrant

In 1895, the aging former commander of the Confederate Fayetteville Arsenal, Lt. Col. Frederick L. Childs, passed away and was buried in the quiet cemetery of the Church of the Holy Cross in Stateburg, South Carolina.[1] The old Confederate veteran went to his grave without ever recovering a treasured piece of his father's military past that had been passed down to him. Childs's gunner's quadrant and other personal belongings fell victim to Sherman's engineers when they razed the Fayetteville Arsenal. Amazingly, almost a century later, the quadrant was returned to the Childs family under the most curious of circumstances.

Col. Frederick L. Childs
Fayetteville Observer, November 4, 1962

Frederick L. Childs was the only son of an American military hero, Bvt. Brig. Gen. Thomas Childs. Thomas Childs entered the United States Army in 1814 at the tender age of 16, while the country was at war with England. While a cadet at West Point, Thomas accepted an early commission from the Army to help meet the needs of the service. The teenager led his detachment against British forces at the 1814 Battle of Fort Erie. The young lieutenant distinguished himself during the battle by capturing British Artillery Battery No. 3. After killing or capturing the British soldiers manning the battery, Childs and his men spiked the guns and destroyed the powder magazine. The valuable ordnance materièl seized by young lieutenant's detachment was then turned over to the War Department.

Congress commended the bravery of Lieutenant Childs during the battle by having one of the captured brass gunner's quadrants engraved and presented to the young officer. The inscription read as follows:

> Captured from the British at the Sortie from Fort Erie on the 17th of September, 1814, by Lieutenant Thomas Childs, who commanded the detachment that spiked the guns and blew up the magazine of Battery No. 3, at the age of 16.

Childs served in the Army for another 39 years, rising to the rank of brevet brigadier general. He died in 1853 while serving in Tampa, Florida. Following his death, his only son, Frederick L. Childs, became the steward for the treasured quadrant. Unlike his father, Frederick graduated from West Point before joining the ranks of the United States Artillery.

Throughout his service in the United States Army and the Confederate Army, Frederick Childs carried the quadrant with him. As Sherman approached Fayetteville in March 1865, Childs accompanied the matériel and equipment evacuated from the Arsenal, leaving the quadrant in the care of his mother and sister at their residence on the Arsenal grounds. Following Sherman's arrival at the Arsenal, Mrs. Childs approached the general, seeking protection for the family's property. She hoped Sherman would show leniency to her based on the Union commander's relationship with her late husband years earlier. Rebuffed by Sherman for her son's traitorous acts, Mrs. Childs was left to the mercy of Sherman's men, who showed little sympathy for the aging widow. Their quarters and all of their personal belongings were either destroyed by fire or dumped into the Cape Fear River along with other items from the Arsenal.

From 1865 on, only the story of the quadrant was passed down through the Childs family. But this story had a happy ending. In 1932 a night watchman at the Norfolk Naval Hospital named Paul Watson learned that a patient, Marine Corps Lt. W. W. Childs, had been in a traffic accident and had been admitted for treatment. The curious Watson gained permission to visit Childs from the hospital staff.

Watson introduced himself to the lieutenant and informed him that his father, a salvage diver, had dived the Cape Fear River in the early 1900s in an effort to recover scrap metal from the Arsenal dumped there by Sherman's men. His father discovered an engraved brass gunner's quadrant inscribed to a Lt. Thomas Childs. The elder Watson decided to hold onto it in the hope of one day identifying its rightful owner. The years passed, and the quadrant was handed down to another generation.

After hearing Watson's story, Lieutenant Childs informed him that Lt. Thomas Childs was his great-grandfather. Coincidentally, Childs happened to have the military commissions of his great grandfather and grandfather in the car with him on the day of the accident. He showed the two commissions to Watson, who did the noble thing and returned the quadrant to its rightful owners, his family's mission finally completed. One can only imagine the delight felt by Lieutenant Childs to have so treasured and storied a military item back in the family's possession after so many years.[2]

Endnotes

Chapter 1

1. Mark L. Bradley, *Last Stand in the Carolinas: The Battle of Bentonville* (Campbell, Cal.: Savas Publishing Company, 1995), 1–2; William T. Sherman, *Memoirs of W. T. Sherman by Himself*, 2 vols. (New York: Charles L. Webster and Co., 1891), 2:181, 190, 219, 231, and 227–228; Maj. Johnny W. Sokolosky, "The Role of Union Logistics: Sherman's Carolinas Campaign of 1865," Masters Thesis (Fort Leavenworth, Kan.: U.S. Army Command & General Staff College, 2000), 3.

2. Ulysses S. Grant, *Personal Memoirs of Ulysses S. Grant*, 2 vols. (New York: Charles Webster and Company, 1885), 2:529.

3. Sherman, *Memoirs*, 2:253, 259–261, and 269; Grant, *Memoirs*, 2:529; Sokolosky, "The Role of Union Logistics," 9.

4. Sherman, *Memoirs*, 2:224–225; Bradley, *Last Stand*, 2.

5. Sherman, *Memoirs*, 2:238.

6. Ezra J. Warner, *Generals in Blue*, (Baton Rouge: Louisiana State University Press, 1992) 441–444.

7. Ibid.

8. Bradley, *Last Stand*, 2; Sherman, *Memoirs*, 2:213, 238, and 271.

9. Sherman, *Memoirs*, 2:263; Sokolosky, "The Role of Union Logistics," 10; and *The War of the Rebellion: A Compilation of the Official Records of the Union and Confederate Armies*, 128 vols. in 4 series (Washington, D.C.: U.S. Government Printing Office, 1889–1904), series 1, vol. 47, part 1, 136 (unless otherwise noted, all future references to the Official Records will be to series 1) (hereinafter referred to as "*O.R.*").

10. Bradley, *Last Stand*, 4. A detailed examination of the Wilmington Campaign goes far beyond the scope of this study. For those interested in a detailed evaluation of the Union efforts to capture Fort Fisher and against the critical port city of Wilmington, see Chris E. Fonvielle, Jr.'s superb *The Wilmington Campaign: Last Departing Rays of Hope* (Mechanicsburg, Pa.: Stackpole, 1997).

11. Fonvielle, *The Wilmington Campaign,* 197–198 and 473–475.

12. Ibid., 331–332; Sherman, *Memoirs,* 2:258–259.

13. Bradley, *Last Stand,* 2–4; Sherman, *Memoirs,* 2:225.

14. Sherman, *Memoirs,* 2:239–40.

15. Ibid., 2:268–9 and 227.

16. John G. Barrett, *Sherman's March Through the Carolinas* (Chapel Hill: University of North Carolina Press, 1956), 45 and 47; Sherman, *Memoirs,* 2:255.

17. Sherman, *Memoirs,* 2:258.

18. Nathaniel Chears Hughes, *Bentonville: The Final Battle of Sherman and Johnston* (Chapel Hill: University of North Carolina Press, 1996), 2.

19. Sherman, *Memoirs,* 253 and 259; *O.R.* vol. 47, pt. 1, 18, and 392–3 and pt. 2, 154; Sokolosky, The Role of Union Logistics," 49.

20. Sokolosky, The Role of Union Logistics, 51; *O.R.* vol. 47, pt. 2, 78–80 and 97; Sherman, *Memoirs,* 2:272. The Atlantic & North Carolina Rail Road extended 95 miles from Morehead City to Goldsboro. At the start of the campaign, only 44 miles of track was serviceable. *O.R.* series III, vol. 5, part 1, 963.

21. Sherman, *Memoirs,* 2:272–274; Bradley, *Last Stand,* 3–4.

22. Bradley, *Last Stand,* 21–22.

23. Ibid., 23. The peace negotiations were called the "Hampton Roads Conference," and were held aboard President Lincoln's steamer *River Queen* on February 3, 1865.

24. Sherman, *Memoirs,* 2:274; Barrett, *Sherman's March,* 55.

25. Barrett, *Sherman's March,* 56. For a more detailed examination of the Battle of Aiken, see Tom Elmore, "Head to Head," *Civil War Times Illustrated* 40 (Feb 2001): 44–52 and 54–55.

26. Warner, *Generals in Blue,* 266–7; Bradley, *Last Stand,* 20.

27. Warner, *Generals in Gray: Lives of Confederate Commanders,* (Baton Rouge: Louisiana State University Press, 1992) 332–3.

28. Bradley, *Last Stand,* 83; Warner, *Generals in Gray,* 333.

29. Bradley, *Last Stand,* 84.

30. Ibid.

31. Barrett, *Sherman's March,* 59–60; Bradley, *Last Stand,* 23; and Sherman, *Memoirs,* 2:274–276.

32. Bradley, *Last Stand*, 81–82; Warner, *Generals in Gray*, 122.

33. Bradley, *Last Stand*, 81–2.

34. Ibid., 82.

35. Sokolosky, "The Role of Union Logistics," 68; Barrett, *Sherman's March*, 91; and Sherman, *Memoirs*, 2:281.

36. Sherman, *Memoirs*, 2:280–8; and Barrett, *Sherman's March*, 89–90. For a more detailed account of the burning of Columbia, see Marion Brunson Lucas, *Sherman and the Burning of Columbia* (College Station, Texas: Texas A&M University Press, 1976).

37. Barrett, *Sherman's March*, 93; *O.R.* vol. 47, part 1, 228; and Sherman, *Memoirs*, 2:244–45.

38. Barrett, *Sherman's March*, 106. McLaws assumed temporary command on February 18 when Hardee became ill. McLaws oversaw the evacuation of Charleston.

39. Ibid., 60; and Sherman, *Memoirs*, 2:274–6.

40. Bradley, *Last Stand*, 59–65.

41. Ibid, 30–31.

42. *O.R.* vol. 47, part 2, 1247.

43. Warner, *Generals in Gray*, 161–2.

44. Bradley, *Last Stand*, 24–27 and 45.

45. Sherman, *Memoirs*, 2:299; Bradley, *Last Stand*, 71–2.

46. *O.R.* vol. 47, part 2, 1247, 1257, and 1274; Bradley, *Last Stand*, 73.

47. Ibid., 1271; Bradley, *Last Stand*, 28–9.

48. Ibid., 1320, 1330, 1332–1333, 1336, and 1337; Bradley, *Last Stand*, 71–2.

49. Sherman, *Memoirs*, 2:292.

50. Ibid., 2:292–93.

51. Bradley, *Last Stand*, 78; Barrett, *Sherman's March*, 122.

Chapter 2

1. *Raleigh Progress*, January 21, 1865; Raleigh *North Carolina Standard*, March 1, 1865; and Barrett, *Sherman's March*, 117.

2. Thomas W. Belton, "A History of The Fayetteville Arsenal and Armory," Master's Thesis, North Carolina State University, Raleigh, North Carolina, i.

3. Belton, "A History of The Fayetteville Arsenal and Armory," i–ii.

4. *O.R.* vol. 47, part 1, 744–45.

5. Ibid., part 2, 1257, 1320, and 1328; Bradley, *Last Stand,* 73; and Joseph E. Johnston, *Narrative of Military Operations, Directed, During the Late War Between the States* (New York: D. Appleton and Co., 1874), 378. Bragg did not approve of Johnston's appointment to command and immediately asked to be relieved of field duty. He later relented and remained in command through the Battle of Bentonville.

6. Bradley, *Last Stand,* 72; Sherman, *Memoirs,* 2:292; *O.R.* vol. 47, part 2, 1320.

7. Bradley, *Last Stand,* 4.

8. Ibid., 73; Fonvielle, *The Wilmington Campaign,* 434.

9. Capt. James W. Strange to his brother, March 9, 1865, Robert Strange Papers, Southern Historical Collection, Wilson Library, University of North Carolina, Chapel Hill, N.C.

10. *O.R.* vol. 47, part 2, 1245 and 1250.

11. Bvt. Maj. Gen. George W. Cullum, *Biographical Register of the Officers and Graduates of the U. S. Military Academy at West Point, N.Y.,* 2 vols. . (Boston and New York: Houghton, Mifflin and Company, 1891), 2:615; Belton, "A History of The Fayetteville Arsenal and Armory," 55–56.

12. Belton, "A History of The Fayetteville Arsenal and Armory," 57; *Fayetteville Observer,* July 16, 1863.

13. *Fayetteville Observer,* July 16, 1863; Mrs. John B. Anderson, "What Sherman Did to Fayetteville, N.C.," *Confederate Veteran* 32, (April 1924), 139.

14. Louis H. Manarin and Weymouth T. Jordan, Jr., eds., *North Carolina Troops 1861–1865 A Roster* (Raleigh: North Carolina Division of Archives and History, 1968), 3:342; Matthew P. Taylor, "Fayetteville Arsenal: History of the Sixth (N.C.) Battalion Armory Guards," *Southern Historical Society Papers* 24. (1896), 235. One can still see portions of the remaining breastworks on the grounds of the Veterans Hospital in Fayetteville. In the November 19, 1863, issue of the *Fayetteville Recorder,* Childs had offered a $100 bounty for those men willing to enlist. Recruits were required to provide their own horses. The men received monthly pay of $12, plus 40 cents per day for their horses.

15. *O.R.* vol. 47, part 2, 1250.

16. Ibid.; Manarin and Jordan, *North Carolina Troops 1861–1861*, 3:342.

17. *O.R.* vol. 47, part 2, 1264.

18. Fonvielle, *The Wilmington Campaign*, 466 and 478; Taylor, "Fayetteville Arsenal," 234. Whether DeRosset remained in Wilmington with Co. G is open to question. In his short history on the battalion, Taylor states that DeRosset remained with both Cos. B & G. Volume 3 of the North Carolina roster of troops states that only Co. B remained in Wilmington. Because Major Taylor was second in command of the battalion, and because Bragg stated that two companies of infantry and an artillery battery were sent to Elizabethtown, the authors believe that DeRosset's force consisted of both Cos. B & G.

19. *O.R.* vol. 47, part 2, 1264.

20. Fonvielle, *The Wilmington Campaign*, 337.

21. *O.R.* vol. 47, part 2, 1265.

22. Ibid., 1289; Fonvielle, *The Wilmington Campaign*, 478; Anderson, "Confederate Arsenal at Fayetteville, N.C.," 223. Samuel A. Ashe, a native North Carolinian, became a noted writer and historian in the postwar years. Lt. Cdr. George W. Young, U.S. Navy, reported that the obstructions emplaced in the upper part of the Cape Fear River proved to be ineffective due to the river's strong current. U.S. Navy *O.R.* vol.12, 70.

23. *O.R.* vol. 47, part 2, 1264. In an effort to reinforce Lt. Col. Childs's force at the arsenal, the state military authorities published an order in the March 2 edition of the *Fayetteville Observer*. The order instructed all men who had so far failed to muster with their designated companies of Cumberland County's Battalion of Detailed Men to report to Lieutenant Colonel Childs immediately for assignment in Company B of the Arsenal Battalion. The order specified that "disobedience... will insure not only disgrace but punishment by arrest." *Fayetteville Observer, March 2, 1865.*

24. Ibid., 1289 and 1303.

25. Ibid., 1319 and 1335.

26. Ibid., 1264, 1279, and 1294.

27. Manarin and Jordan, *North Carolina Troops 1861–1865*, 3:342. Co. F, 2nd Battalion North Carolina Local Defense Troops, was a cavalry unit commanded by Capt. James W. Strange. Shortly after its organization, the company was transferred to other regions in the state where it was more needed.

28. Strange to his brother, March 9, 1865.

29. *O.R.* vol. 47, part 2, 1289, 1294; Belton, "A History of the Fayetteville Arsenal," 67; *Fayetteville Observer,* February 27, 1865.

30. *O.R.* vol. 47, part 2, 1294, 1295, and 1302; Fonvielle, *The Wilmington Campaign,* 414–416.

31. *O.R.* vol. 47, part 2, 1294–95.

32. Ibid., 1344–45; Clark, "Fayetteville Arsenal," 234–35.

33. Bradley, *Last Stand,* 73.

34. Ibid., 85; *O.R.* vol. 47, part 2, 1344–45, 1348, and 1352; *Tennesseans in the Civil War: A Military History of Confederate and Union Units with Available Rosters of Personnel,* 2 vols. (Nashville, Tenn.: Civil War Centennial Commission, 1964), 1:66.

35. *Fayetteville Observer,* March 2, 1865.

36. Barrett, *The Civil War in North Carolina,* 313; Anderson, "Confederate Arsenal at Fayetteville, N. C.," 223; *O.R.* vol. 47, part 2, 1289; Belton, "A History of The Fayetteville Arsenal and Armory," 69.

37. *O.R.* vol. 47, part 2, 1344.

38. Ibid., 1345.

39. Ibid., part 1, 171.

40. Ibid., part 2, 1352.

41. Pvt. Joseph H. Lanier, Co. A, was captured at Rockfish Creek on March 10.

42. *O.R.* vol. 47, part 2, 1351.

43. Ibid., 1361, 1369–70.

44. Ibid., part 1, 932, 976, 1078, and 1086; Bradley, *Last Stand,* 75–77.

45. Thomas W. Osborn, *Fiery Trail: A Union Officer's Account of Sherman's Last Campaigns,* (Knoxville: University of Tennessee Press, 1986), 179.

46. James Pike, *The Scout and Ranger: Being the Personal Adventures of Corporal James Pike* (Cincinnati: J. R. Hawley & Co., 1865), 385–87; L. G. Bennett & W. M. Haigh, *History of the Thirty-Sixth Regiment Illinois Volunteers, During the War of the Rebellion,* (Aurora, Ill.:Knickerbocker & Hodder, 1876), 788.

47. Huguenin journal, March 9–10, 1865.

48. Phoebe Pollitt & Camille N. Reese, "War Between the States: Nursing in North Carolina," *Confederate Veteran* 2 (1892), 28.

49. The Monroe's Crossroads battlefield is nestled among the drop zones at Fort Bragg, and is one of the most pristine civil war battlefields in existence.

50. Bradley, *Last Stand,* 92–104. For a more detailed account of the Battle of Monroe's Crossroads, see Eric J. Wittenberg, *An Infernal Surprise: The Battle of Monroe's Crossroads, March 10, 1865* (Cincinnati, Ohio: Ironclad Publishing, 2005).

51. Mrs. Josephine Worth, "Sherman's Raid," *War Days in Fayetteville, N.C.* (Fayetteville, N.C.: Judge Printing Co., 1910), 46.

52. Ibid.

53. Ibid., 47.

54. Anthony W. Riecke, "Recollections of a Confederate Soldier," March 10, 1865; Arthur P. Ford, *Life in the Confederate Army: Being Personal Experiences of a Private Soldier in the Confederate Army,* (New York: Neale Publishing Company, 1905), 45.

55. H. W. Graber, *The Life Record of H. W. Graber: A Terry Texas Ranger 1861–1865,* (Privately published, 1918), 234.

56. *O.R.* vol. 47, part 2, 1370; *Dunn Dispatch,* February 15, 1965. On March 16, Bragg sent a message to Hoke, notifying him that the two companies of infantry and the artillery battery that had previously been ordered to evacuate Elizabethtown and report to Hardee at Fayetteville were now to rejoin Hoke's command as soon as possible. It is not known whether DeRosset's arsenal personnel or Mosely's battery ever complied with the order. *O.R.* vol. 47, part 2, 1404–1405.

57. Ibid., 1356.

58. Ibid., 1362 and 1372.

59. Graber, *The Life Record of H. W. Graber,* 234.

60. Anderson, "Confederate Arsenal at Fayetteville, N.C.," 223; Osborn, *The Fiery Trail,* 179. Bragg's decision to withdraw the small Elizabethtown detachments to Fayetteville proved wise. Terry had ordered the 13th Pennsylvania Cavalry to travel north from Wilmington toward Elizabethtown and then on to Fayetteville along the west bank of the Cape Fear River. The Union cavalryman reached Elizabethtown on March 13.

61. Eliza T. Stinson, "Taking of the Arsenal," *War Days of Fayetteville, N.C.* (Fayetteville, N.C.: Judge Printing Co., 1910), 16–17.

62. Eric Wittenberg, "*Giant In Gray: Wade Hampton at Fayetteville,*" *North & South*, vol. 6, num. 6, page 82.

63. Bradley, *Last Stand*, 80.

64. George W. Pepper, *Personal Recollections of Sherman's Campaign in Georgia and the Carolinas* (Zanesville, Ohio: Hugh Dunne, 1866), 361.

65. Charles W. Willis, *Army Life of an Illinois Soldier* (Washington, D.C.: Globe Printing Company, 1906), 360–361.

66. Bradley, *Last Stand*, 107–108; and Barrett, *Sherman's March*, 132.

67. Bradley, *Last Stand*, 107–108.

68. Ibid., 108; Eric Wittenberg, "*Giant In Gray: Wade Hampton at Fayetteville,*" North & South, vol. 6, no. 6, page 85.

69. Anderson, "Confederate Arsenal at Fayetteville, N.C.," 139; Huguenin journal, March 9–10, 1865.

70. Bradley, *Last Stand*, 108–109.

71. Pepper, *Personal Recollections*, 344.

72. Bradley, *Last Stand*, 109.

Chapter 3

1. Pollitt & Reese, "War Between the States: Nursing in North Carolina," 28. One of the temporary hospitals in Fayetteville was on Mrs. Fatima W. Worth's plantation, known as "the Old Worth Place." Mrs. Worth's support of the Confederate war effort was typical of many prominent North Carolina families. Earlier in the war, Mrs. Worth had converted 26 acres of land for use in the production of opium. During the war, opium was a precious medical commodity.

2. Ibid., 30; Anderson, "War Days In Fayetteville," 43.

3. Anderson, "What Sherman Did to Fayetteville," 139; Pepper, *Personal Reflections of Sherman's Campaign*, 343.

4. Bradley, *Last Stand*, 110; Lloyd Lewis, *Sherman: Fighting Prophet* (New York: Harcourt, Brace & World, 1960), 514.

5. Sherman, *Memoirs*, 2:294–295.

6. Alexander McClurg, "The Last Chance of the Confederacy," 370.

7. William Wirt Calkins, *The History of the One Hundred and Fourth Regiment of Illinois Volunteer Infantry* (Chicago: Donohue and Hennebery, 1895), 296; Sherman's men received no mail during their stay at Fayetteville. The mail had been forwarded to Beaufort, North Carolina, in anticipation of the army's arrival at Goldsboro.

8. Henry Hitchcock, *Marching with Sherman* (Lincoln: University of Nebraska Press, 1995), 270.

9. Thomas Higgins Wentworth, *Harvard Memorial Biographies* (Cambridge: Sever and Francis, 1866), 471–472.

10. Joseph E. Fiske, *War Letters of Capt. Joseph E. Fiske Written to His Parents During the War of the Rebellion from Andover Theological Seminary and Encampments in North Carolina and From Southern Prisons* (Wellesley, Mass.: The Maugus Press, n.d.), 59.

11. Taylor, "Fayetteville Arsenal," 231–232.

12. Anderson, "What Sherman Did to Fayetteville," 139.

13. Goodhue, Journal March 16, 1865.

14. Anderson, "Confederate Arsenal at Fayetteville, N.C.," 238.

15. Bradley, *Last Stand,* 109; The mills at Phoenix, Blount Creek, Union Mills, Cross Creek, Beaver Creek and Little River, among others, fell victim to Sherman's torch. Harold S. Wilson, *Confederate Industry: Manufacturers and Quartermasters in the Civil War* (Jackson: University Press of Mississippi, 2002), 217.

16. Wilson, *Confederate Industry,* 217.

17. Samuel Merrill, *The Seventieth Indiana Volunteer Infantry in the War of the Rebellion* (Indianapolis: Bowen-Merrill Company, 1900), 256–257.

18. Barrett, *Sherman's Campaign,* 143.

19. William Grunert, *History of the One-Hundred and Twenty-ninth Illinois Regiment Volunteer Infantry* (Winchester, Ill.: R. B. Dedman, 1866), 212.

20. *O.R.* vol. 47, part 1, 169.

21. Gilbert R. Stormont, ed., *History of the Fifty-Eighth Regiment of Indiana Volunteer Infantry. Its Organization, Campaigns and Battles from 1861 to 1865. From the Manuscript Prepared by the Late Chaplain John J. Hight, During His Service with the Regiment in the Field* (Princeton: Press of the Clarion, 1895), 498; *O.R.,* vol. 47, part 1, 428 and 204.

22. John C. Oeffinger, ed., *A Soldier's General: The Civil War Letters of Major General Lafayette McLaws* (Chapel Hill: University of North Carolina Press, 2002), 264.

23. K. Jack Bauer, ed., *Soldiering: The Civil War Diary of Rice C. Bull* (San Rafel, Cal.: Presidio Press, 1977), 224–225.

24. P. D. Branum, *Letters of Lieut. J. M. Branum* (Sewickly, Pa.: n.p. 1897), 45.

25. *O.R.* vol. 47, part 1, 799. To the soldiers' surprise, they found a brass 6-pounder, named the "Star of the West," in the millpond. This gun was supposedly captured with the U.S. steamer of that name.

26. Ibid., part 2, 1124–26.

27. Ibid., part 1, 1375.

28. Ibid.

29. Thomas Abram Hugenin, *The Journal of Thomas Abram Huguenin: Last Confederate Commander of Fort Sumter,* page 36.

30. Bradley, *Last Stand,* 114; Hardee, "Memoranda" March 16, 1865, JO 843, J. E. Johnston Papers.

31. *O.R.* vol. 47, part 1, 823.

32. Ibid., 823–824, 832–833, 835–838.

33. Ibid., 823–824, 840–841.

34. *O.R.* vol. 47, part 2, 821–822.

35. Bradley, *Last Stand,* 112.

36. *O.R.* vol. 47, part 2, 803, 861.

37. Branum, *Letters of Lieut. J. M. Branum,* 44; Robert P. Broadwater, *Battle of Despair: Bentonville and the North Carolina Campaign* (Macon, Ga.: Mercer University Press, 2004), 44; Bauer, *Soldiering:* 224; John Richard Boyle, *Soldiers True: The Story of the One Hundred and Eleventh Regiment Pennsylvania Veteran Volunteers* (New York: Eaton & Sons, 1903), 287.

38. Sherman, *Memoirs,* 2:300; *O.R.* vol. 47, part 1, 807.

39. Goodhue, Journal March 16, 1865.

40. Ibid.

41. *O.R.* vol. 47, part 2, 807.

42. Illinois Adjutant General's Office, *Report of the Adjutant General of the State of Illinois* (Springfield: Phillips Bros., 1900–1902), 4:30–34; *The*

New York Times, April 3 1865. The fire aboard the vessel originated in the engine-room. Hurricane-force winds and rough seas buffeted the ship, causing several barrels of kerosene oil to fall from their storage shelves on top of the hot boilers.

43. *The New York Times*, April 14, 1865; Robert S. Orrell, www.rootsweb.com/~nccumber/civilwar.htm.

44. Fonvielle, *The Wilmington Campaign*, 450–451.

45. Bradley, *Last Stand*, 112.

46. Samuel Toombs, *Reminiscences of the War, Comprising a Detailed Account of the Experiences of the Thirteenth New Jersey Regimental Volunteers* (Orange, N.J.: Journal Office, 1878), 14.

Chapter 4

1. Grunert, History of the One-Hundred and Twenty-ninth Illinois Regiment Volunteer Infantry, 213.

2. Diary of Robert Morris McDowell, entry for March 15, 1865, Chemung County Historical Society, Elmira, New York.

3. *O.R.* vol. 47, part 2, 1362.

4. Hardee, "Memoranda," March 16, 1865; Bradley, *Last Stand in the Carolinas*, 115.

5. Oeffinger, *A Soldier's General*. 265.

6. Bradley, *Last Stand in the Carolinas*, 115. Mark Bradley offers an interesting explanation for Hardee's stand at Averasboro.

7. *O.R.* vol. 47, part 2, 1372.

8. *Ibid.*, 1298, 1386, 1397; Joseph E. Johnston Papers, "Return of Effective Strength dated March 17, 1865," (Hardee's Corps strength as of March 14, 1865).

9. Joint Publication 1–02. *Department of Defense Dictionary of Military and Associated Terms*, 12 April 2001 (as amended through 15 October 2001), 146.

10. *O.R.* vol. 47, part 2, 1386–87; Joseph Johnston Papers, "Return of Effective Strength dated March 17, 1865," (Hardee's Corps strength as of March 14, 1865).

11. Hughes, *General William J. Hardee*, 285; *Blue and Gray Magazine*, Volume XVI, Issue 1, 10. This article offers an insightful comparison

between Hardee's defensive plan at Averasboro and that of American commander Brig. Gen. Daniel Morgan at the Battle of Cowpens during the Revolutionary War.

12. "Memoir of Major Thomas Young, a Revolutionary Patriot of South Carolina," 100–102. Obviously, a detailed discussion of the Battle of Cowpens strays far beyond the scope of this book. However, if the reader is interested in learning more about Morgan's well-designed and well-fought defense in depth at Cowpens, see Lawrence E. Babits, *A Devil of a Whipping: The Battle of Cowpens* (Chapel Hill: University of North Carolina Press, 1998), which is the best tactical treatment of this critical battle yet written.

13. Williams, *Rhett,* 507.

14. *Ibid,* 517.

15. Huguenin Journal, entries for March 15–16, 1865.

16. *O.R.* vol. 47, part 1, 1084.

17. *Ibid.*

18. *Ibid.*

19. *Ibid,* 24.

20. Middleton Diary, March 15, 1865.

21. *O.R.* vol. 47, part 1, 1084

22. Huguenin Journal, entries for March 15–16, 1865.

23. It should be remembered that the act of dismounting cavalry automatically reduces the effective strength of the cavalry by twenty-five percent. One of every four men is detailed to hold his own horse as well as the horses of three other troopers. The led horses were kept nearby so that the dismounted troopers could quickly remount and move out.

24. *O.R.* vol. 47, part 1, 880.

25. *Ibid.*

26. Committee of the Regiment, *Ninety-second Illinois Regiment,* 229.

27. *Ibid.*

28. Theodore F. Northrop, "Incidents of Sherman's March in N.C.," *Confederate Veteran* 21 (1913), 341.

29. *Ibid.*

30. Pepper, *Personal Recollections,* 257 and 259.

31. Northrop, "Incidents of Sherman's March in N.C.," 341.

32. *Ibid*, 342.

33. Hamilton, *Recollections of a Cavalryman*, 191.

34. Theo. F. Northrop, "General Rhett's Capture," *National Tribune*. April 23, 1891. Kilpatrick and Northrop probably were referring to Mosby's capture of Brig. Gen. Edwin S. Stoughton in March 1863.

35. Hamilton, *Recollections of a Cavalryman*, 191. Hamilton is clearly exaggerating, for no Confederate regiments were captured en mass at Averasboro.

36. Hitchcock, *Marching With Sherman*, 289.

37. Morris Holt. "A True Story of the Capture of Col. Rhett," *National Tribune*, May 31, 1906.

38. Hamilton, *Recollections of a Cavalryman*, 193.

39. H. P. McCain to the Assistant Secretary of War, March 31, 1917, RG 94, Records of the Adjutant General's Office 1780–1917, Theodore F. Northrop File, File No. 1674 vs. 1676, Box 1200, National Archives, Washington, D.C.

40. Toombs, *Reminiscences of the War*, 209.

41. McDowell diary, entry for March 15, 1865.

42. Bryant, *History of the Third Regiment of Wisconsin Veteran Volunteer Infantry*, 316.

43. Toombs, *Reminiscences of the War*, 209.

44. Daniel Oakey, "Marching Through Georgia and the Carolinas," *The Century* (October 1887), 926.

45. Bryant, *History of the Third Regiment of Wisconsin Veteran Volunteer Infantry*, 315.

46. Oakey, "Marching Through Georgia and the Carolinas," 926.

47. *Ibid*; Toombs, *Reminiscences of the War*. 209.

48. Huguenin Journal, entry for March 15, 1865.

49. Middleton Diary, entry for March 15, 1865.

50. Huguenin Journal, entry for March 15, 1865.

Chapter 5

1. Edwin E. Bryant, *History of the Third Regiment of Wisconsin Veteran Volunteer Infantry, 1861–1865*. (Cleveland: The Arthur H. Clark Company,

1891), 316; Daniel Oakey, "A Howling Waste...Marching Through Georgia and the Carolinas," included in Robert U. Johnson and Clarence C. Buel, eds. *Battles and Leaders of the Civil War.* 4 vols. (New York: Century Publishing Co., 1884–1888): 4:598–599.

2. *Ibid.*

3. Middleton diary, entry for March 16, 1865.

4. Huguenin journal, entry for March 16,1865.

5. Oakey, "Marching Through Georgia and the Carolinas," 926.

6. *O.R.* vol. 47, part 1, 585 and 862.

7. Warner, *Generals in Blue,* 560.

8. Williams, *From the Cannons Mouth,* 380.

9. *O.R.* vol. 47, part 1, 907. There is a disagreement over who actually destroyed the limber and gun on the Confederate first line. The XX Corps artillery claimed that they dislodged the gun and destroyed the limber.

10. *Ibid,* 1084–1085.

11. Huguenin journal, March 16, 1865.

12. *O.R.* vol. 47, part 1, 1084–1085.

13. Huguenin journal March 16,1865. Lt. Col. Robert Detreville, commander of the 1st South Carolina Regular Infantry, fell mortally wounded early in the battle. Detreville's body now rests in the Confederate cemetery on the third line.

14. James Miller, "With Sherman Through the Carolinas," *Civil War Times Illustrated* Vol. VIII, No. 6 (October 1969), 37.

15. Bryant, *History of the Third Regiment,* 317.

16. *O.R.* vol. 47, part 2, 867.

17. Spencer diary, entry for March 16,1865.

18. Bauer, *Soldiering: The Civil War Diary of Rice C. Bull,* 226.

19. Ford, *Life in the Confederate Army,* 50.

20. *O.R.* vol. 47, part 1, 1084–1085.

21. Northrop, "Incidents of Sherman's March in N.C.," 342.

22. *O.R.* vol. 47, part 1, 846–47.

23. Hartwell Osborn, *Trials and Triumphs. The Record of the Fifty-Fifth Ohio Volunteer Infantry.* (Chicago: A. C. McClurg and Co., 1904), 199.

24. Samuel W. Ravenel, "Ask the Survivors of Bentonville," *Confederate Veteran* 18 (March 1910), 124. The sergeant of the piece was later identified simply as Guibet.

25. *O.R.* vol. 47, part 1, 789.

26. *Ibid.*

27. Thomas Simpson diary, entry for March 16, 1865.

28. Charles H. Dickinson diary, entry for March 16, 1865.

29. J. E. Brant, *History of the Eighty-Fifth Indiana Volunteer Infantry: Its Organization, Campaigns and Battles* (Bloomington, Indiana: Craven Brothers, Printers and Binders, 1902), 105.

30. *O.R.* vol. 47, part 1, 789; Thomas Finley diary, entry for March 16, 1865.

31. Samuel Merrill, *The Seventieth Indiana Volunteer Infantry in the War of the Rebellion* (Indianapolis: The Bowen-Merrill Company, 1900), 257.

32. Oakey, "Marching Through Georgia and the Carolinas," 927.

33. Huguenin journal, entry for March 16, 1865; Boylston, *Edisto Rebels at Charleston*, 43.

34. Finley diary, entry for March 16, 1865; Dickinson diary, entry for March 16, 1865; William M. Anderson, *They Died to Make Men Free: A History of the 19th Michigan Infantry in the Civil War* (Berrien Springs, Mich.: Hardscrabble Books, 1980), 249.

35. Lyman S. Widney, "From the Sea to the Grand Review," *National Tribune*, August 20, 1903.

36. *O.R.* vol. 47, part 1, 852.

37. Thomas B. Roy diary, entry for March 16, 1865; Samuel W. Ravenel, "The Boy Brigade of South Carolina," *Confederate Veteran* 29 (1921), 418; *O.R.* vol. 47, part 1, 789–90.

38. *O.R.* vol. 47, part 1, 586. On April 13, 1865, the *Charleston Courier* listed six officers killed on the first line from the 1st South Carolina Regulars, including Lieutenant Colonel Detreville, Lieutenant Glover, Captain Quattlebaum and, from the 1st South Carolina Artillery, Captain Lesesne, Lieutenant Laborde, Lieutenant Stewart. No listing was given for Lucas's Battalion, although the seventh officer mentioned in Williams's report must have been from that battalion.

39. *O.R.* vol. 47, part 1, 586; Oeffinger, *A Soldier's General*, 267.

40. *Charleston Courier*, April 13, 1865. One of the wounded officers from the 1st South Carolina Heavy Artillery was Lt. Eldred Simkins Fickling, reportedly the tallest officer in the Confederate army at 6' 9".

41. Huguenin journal, entry for March 16, 1865; Oeffinger, *A Soldier's General*, 266.

42. Ford, *Life in the Confederate Army*, 54. According to Ford, a few men had been guilty of misconduct at Averasboro.

43. *Atlanta Daily Constitutionalist*, April 20, 1865

44. Robert W. Sanders letter, n.d., Eugene Smith collection, _____.

45. Graham Daves, "The Battle of Averasboro," *Southern Historical Society Papers* VII (1879), 125–26.

46. Huguenin journal, entry for March 16, 1865

47. *Atlanta Journal*, December 14, 1901.

48. *O.R.* vol. 47, part 1, 889.

49. Oeffinger, *A Soldier's General*. 266. W. H. Andrews, *Footprints of a Regiment: A Recollection of the First Georgia Regulars 1861–1865*, edited by Richard M. McMurry (Marietta, Ga.: Longstreet Press, 1992), 171. Hardee did not believe that Taliaferro's Division had the experience to delay the Union advance during the retrograde and chose a veteran regiment, the 2nd South Carolina infantry, to perform this task.

50. *O.R.* vol. 47, part 1, 784.

51. *Ibid.* 889–90. Andrews, *Footprints of a Regiment*, 171.

52. *O.R.* vol. 47, part 1, 890.

53. *Ibid.*, 868–69.

54. *Ibid.*, 1084–1085.

55. Oeffinger, *A Soldier's General*, 266.

56. *Ibid.*, 266–67.

57. Andrews, *Footprints of a Regiment*, 172.

58. *O.R.* vol. 47, part 1, 784.

59. Charles M. Castle, "In North Carolina. How Harrison's Brigade Put Rhett's Artillery to Flight," *National Tribune*, May 28, 1891; Charles M. Castle, "Averysboro," *National Tribune*, March 25, 1886.

60. *O.R.* vol. 47, part 1, 825.

61. *Ibid.*, 533.

62. *Ibid.*, 433.

63. *Ibid.*, 1084–85, 1126. Details are sketchy on exactly how many troops Wheeler had at Averasboro. In a dispatch written by Hardee to Johnston at 4:30 A.M. on 17 March, Hardee claimed that Wheeler had only 500 to 600 men with him that morning.

64. *Ibid*, 496.

65. William B. Westervelt, *Lights and Shadows of Army Life, as Seen by a Private Soldier* (Marlboro, New York,: C. H. Cochrane, 1886), 98.

66. *O.R.* vol. 47, part 1, 496; Styple, *Writing and Fighting the Civil War*, 345.

67. *O.R.* vol. 47, part, 484, 496, and 508; Styple, *Writing and Fighting the Civil War*, 345.

68. *Atlanta Journal*, December 14, 1901.

69. *O.R.* vol. 47, part 1, 1084–85.

70. *O.R.* vol. 47, part 1, 1074.

71. *Ibid.*

72. *O.R.* vol. 47, part 1, 586.

73. *Ibid.*, part 2, 851.

74. *Ibid.*, 24–25, 1074.

75. *Ibid.*, 1411 and 1415.

76. *Ibid.*, 1429; Hampton, "The Battle of Bentonville," 710.

77. *O.R.* vol. 47, part 2, 908.

78. Bradley, *Last Stand*, 154 and 159; Slocum, "Sherman's March from Savannah to Bentonville," 692.

79. *O.R.* vol. 47, part 1, 25; Sherman, *Memoirs*, 2:303; Slocum, "Sherman's March from Savannah to Bentonville," 692.

Chapter 6

1. Sherman, *Memoirs*, 2:306–7.

2. Bradley, *Last Stand*, 115.

3. *Hillsborough Recorder*, March 29, 1865.

4. *O.R.* vol. 47 part 2, 1392.

5. Tedder, "Fort Sumter to Bentonville," 54.

6. *O.R.* vol. 47, part 1, 1084.

7. Oeffinger, *A Soldier's General*, 265.

8. Army Field Manual (FM 7–8), 2–8.

9. Oeffinger, *A Soldier's General,* 265.

10. *O.R.* vol. 47, part 1, 1084.

11. Shiman, "Engineering Sherman's March," 106.

12. Huguenin journal, entry for March 19, 1865.

13. *O.R.* vol. 47, part 2, 1411.

14. Oeffinger, *A Soldier's General,* 266.

Appendix B

1. Sokolosky, "The Role of Union Logistics," iii.

2. James M. McPherson, *Battle Cry of Freedom: The Civil War Era* (New York: Oxford University Press, 1988), 827.

3. Barrett, *Sherman's March Through the Carolinas,* vii.

4. *The Surrender of Johnston's Army and the Closing Scenes of the War in North Carolina,* (Cincinnati: Robert Clarke and Co., 1888), 256.

5. Martin Van Creveld, *Supplying War* (Cambridge, Mass.: Cambridge University Press, 1977), 1.

6. Sokolosky, "The Role of Union Logistics," 1–2.

7. Sokolosky, "The Role of Union Logistics," iii.

8. *O.R.* vol. 44, part 1, 637.

9. Sherman, *Memoirs,* 2:174–176; Sokolosky, "The Role of Union Logistics," 3–4.

10. Sherman, *Memoirs,* 2:174–177.

11. James A. Houston, *The Sinews of War: Army Logistics, 1775–1853* (Washington, D.C.: Government Printing Office, 1966), 236.

12. Sokolosky, "The Role of Union Logistics," 5.

13. Sherman, *Memoirs,* 2:174–176.

14. *Ibid.,* 176.

15. *Ibid.,* 176.

16. Houston, *The Sinews of War,* 236.

17. Sherman, *Memoirs,* 2:172.

18. *Ibid.,* 171; Sokolosky, "The Role of Union Logistics," 8.

19. Sherman, *Memoirs,* 2:172.

20. *Ibid.,* 260.

21. Joseph T. Glatthar, "Union Soldiers and Their Attitudes on Sherman's Savannah and Carolina Campaigns" (PhD. diss., University of Wisconsin-Madison, 1983), 200.

22. *Ibid.*, 197.

23. *Ibid.*, 210.

24. *O.R.* vol. 47, part 2, 440, 464, 474–475.

25. *O.R.* vol. 47, part 2, 744, 768.

26. *O.R.* vol. 47, part 2, 736.

27. *Ibid.*, series 3, vol. 5, part 1, 33.

28. Surgeon General's Office, United States Army, *The Medical and Surgical History of the Civil War*, vol. 2 (formerly *The Medical and Surgical History of the War of the Rebellion*), (Wilmington: Broadfoot Publishing Co., 1990), 240.

29. *Ibid.*, 240.

30. *O.R.* vol. 47, part 2, 799–800; Sokolosky, "The Role of Union Logistics," 78–79.

31. *O.R.* vol. 47, part 2, 795.

32. *Ibid.*

33. Sokolosky, "The Role of Union Logistics," 84.

34. *O.R.* vol. 47, part 1, 890.

35. *Ibid.*, 693.

36. *Ibid.*, 63–66.

37. *Ibid.*, 693.

38. *Ibid.*

39. John Randall McBride, *History of Thirty-Third Indiana Veteran Volunteer Infantry During the Four Years of the Civil War, from Sept. 16, 1861 to July 21, 1865.* (Indianapolis: Wm. R. Buford, 1900), 173.

40. *O.R.* vol. 47, part 2, 878.

41. Abel C. Stelle, *History of the Thirty-First Regiment Wisconsin Volunteer Infantry* (New Albany, Ind.: n.p., 1904), 36.

42. Jessie S. Smith, "On the Battlefield of Averasboro, N.C.," *Confederate Veteran* 34 (February 1926), 49.

43. Sokolosky, "The Role of Union Logistics," 112.

44. Sokolosky, "The Role of Union Logistics," 112

45. *O.R.* series 3, vol. 5, part 1, 227.

Appendix C

1. Diary of Corporal Thomas Simpson, entries for March 16–17, 1865.

2. Sherman, Memoirs, 2, p302; Diary of Charles G. Michael, entry for 17 March 1865.

3. Sherman, *Memoirs*, 302.

4. Robbins autobiography, 1–4.

5. Horace W. Davenport, "Such is Military: Dr. George Martin Trowbridge's Letters from Sherman's Army, 1863–1865," *Bulletin of the New York Academy of Medicine* 63 (November, 1987), 876.

6. Dairy of Corporal Thomas Simpson, entries for March 16–17, 1865.

7. Smith, "When Sherman Came: Southern Women and the Great March," 290.

8. *Ibid.*

9. Oates, *The Story of Fayetteville*, 393–4.

10. *Ibid.*

11. Grunert, "History of the 129th Regiment Illinois Volunteer Infantry," 216.

12. Ward, *Simon Baruch: Rebel in the Ranks of Medicine*, 59–60.

Appendix E

1. "Historic Old Southern Home," Confederate Veteran, vol. 37, April 1919, p. 130.

2. Mrs. Stephen E. Puckett, "Long Lost Present From Congress To Young Officer in War of 1812 Recovered by His Great Grandson," *Columbia S.C. State*, September 4, 1932.

Bibliography

Newspapers:
Advertiser and Tribune (Detroit, Mich.)
Argus (Wadesboro, N.C.)
Atlanta Journal
Charleston Courier
Daily Constitutionalist (Augusta, Ga.)
Fayetteville Observer
Frank Leslie's Illustrated Newspaper (N.Y.)
Hillsborough Recorder
National Tribune (Washington, D.C.)
Peoples Advocate (Fayetteville)
North Carolina Standard (Raleigh)
Raleigh Progress
Richmond Dispatch
The State (Columbia, S.C.)
The Sunny South (Atlanta, Ga.)
Sussex Independent
Sussex Register
Wantage Recorder

Manuscripts:
Chemung County Historical Society, Elmira, New York:
    Robert Morris McDowell Diary
Creston-Dement Public Library, Creston, Illinois:
    Lyle G. Headon Collection:
        Dr. Henry Clay Robbins Autobiography
The Citadel Archives and Museum, Charleston, South Carolina:
    W. A. Johnson Diary
Mrs. Richard E. Coen Collection, Charleston, South Carolina:
    Capt. Thomas Huguenin Journal
Library of Congress, Prints and Photographs Division, Washington, D.C.:
    "Scouts and Guides of the Army of the Potomac at Brandy Station,
    Virginia, March, 1864."

Nathaniel Cheairs Hughes Collection, Chattanooga, Tennessee:
  Thomas Benton Roy Diary
New York State Library, Manuscripts and Special Collections, Albany,
  New York:
  William E. Fisher Letters
  Hiram Wilde Reminiscences
Huntington Library, San Marino, California:
  Joseph Eggleston Johnston Papers
Margaret Yearwood Hutchinson Collection, Olympia, Washington:
  Samuel Dewees Hutchinson Letters
Illinois in the Civil War web site: Thomas Simpson Diary
Indiana Historical Society, William E. Smith Memorial Library,
  Indianapolis, Indiana:
  Charles Gottlieb Michael Diary
National Archives, Washington, D.C.: RG 94, Office of the Adjutant
  General: General Correspondence Volunteer Records.
  Service and Pension Records of Civil War Soldiers
North Carolina Division of Archives and History, Raleigh, North
  Carolina:
  Mrs. Thomas H. Webb Collection:
    Janie Smith Letter
Southern Historical Collection, Wilson Library, University of North
  Carolina at Chapel Hill:
  Arthur P. and Marion J. Ford Book
  Daniel Miles Tedder Book
Pennsylvania Historical Society, Philadelphia, Pennsylvania:
  Thomas J. Jordan Civil War Letters, 1861-1866
George Slaton Collection, Wilmington, North Carolina:
  William Colcock Letter
George Spencer Collection:
  Israel P. Spencer memoirs
South Carolina Historical Society, Charleston, South Carolina:
  Cheves-Middleton Papers:
      Edward B. Middleton Diary
      William F. Goodhue Journal
      Edward P. Pearson, Jr. Letter

Charles and Richard B. Townsend Collection, Minot, North Dakota:
     Anthony W. Riecke Narrative: "Recollections of a Confederate
     Soldier of the Struggle of the Lost Cause"
United States Army Military History Institute, Carlisle, Pennsylvania:
     Civil War Miscellaneous Collection:
          Thomas Y. Finley Diary
          Leander E. Davis Reminiscences
North Carolina Collection, Louis Round Wilson Library, University of
     North Carolina at Chapel Hill:
          North Carolina Clipping File
          Robert Strange Papers
South Caroliniana Library, University of South Carolina, Columbia,
     South Carolina: Frederick L. Childs Collection
Eugene W. Smith Collection, Dunn, North Carolina:
     Robert W. Sanders Letter
State Historical Society of Wisconsin, Madison, Wisconsin:
     Charles H. Dickinson Papers

Published primary sources:
Allen, W. G. "About the Fight at Fayetteville, N.C." *Confederate Veteran*
     19, 1911.
Anderson, Mrs. J. H. "Confederate Arsenal at Fayetteville, N.C."
     Confederate Veteran 36, 1928.
_____. "What Sherman Did to Fayetteville, N.C." *Confederate
     Veteran* 32, April 1924.
Anderson, William M. *The Civil War Letters of Henry Orendorff.*
     Macomb, Ill.: Western Illinois University, 1986.
_____. *They Died to Make Men Free: A History of the 19th Michigan
     Infantry in the Civil War.* Berrien Springs, Mich.: Hardscrabble
     Books, 1980.
Andrews, W. H. *Footprints of a Regiment: A Recollection of the First
     Georgia Regulars 1861-1865.* Edited by Richard M. McMurry.
     Marietta, Ga.: Longstreet Press, 1992.
Aten, Henry J. *History of the Eighty-Fifth Regiment, Illinois Volunteer
     Infantry.* Hiawatha, Kan.: privately published, 1901.

Atkins, Smith D. "General Sherman's March Through the Carolinas." *The State*, June 21, 1908.

Benton, Charles E. *As Seen from the Ranks: A Boy in the Civil War*. New York: G.P. Putnam's Sons, 1902.

Beymer, William Gilmore. *On Hazardous Service; Scouts and Spies of the North and South*. New York: London, Harper & Brothers, 1912.

Bradbury, William H. *While Father Is Away: The Civil War Letters of William H. Bradbury*. Edited by Jennifer C. Bohrnstedt. Lexington: University Press of Kentucky, 2003.

Bradley, G. S. *The Star Corps or, Notes of an Army Chaplain During Sherman's March to the Sea*. Milwaukee: Jermain and Brightman, 1865.

Brant, Jefferson E. *History of the Eighty-Fifth Indiana Volunteer Infantry: Its Organization, Campaigns and Battles*. Bloomington, Indiana: Craven Brothers, Printers and Binders, 1902.

Broadfoot, Andrew. "Interesting Story of Arsenal Recollections." *Fayetteville Observer*, May 15, 1928.

Bryan, R. K. "Sherman's Army in Fayetteville, N.C." *The Peoples Advocate*, July 23, 1925.

Bryant, Edwin E. *History of the Third Regiment of Wisconsin Veteran Volunteer Infantry, 1861-1865*. Cleveland: The Arthur H. Clark Company, 1891.

Bull, Rice C. *Soldiering: the Civil War Diary of Rice C. Bull, 123d New York Volunteer Infantry*. Edited by K. Jack Bauer. San Rafael, Cal.: Presidio Press, 1977.

Burt, R. W. "Foraging For Sherman's Army." *National Tribune*, November 3, 1898.

Burton, E. P. *Diary of E. P. Burton*. Des Moines: The Historical Records Survey, 1939.

Camburn, T. E. "Capture of Col. Rhett." *National Tribune*, August 23, 1906.

Carter, George E., ed. *The Story of Joshua D. Breyfogle, Private, 4th Ohio Infantry (10th Ohio Cavalry) and the Civil War*. Lewiston, N.Y.: The Edward Mellen Press, 2001.

Castle, Charles M. "Averysboro." *National Tribune*, March 25, 1886.

_____. "In North Carolina. How Harrison's Brigade Put Rhett's Artillery to Flight." *National Tribune*, May 28, 1891.

"Cavalryman." "Campaign Through the Carolinas." *National Tribune*, April 28, May 5, and May 12, 1892.

Clark, Walter, ed. *Histories of the Several Regiments and Battalions from North Carolina in the Great War 1861-'65. Written by Members of the Respective Commands.* 5 vols. Goldsboro, N.C.: Nash Brothers, 1901.

Collins, R. "The First to Enter Fayetteville." *National Tribune*, May 13, 1886.

Committee of the Regiment. *Ninety-Second Illinois Volunteers.* Freeport, Ill.: Journal Steam Publishing House and Bookbindery, 1875.

Connelly, James A. *Three Years in the Army of the Cumberland: The Letters and Diary of Major James A. Connelly.* Edited by Paul M. Angle. Bloomington: University of Indiana Press, 1959.

Conner, W. H. "The Guns at Averasboro." *National Tribune*, February 22, 1912.

Conyngham, David P. *Sherman's March through the South With Sketches and Incidents of the Campaign.* New York: Sheldan & Co., 1865.

Cook, S. G., and Benton, Charles E. eds. *The "Dutchess County Regiment" (150th Regiment of New York State Volunteer Infantry) in the Civil War.* Danbury Medical Printing Company, 1907.

Cram, George Franklin. *Soldiering with Sherman: Letters of George F. Cram.* Edited by Jennifer C. Bohrnstedt. DeKalb, Ill.: Northern Illinois University Press, 2000.

Daniels, Orange. "The Averysboro Fight." *National Tribune*, June 21, 1900.

Daves, Graham. "The Battle of Averasboro." *Southern Historical Society Papers* 7 (March 1879).

"Death of Capt. Northrop." *Sussex Independent*, February 1, 1918.

"Death of Civil War Veteran on Sunday." *Wantage Recorder*, February 1, 1918.

Du Bose, John W. "The Fayetteville Road Fight." *Confederate Veteran* 20, 1912.

Elliott, William. "Through The Carolinas." *National Tribune*, March 10, 1887.

Elmore, Willard. "A Comrade of the 147th N.Y. Tells of Averysboro and Bentonville." *National Tribune*, June 3, 1886.

Fallis, Leroy. "Kilpatrick at Averasboro." *National Tribune*, November 17, 1904.

Fanning, T. W. *The Hairbreadth Escapes and Humorous Adventures of A Volunteer in the Cavalry Service By One of Them.* Cincinnati: P. C. Browne, 1865.

Fleharty, S. F. *Our Regiment: A History of the 102nd Illinois Infantry Volunteers.* Chicago: Brewster and Hanscom, 1865.

Ford, Arthur Peronneau. *Life in the Confederate Army.* New York: The Neale Publishing Co., 1905.

Graber, H. W. *The Life Record of H. W. Graber: A Terry Texas Ranger 1861-1865.* Privately published, 1918.

Grant, Ulysses S. *Personal Memoirs of U. S. Grant.* 2 vols. New York: Charles Webster & Co., 1885.

Grunert, William. *History of the 129th Regiment Illinois Volunteer Infantry.* Winchester, Ill.: R. B. Dedman, 1866.

Guild, George B. *A Brief Narrative of the Fourth Tennessee Cavalry Regiment: Wheeler's Corps, Army of Tennessee.* Nashville, Tenn.: privately published, 1913.

Hackett, Henry C. "The Fayetteville Arsenal: The Way it was Destroyed by Union Troops." *National Tribune,* May 18, 1916.

Halsey, Ashley, ed. *A Yankee Private's Civil War by Robert Hale Strong.* Chicago: Henry Regnery Company, 1961.

Hamilton, William Douglas. *Recollections of a Cavalryman After Fifty Years.* Columbus: F. J. Heer Printing Co., 1915.

Hampton, Wade. "The Battle of Bentonville." Included in Robert U. Johnson and Clarence C. Buel, eds., *Battles and Leaders of the Civil War.* 4 vols. New York: The Century Company, 1884-1889.

Hedley, Fenwick Y. *Marching Through Georgia. Pen-Pictures of Every-Day Life in General Sherman's Army from beginning of the Atlanta Campaign Until the Close of the War.* Chicago: R. R. Donnelley and Sons, 1887.

Hibbets, Jeff J. "Fayetteville, N.C." *National Tribune,* June 11, 1885.

Hinkley, Julian Wisner. *A Narrative of Service with the Third Wisconsin Infantry.* Madison: Wisconsin Historical Commission, 1912.

Hinman, Wilbur F. *The Story of the Sherman Brigade, the Camp, the March, the Bivouac, the Battle, and How the Boys Lived and Died During Four Years of Active Field Service.* Alliance, Ohio: privately published, 1897.

Hitchcock, Henry. *Marching With Sherman: Passages From the Letters and Campaign Diaries of Henry Hitchcock.* Edited by M. A. DeWolfe Howe. Lincoln: University of Nebraska Press, 1995.

Holman, Natt. "Participant in the Battle of Fayetteville, N.C."
    Confederate Veteran 19, 1911.

Holt, Morris C. "A True Story of the Capture of Col. Rhett, A South
    Carolina Fire Eater Who Never Fought a Battle." *National Tribune*,
    May 31, 1906.

Inglesby, Charles F. *Historical Sketch of the First Regiment of South Carolina
    Artillery. (Regulars)*. n.p.: Walker, Evans & Cogswell Co., n.d.

Johnston, Joseph E. *Narrative of Military Operations, Directed, During the
    Late War Between the States*. New York: D. Appleton and Co., 1874.

Joint Publication 1-02. *Department of Defense Dictionary of Military and
    Associated Terms*. 12 April 2001 (as amended through 15 October 2001).

Kinnear, J. R. *History of the Eighty-Sixth Regiment, Illinois Volunteer
    Infantry*. Chicago: Tribune Company's Book and Job Printing
    Office, 1866.

Kyle, Anne K. "Incidents of Hospital Life." Included in *War Days of
    Fayetteville, N.C.* Fayetteville, N.C.: Judge Printing Co., 1910.

McBride, John Randolph. *History of Thirty-Third Indiana Veteran
    Volunteer Infantry During the Four Years of the Civil War*.
    Indianapolis: Wm. R. Buford, 1900.

Merrill, Samuel. *The Seventieth Indiana Volunteer Infantry in the War of the
    Rebellion*. Indianapolis: The Bowen-Merrill Company, 1900.

Meagher, Peter. "The 17th New York." *National Tribune*, October 28, 1886.

Miller, James, "With Sherman Through the Carolinas." *Civil War Times
    Illustrated* VIII (October 1969).

Moore, James, M. D. *Kilpatrick and Our Cavalry: Comprising a Sketch of the Life
    of General Kilpatrick, With an Account of the Cavalry Raids, Engagements, and
    Operations Under His Command, From the Beginning of the Rebellion to the
    Surrender of Johnston*. New York: W. J. Widdleton, 1865.

Morhous, Henry C. *Reminiscences of the 123d Regiment, N. Y. S. V., Giving
    a Complete History of Its Three Years Service in the War*. Greenwich,
    N.Y.: People's Book and Job Office, 1879.

Morris, W. H. "The Other Side of Fayetteville." *Confederate Veteran*
    20, 1912.

Morse, Charles Fessenden. *Letters Written During the Civil War, 1861-
    1865*. Boston: privately published, 1898.

Nichols, George Ward. *The Story of the Great March.* New York: Harper
and Brothers, 1866.

Northrop, Theo F. "Incidents of Sherman's March in North Carolina."
Confederate Veteran 21, 1913.

_____. "Capture of Gen. Rhett." *National Tribune*, January 18, 1906.

_____. "Gen Rhett's Capture. As Told by the One Who Took
Him to Sherman." *National Tribune*, April 23, 1891.

_____. "Other Side of the Fayetteville Road Fight." *Confederate
Veteran* 20, 1912.

_____. "The Capture of Col Rhett. The Captor Tells the Story of
its Occurrence." *National Tribune*, December 7, 1911.

Oakey, Daniel. "A Howling Waste...Marching Through Georgia and the
Carolinas." Included in Robert U. Johnson and Clarence C. Buel,
eds. *Battles and Leaders of the Civil War.* 4 vols. (New York: Century
Publishing Co., 1884-1888).

_____. "Marching Through Georgia and the Carolinas." *The
Century* 34 October 1887.

Osborn, Hartwell and others. *Trials and Triumphs. The Record of the Fifty-
Fifth Ohio Volunteer Infantry.* Chicago: A. C. McClurg and
Company, 1904.

Osborn, Thomas W., *The Fiery Trail: A Union Officer's Account of Sherman's
Last Campaigns,* Knoxville: University of Tennessee Press, 1986.

Pepper, George W. *Personal Recollections of Sherman's Campaigns in
Georgia and the Carolinas.* Zanesville, Ohio: Hugh Dunne, 1866.

Pike, James. *The Scout and Ranger, Being the Personal Adventures of
Corporal Pike, of the Fourth Ohio Cavalry.* Cincinnati: J. R. Hawley &
Co., 1865.

Potter, John. *Reminiscences of the Civil War in the United States.*
Oskaloosa, Iowa: The Globe Press, 1897.

Quint, Alonzo H. *The Record of the Second Massachusetts Infantry, 1861-
1865.* Boston: James P. Walker, 1867.

Ravenel, Samuel W. "Ask the Survivors of Bentonville." *Confederate
Veteran* 18, March 1910.

_____. "The Boy Brigade of South Carolina." *Confederate Veteran*
29, November-December 1921.

Reynolds, Donald E. and Kele, Max H., eds. "A Yank in the Carolinas Campaign: The Diary of James W. Chapin, Eighth Indiana Cavalry." *North Carolina Historical Review* vol. 46, no. 1,Winter 1969.

Riecke, Anthony W. *Recollections of a Confederate Soldier of the Struggle for the Lost Cause.* n.p.: 1879.

Robertson, John I. "Cheraw and Fayetteville. Work of Destruction Carried on by the 1st Mich. Engineers." *National Tribune,* July 1, 1920.

Sanders, Robert W. "The Battle of Averasboro." *Confederate Veteran* 34, 1926.

Shaw, Alfred J. "At Averasboro, N. C." *National Tribune,* July 16, 1914.

Sherman, William T. *Memoirs of General William T. Sherman.* 2 vols. New York: D. Appleton, 1875.

Slocum, Henry W. "Sherman's March from Savannah to Bentonville." Included in Robert U. Johnson and Clarence C. Buel, eds. *Battles and Leaders of the Civil War.* 4 vols. New York: Century Publishing Co., 1884-1889.

Smith, Jessie Slocumb. "When Sherman Came: Women and the Great March." *Confederate Veteran* 34, 1926.

Stelle, Abel C. *Memoirs of the Civil War: History of the Thirty-First Regiment Wisconsin Volunteer Infantry.* New Albany, Ind.: n. p., 1904.

Stinson, Eliza T. "Taking of the Arsenal." Included in *War Days of Fayetteville, N.C.* Fayetteville, N.C.: Judge Printing Co., 1910.

Storrs, John W. *The Twentieth Connecticut. A Regimental History.* Ansonia, Conn.: Press of the Naugatuck and Valley Sentinel, 1886.

Styple, William B., ed. *Writing and Fighting the Civil War: Soldier Correspondence to the New York Sunday Mercury.* Kearny, N.J.: Belle Grove Publishing, 2000.

Swordberg, Claire E., ed. *Three Years With the 92nd Illinois: The Civil War Diary of John M. King.* Mechanicsburg, Pa.: Stackpole Books, 1999.

Taylor, Matthew P. "Fayetteville Arsenal: History of the Sixth (N.C.) Battalion Armory Guards." *Southern Historical Society Papers* 24, 1896.

The Official Military Atlas of the Civil War. Washington D.C.: Government Printing Office, 1891-95.

The War of the Rebellion: A Compilation of the Official Records of the Union and Confederate Armies. 128 vols. in 3 series. Washington, D.C.: U.S. Government Printing Office, 1891-95.

Toombs, Samuel. *Reminiscences of the War, Comprising a Detailed Account of the Experiences of the Thirteenth Regiment New Jersey Volunteers.* Orange, N.J.: Printed at Journal Office, 1878.

Underwood, Adin B. *The Three Years' Service of the Thirty-Third Mass. Infantry Regiment 1862-1865.* Boston: A. Williams and Company, 1881.

Wells, Edward L. "Hampton at Fayetteville." *Southern Historical Society Papers* 13, 1885.

Westervelt, William B. *Lights and Shadows of Army Life, as Seen by a Private Soldier.* Marlboro, N.Y.: C. H. Cochrane, 1886.

Williams Alpheus S. *From the Cannon's Mouth: The Civil War Letters of Alpheus S. Williams.* Edited by Milo S. Quaife. Lincoln: University of Nebraska Press, 1995.

Wills, Charles W. *Army Life of an Illinois Soldier.* Washington, D.C.: Globe Printing Company, 1906.

Winkler, William K., ed. *Letters of Fredrick C. Winkler, 1862-1865.* Privately published, 1963.

Winther, Oscar Ogburn, ed. *With Sherman to the Sea. The Civil War Letters, Diaries, and Reminiscences of Theodore F. Upson.* Baton Rouge: Louisiana State University Press, 1943.

"With Hampton in Battle: A Brilliant Cavalry Charge at Fayetteville." *The Sunny South*, December 5, 1897.

Worth, Josephine Bryan. "Sherman's Raid." Included in *War Days in Fayetteville, N.C.* Fayetteville, N.C.: Judge Printing Company, 1910.

Young, Thomas. "Memoir of Major Thomas Young." *Orion Magazine*, October and November, 1843.

Published Secondary Sources:

Angley, Wilson, Jerry L. Cross, and Michael Hill. *Sherman's March through North Carolina: A Chronology.* Raleigh: North Carolina Division of Archives and History, 1995.

Barrett, John G. *Sherman's March Through the Carolinas.* Chapel Hill: University of North Carolina Press, 1956.

_____. *The Civil War in North Carolina.* Chapel Hill: University of North Carolina Press, 1963.

Boylston, Jr., Raymond P. *Edisto Rebels at Charleston*. Raleigh: Boylston Enterprises, 2003.

Bradley, Mark L. *Last Stand in the Carolinas: The Battle of Bentonville*. Campbell, Cal.: Savas Woodbury Publishers, 1996.

_____. *Old Reliable's Finest Hour: The Battle of Averasboro, North Carolina, March 15-16, 1865*. Columbus, Ohio: Blue and Gray Magazine, 1998.

_____. *This Astounding Close: The Road to Bennett Place*. Chapel Hill: University of North Carolina Press, 2000.

Broadwater, Robert P. *Battle of Despair: Bentonville and the North Carolina Campaign*. Macon: Mercer University Press, 2004.

Burne, Alfred H. *Lee, Grant and Sherman: A Study in Leadership in the 1864-65 Campaign*. New York: Charles Scribner's Sons, 1939.

Civil War Centennial Commission. *Tennesseans in the Civil War, Part I*. Nashville, Tenn.: 1964.

Connelly, Thomas L. *Autumn of Glory: The Army of Tennessee, 1862-1865*. Baton Rouge: Louisiana State University Press, 1971.

Cullum, Bvt. Maj. Gen. George W. *Biographical Register of the Officers and Graduates of the U. S. Military Academy at West Point, N.Y.* 2 vols. Boston: Houghton, Mifflin and Company, 1891.

Daiss, Timothy. *In the Saddle: Exploits of the 5th Georgia Cavalry During the Civil War*. Atglen, Pa.: Schiffer Publishing, 1999.

Davenport, Horace W. "Such Is Military: Dr. George Martin Trowbridge's Letters from Sherman's Army, 1863-1865." *Bulletin of the New York Academy of Medicine* 63, November 1987.

Davis, Burke. *Sherman's March*. New York: Random House, 1980.

Davis, William C. *Rhett: The Turbulent Life and Times of a Fire-Eater*. Columbia: University of South Carolina Press, 2001.

DeLeon, T. C. *Joseph Wheeler; the Man, the Statesman, the Soldier, Seen in Semi-Biographical Sketches*. Atlanta: Byrd Printing, 1899.

Dyer, John P. *Fightin' Joe Wheeler*. Baton Rouge: Louisiana State University Press, 1941.

Fitzhugh, Lester. *Terry's Texas Rangers*. Houston: Civil War Roundtable, 1958.

Fonvielle, Chris E., Jr. *The Wilmington Campaign: Last Rays of Departing Hope*. Campbell, Cal.: Savas Publishing, 1997.

Foote, Shelby. *The Civil War, A Narrative, Vol. III.* New York: Random House, 1974.

Fowler, Malcom. "Battle of Averasboro." *Dunn Dispatch,* February 15, 1965.

Gibson, John M. *Those 163 Days: A Southern Account of Sherman's March from Atlanta to Raleigh.* New York: Van Rees Press, 1961.

Glatthaar, Joeseph T. *The March to the Sea and Beyond: Sherman's Troops in the Savannah and Carolinas Campaigns.* New York: New York University Press, 1985.

Hughes, Michael J. *Sherman's 1864-65 Campaigns: Strategic Assessment and Lessons for Today.* Newport, R.I.: U. S. Naval War College, 1994.

Hughes, Nathaniel C. *Bentonville: The Final Battle of Sherman and Johnston.* Chapel Hill: University of North Carolina Press, 1996.

_____. *General William J. Hardee: Old Reliable.* Baton Rouge: Louisiana State University Press, 1965.

Houston, James A. *The Sinews of War: Army Logistics, 1775-1953.* Washington, D.C.: U.S. Government Printing Office, 1966.

Hunt, Roger D. *Brevet Brigadier Generals in Blue.* Gaithersburg, Md.: Olde Soldier Books, 1990.

Manarin, Louis H., and Jordan, Weymouth T., Jr., eds. *North Carolina Troops 1861-1865 A Roster.* Vol. 3. Raleigh: North Carolina Division of Archives and History, 1968.

Martin, Samuel J. *Kill-Cavalry: Sherman's Merchant of Terror–The Life of Union General Hugh Judson Kilpatrick.* Madison, N.J.: Fairleigh-Dickinson University Press, 1996.

McPherson, James M. *Battle Cry of Freedom: The Civil War Era.* New York: Oxford University Press, 1988.

Moore, Mark A. *Moore's Historical Guide to the Battle of Bentonville.* Mason City, Iowa: Savas Publishing, 1997.

_____. *Moore's Historical Guide to the Wilmington Campaign and the Battles for Fort Fisher.* Mason City, Iowa: Savas Publishing, 1999.

Morrill, Dan. *The Civil War in the Carolinas.* Charleston, S.C.: The Nautical and Aviation Publishing Co. of America, 2002.

Nevin, David. *Sherman's March: Atlanta to the Sea.* Alexandria, Va.: Time-Life Books, 1986.

Oates, John A. *The Story of Fayetteville and the Upper Cape Fear*. Charlotte, N.C.: The Dowd Press, 1950.

Oeffinger, John C., ed. *A Soldier's General: The Civil War Letters of Major General Lafayette McLaws*. Chapel Hill: University of North Carolina Press, 2002.

"Patriotic Mrs. Armand J. DeRosset." *Confederate Veteran* 3, July 1895.

Pollitt, Phoebe, and Reese, Camille N. "War Between the States, Nursing in North Carolina," *Confederate Veteran* 2, 1892.

Surgeon General's Office, United States Army. *The Medical and Surgical History of the Civil War*. Vol. 2. Wilmington, N.C.: Broadfoot Publishing Co., 1990.

Spencer, Cornelia Phillips. *The Last Ninety Days of the War in North Carolina*. New York: Watchman Publishing Co., 1866.

Starr, Stephen Z. *The Union Cavalry in the Civil War: The War in the West 1861-1865*. 3 vols. Baton Rouge: Louisiana State University Press, 1977-1985.

Van Creveld, Martin. *Supplying War*. Cambridge, Mass.: Cambridge Press, 1977.

Vandiver, Frank E., ed. *Narrative of Military Operations by Joseph E. Johnston*. Bloomington, Ind.: University of Indiana Press, 1959.

Ward, Patricia Spain. *Simon Baruch: rebel in the ranks of medicine, 1840-1921*. Tuscaloosa: University of Alabama Press, 1994.

Warner, Ezra J. *Generals in Blue: The Lives of the Union Commanders*. Baton Rouge: Louisiana State University Press, 1964.

_____. *Generals in Gray: The Lives of the Confederate Commanders*. Baton Rouge: Louisiana State University Press, 1959.

Wilson, Harold S. *Confederate Industry: Manufacturers and Quartermasters in the Civil War*. Jackson: University Press of Mississippi, 2002.

Wittenberg, Eric J. *An Infernal Surprise: The Battle of Monroe's Crossroads, March 10, 1865*. Cincinnati, Ohio: Ironclad Publishing, 2005.

Theses and Dissertations:

Belton, Thomas W. "A History of The Fayetteville Arsenal and Armory." Master's thesis, North Carolina State University, 1979.

Fonvielle, Chris E. Jr. "'The Last Rays of Hope': The Battles of Fort Fisher, the Fall of Wilmington, North Carolina, and the End of the Confederacy." Ph.D. diss. University of South Carolina, 1994.

Glatthaar, Joseph T. *"Union Soldiers and Their Attitudes on Sherman's Savannah and Carolina Campaigns."* Ph.D. diss. University of Wisconsin-Madison, 1983.

Shiman, Philip Lewis. "Engineering Sherman's March: Army Engineers and the Management of Modern War, 1862-1865." 2 Vols. Ph.D. diss. Duke University, 1991.

Sokolosky, Maj. Johnny W. "The Role of Union Logistics During Sherman's Carolinas Campaign of 1865." M.A. thesis, United States Army Command and General Staff College, 2002.

Index

(m), (p), (d) after page numbers indicate maps (m), photos (p), and drawings (d).